OUTSIDE LITERATURE

Tony Bennett

London and New York

To Sue, with all my
love and thanks

First published 1990
by Routledge
11 New Fetter Lane, London EC4P 4EE
Simultaneously published in the USA and Canada by Routledge
a division of Routledge, Chapman and Hall, Inc.
29 West 35th Street, New York, NY 10001

© 1990 Tony Bennett

Typeset in 11/12pt Garamond by
Columns Ltd, Reading, Berks
Printed in Great Britain by
Clays Ltd, St. Ives plc

British Library Cataloguing in Publication Data
Bennett, Tony.
Outside literature.
1. Literature. Theories.
I. Title
801.95

Library of Congress Cataloging in Publication Data
Bennett, Tony
Outside literature / Tony Bennett.
p. cm.
Includes bibliographical references.
1. Marxist criticism. 2. Literature–Aesthetics.
3. Postmodernism. 4. Structuralism (Literary analysis) I. Title.
PN98.C6B37 1990
801'.95–dc20 90–8167
0 415 01093 4
0 415 01094 2 (Pbk)

CONTENTS

Part III

Part IV

ACKNOWLEDGEMENTS

The author and publishers wish to thank the following who have kindly given permission for the use of copyright material: New Left Books for excerpts from Terry Eagleton, *Criticism and Ideology* and from Ernesto Laclau and Chantal Mouffe, *Hegemony and Socialist Strategy: Toward a Radical Democratic Politics*; Harvard University Press for excerpts from John Frow, *Marxism and Literary History*; Basil Blackwell for excerpts from Ludwig Wittgenstein, *Philosophical Investigations*; Chatto & Windus Ltd for excerpts from Ian Watt, *The Rise of the Novel*; Oxford University Press for excerpts from Immanuel Kant, *The Critique of Judgement*; Bobbs-Merrill Co Ltd, for excerpts from David Hume, *Of the Standard of Taste, and Other Essays*; Macmillan Publishing Company for excerpts from Ian Hunter, *Culture and Government: The Emergence of Modern Literary Education*; Faber & Faber for excerpts from Edward Said, *The World, the Text and The Critic*, and Routledge for excerpts from Fredric Jameson, *The Political Unconscious*.

PREFACE

This book has been a long time in the making. I first began work on it in 1983. Owing to other pressures, however, I have rarely been able to devote more than a few days at a time to this work and, on occasions, have been obliged to put it to one side – festering malignantly in my filing cabinet – for several months.

These remarks have a bearing on the form of the book. When it became clear that I should have to accommodate the book's conception to these circumstances of working or abandon the project entirely, I determined on an episodic principle of organisation. Thus, rather than offering a continuing argument which develops cumulatively from chapter to chapter, I have sought, in each chapter, to deal with a relatively discrete problem. While chapters 1 and 2 constitute necessary starting points in situating the concerns of the book as a whole, the reader will find that, thereafter, each chapter can be read relatively independently of those adjacent to it. On the whole, however, I think that the chapters are best read in the order in which I have placed them.

For there is a consistency of purpose running through the book: to contribute to the development of a logic for literary analysis that will be adequately social and historical in its orientations. While I have assumed that the commitment to such a project is now sufficiently shared for this purpose to require no extensive elaboration or defence, my study is also premised on the conviction that this intention is not so easily realised as is commonly supposed. Even where a socialising and historicising logic is espoused, it is often incompletely sustained owing to the inherited weight of formalist and idealist categories and procedures which, when they are not carefully scrutinised, insinuate their way into the analysis, deflecting it from its objectives.

It is partly for this reason that the book takes the form of a critical dialogue with the concerns of Marxist literary theory. Whatever its shortcomings, this remains the most fully developed and sustained tradition of theorising concerned with literary practices in their social and historical connections. Indeed, I had originally envisaged my intention as that of offering a revised version of Marxist literary theory, one which would better equip it to realise its socialising and historicising aspirations. In the course of writing, however, it became increasingly clear that Marxism's claim to provide a framework for the development of a comprehensive social and historical theory of literature can no longer be sustained. While, in thus rejecting Marxism's totalising pretensions, my arguments are post-Marxist in conception, they are certainly not intended as anti-Marxist − although I have no doubt some die-hards will see them that way − but rather aim for a more selective and localised use of Marxist concepts and categories.

However, little purpose is served by my seeking to anticipate the reader's judgement on these matters. It will perhaps be more helpful if, instead, I outline the organising principles of the book. Part I offers a general review of a range of connected problems within Marxist literary theory viewed in the light of their relations to some of the more generally problematic aspects of Marxist thought as a whole. Each of the following sections then focuses on a particular region of Marxist literary–theoretical debate. The chapters comprising part II thus deal with difficulties associated with Marxist conceptions of the social determination of literary forms. Part III then addresses the problems associated with Marxist theories of the specificity of literature and of the aesthetic, while the chapters comprising part IV focus on Marxist conceptions of criticism, and the reasons for considering these incapable of supporting much beyond a politics of grand gestures.

I do not, in developing these concerns, offer a comprehensive history of Marxist literary theory or attempt to differentiate its various sub-branches in any detail. While not denying the importance of either consideration, my purpose has rather been to identify those difficulties which subtend the main schools of Marxist literary theory in spite of their differences in other respects. Nor have I attempted an overall assessment of Marxist contributions to literary theory considered in their relations to contending bodies of literary theory. Rather, I have drawn on these where relevant to the point under discussion, and usually as a means of providing a critical perspective on, or alternative to, Marxist formulations. While the reader will find that my arguments are informed by perspectives culled (often opportunistically) from post-structuralism, deconstruction and Foucaultian theory, there is no attempt to buy in to these positions as totalities or to oppose, and prefer them, to Marxist thought in some holistic way. For reasons outlined as the study develops, there are good grounds for resisting this type of theorising.

The period of writing this book coincided with a major change in my working circumstances. The early stages of research and drafting were begun while I worked at the Open University in Britain. The bulk of the writing, however, was completed while working at Griffith University in Australia. My work, for better or worse, has undoubtedly been influenced by these changed circumstances, and particularly by the (in my experience) uniquely invigorating climate of literary–theoretical debate which prevails at Griffith. Although I have not explicitly discussed the contents of this book as a whole with any of my Griffith colleagues, it has, in part, been shaped as a result of conversations on the topics it addresses as well as by the practical experience of working together in planning and designing courses. I have learned much from David Saunders's developing work on the relations between law and literature, as also from Colin Mercer's work on the cultural technologies of popular entertainment. I am especially grateful to Dugald Williamson whose scrupulous criticisms of Lacan helped convince me that, at least for my purposes, I could leave this body of theory by the wayside. I am also indebted to Jeffrey Minson and Ian Hunter whose work has obliged me to approach Foucault's work and its implications for literary scholarship more seriously and open-mindedly than I was previously wont to.

Working in Australia has also allowed me to come to know and share ideas with John Frow, a rewarding experience on both counts. Special mention should also be made of Anne Freadman, whose work on genre I draw on substantially in chapter 4, and of Noel King, whose critical comments and encouraging support I have greatly valued. I am especially grateful to both Frow and King for obliging me to be more circumspect in interpreting my title.

Many of the chapters which follow were first presented in draft form at more places than I can remember. As is always the case, I have learned much from these occasions. Particular thanks, however, are due to Stephen Knight and Ken Ruthven, both for their comments on two such occasions as well as for their help and support in other matters. Special thanks, also, to those who commented on an early version of chapter 4 as a result of its presentation at the 1988 conference of the Australian and South Pacific Association of Comparative Literary Studies.

There are some longer-term debts which should be acknowledged, too. To Graham Martin, a special thanks for his interest, help, encouragement and friendship over the years. And, to Terry Eagleton, a tribute to his unending ability to keep the doors of debate and communication open in spite of disagreements. I should also like to thank James Donald for his editorial input to chapter 9 which – although I resisted his suggestions at the time – is considerably improved as a consequence.

I should like, finally, to express my deep appreciation of Raymond Williams's work. His death, in early 1988, was an incalculable loss. Although, now, their limitations are apparent, his early studies still rank as pioneering in the work they have subsequently made possible. Just as important, he was always prepared to respond positively to new intellectual and political challenges, and, in doing so, played a crucial role in helping prevent debate polarise around entrenched positions. Along with many of my generation, my debt to Williams is inestimable – all the more so for the fact that, at times, his help took a personal rather than just theoretical form. His ability to dismantle himself of the robes of his prestige and to show, to all who came into contact with him, an unfailing democratic consideration and kindness is as worthy of commemoration as his writings.

Some of the chapters published here have appeared elsewhere. Chapter 6 was first published in *Thesis Eleven*, no. 12, 1985. Chapter 8 first appeared in a special issue of *Poetics* on *Literary Theory in Australia*, published in 1988, while chapter 9 was first published in *New Formations*, no. 2, summer, 1987. I am grateful to the editors and publishers of these journals for their permission to reprint these materials here. While I have avoided the temptation to modify these articles for the occasion of their publication in this volume I should perhaps indicate that the opening tone of chapter 6 now strikes me as regrettably iconoclastic.

The process of writing, of course, accounts for only a part of the work involved in making a book. My special thanks, therefore, to

Judith Davies, Robyn Skaar and Karen Yarrow in the Division of Humanities at Griffith University for translating my initial scribblings and subsequent revisions into a presentable form. Thanks, also, to the administrative staff of the Division for making this kind of support possible. And books need publishers. Thanks, therefore, to Janice Price for her work in creating a publishing context which has promoted the concerns of literary theory so well, and for her patience in waiting for this book to be produced.

There are, finally, some debts which can never be properly acknowledged. I owe Sue far more than a note of thanks for supporting and encouraging me in completing this book. But she knows that. So it will be enough, here, to record that without her help and understanding, there would have been nothing to write a preface for.

And, to Tanya, Oliver and James: thanks for *not* staying out of the study and for making life infinitely richer and more rewarding than it would otherwise be.

Tony Bennett
Brisbane, 1989

Part I

1

OUTSIDE 'LITERATURE'

Racine lends himself to several languages: psychoanalytic, existential, tragic, psychological (others can be invented, others will be invented); none is innocent. But to acknowledge this incapacity to *tell the truth* about Racine is precisely to acknowledge, at last, the special status of literature. It lies in a paradox: literature is that ensemble of objects and rules, techniques and works, whose function in the general economy of our society is precisely to *institutionalise subjectivity*. To follow this movement, the critic must himself become paradoxical, must lay the fatal bet and talk about Racine in one way and not in another: he too belongs to literature.[1]

In this passage, which occurs toward the end of his essay 'History or literature?', Barthes prepares the ground for finally specifying the distinction between two approaches to literature which it had been his concern, in the preceding pages, to disentangle: the history of literature, concerned with literature as an institution, and criticism, concerned with literature as a creation.

With regard to the former, Barthes argues that literary history, properly conceived and executed, should concern itself with the examination of literary functions – of production, communication, consumption – and their determining institutional conditions. 'In other words,' as he puts it, 'literary history is possible only if it becomes sociological, if it is concerned with activities and institutions, not with individuals.'[2] When posed in this way – historically, institutionally, functionally – the question of literature's being is radically transformed. For a historical ontology of literature, Barthes contends, dissolves its object. 'Now literature's very being,' he writes, 'when restored to history, is no longer a being.'[3] Its place is occupied by a series of dispersed and historically variable functions which exceed the compass of any and all conceptions of literature as an eternity imbued with an unchanging being of its own. From the point of view of these concerns, the study of literature becomes 'the study of techniques, rules, rites and collective mentalities'.[4]

If, however, one takes up the position of the critic inside literature – if, as Barthes puts it, 'one wants to install oneself inside Racine . . . to speak, even if only a word, about the Racinian *self*' – then one must expect to see 'the most prudent critic reveal himself as an utterly subjective, utterly historical being'.[5] For the critic who takes up such a position, there is no truth of literature to be said but merely different ways of speaking about literature within the regimes for the institutionalisation of subjectivity of which criticism forms a part.

Two approaches to literature, then: one which occupies a place within the space of the literary and which works with it as a terrain of practices implicated in the formation of subjectivities, and a second, adopting a position outside literature in order to write its history as a history of functions, rules, techniques and institutions – in short, a history like any other, a history of surfaces without any hidden depths or secreted interiors to fathom.

Perhaps, however, the delineation of these two approaches is not – cannot be – quite so clear as Barthes pretends, and not least because it has a discomfortingly familiar ring about it. For Barthes's formulation bears a striking resemblance to the mutually tolerable division of labour that is often proposed for the relations between criticism and the sociology of literature. The latter is often freely granted sovereignty over what criticism typically construes as the sociological penumbra of literary production (the organisation of literary markets, the structure of the literary profession, and so forth). Yet this is usually at the price of being called on to concede that such considerations bear only tangentially on the 'real stuff' of literature where, accordingly, criticism retains an undisputed monopoly.

The more compelling difficulty, however, is that any construction of an inside/outside polarity in relation to literature can too easily be deconstructed. For what else can such a polarity mark but an impossible boundary between two spaces which, in being posited as interdependent, must seep into and contaminate one another, thus undoing their separateness? Indeed: what can be its purpose but to establish a zone of mutual transgressions? Just as, to bend Derrida, '*Il n'y a pas de hors-texte*', then so there is no outside of literature – no way of writing about it that can be external to it in the sense of being unaffected by, or without consequences for, the way in which the field of literature is currently constituted. Nor, even supposing one could be fashioned, would there be any point in writing from such a position. For if, as Barthes contends, literature is 'that ensemble of objects and rules, techniques and works' whose function is to 'institutionalise subjectivity', what purpose could there be to writing about literature except to contribute to or modify its functioning in this regard? And how could this be done from anywhere else except within, or in some productive relation to, the institutions and discourses which currently comprise the field of literature? Stephen Heath thus notes that while Terry Eagleton 'continually inscribes an "outside" into his work, appealing to political reality, class struggle, as a necessary limit and focus on what he has to say,' his 'gestures away from literature and literary theory, the professional field, . . . are themselves in the field'.[6] Although denying the existence of literature, Eagleton cannot, Heath argues, avoid the contradiction that that very denial is 'a contribution to literary studies' which operates 'in support of those studies and their institution, which are after all the very basis of his intervention, the very condition of its possibility'.[7] There are, of course, many fields of politics outside literature; but no literary politics. And so, of course, no literary theory either; not even of a historical or sociological kind. If literature has no political outside, so it also lacks a theoretical outside, a position from which the history of its functions might be written that is not implicated in the theoretical and political constitution of the prevailing field of literary institutions, practices and debates.

Let me be clear, then, that the literature which, in this study, I seek to distance myself from is not the whole of the existing field of literary practices, institutions and discourses. For these do not add up to a single and unified 'inside' in relation to which an 'outside' might be constituted. Rather, it is the particular *way of thinking* about these which proceeds from the assumption that literature comprises a special kind of writing that is to be understood aesthetically. The distinction is not, of course, a clear one. For this sense of literature – 'literature', that is, as a category of aesthetic discourse – forms a part of the existing constitution and functioning of literary practices, institutions and discourses. None the less, it has a certain strategic and polemical value, suggesting the respects in which – as it is my purpose to argue – an approach which distances itself from 'literature' in this second sense may be better able to understand the organisation of the existing field of literary practices, institutions and discourses and therefore be better equipped, politically, to take advantage of the contradictions within and between these.

Yet the production of a position outside 'literature' is not a matter of mere say-so. There is no ready-made theoretical position outside aesthetic discourse which can simply be taken up and occupied. Such a space requires a degree of fashioning; it must be organised and, above all, won – won from the preponderant cultural weight of aesthetic conceptions of the literary. And won not just for its own sake. The prospect must also be entertained that such a position, when properly fashioned, would significantly modify our understanding as to precisely how literary discourses and practices function as instruments for the formation of subjectivities. This may also engender a clearer understanding of the conditions which must be taken into account in attempts to change the political contexts in which these instruments are deployed. The result may well be, so to speak, to dismantle 'the space of Racine' so that no practice might install itself there while organising new conceptions of the literary in relation to which new practices – of commentary, use and articulation – might be formed and developed. Such, at any rate, it is my purpose to argue and, in so doing, to contribute to the formation of a set of positions outside 'literature' which would allow the theoretical, political and critical concerns prompted by aesthetic conceptions to be significantly recast – or, in some cases, just abandoned.

If such a project is possible today – indeed, is already well underway – it is because the space of literature, its functioning as an institution, is itself undergoing profound transformation. Far from being a natural horizon, the aesthetic conception of 'literature' is now clearly visible as one whose social and historical co-ordinates and institutional and discursive rims are becoming ever more readily perceptible. As customary contrasts – between the 'literary' and the non-literary, for example – lose their purchase, it is now possible to see not merely their edges but beyond their edges and, in realising the full implications of their historicality, to glimpse the possibility of a situation in which they may no longer order and organise the terms of literary production and reception. This is not merely to query the effect of a category ('literature') but concerns its functioning within and across an array of institutions and, accordingly, the challenge of organising positions — discursive and institutional — which will be not just outside 'literature' but beyond it in the sense of opening up new fields of knowledge and action.

Yet such positions cannot be produced *ex nihilo*, as if by magic. They must be worked for and this, like any practice, requires that use be made of the resources to hand — resources which, for the most part, have been shaped and fashioned by and within aesthetic discourse. There can be no question, then, of proceeding as if it were a matter of laying entirely new foundations capable of supporting a brand new theoretical edifice sculpted out of pristine raw materials. Rather, such positions can be organised only by *prising* them away from aesthetic conceptions of literature. Their construction is dependent on a process of extrication through which concepts and methods formed in the sphere of aesthetic discourse are drawn forth from that sphere in order that they might be re-assembled in new theoretical configurations.

It is to this process of extricating — wresting — from aesthetic discourse materials which might be of service in constructing a discursive space external to it that this study addresses itself. It does so via a series of critical engagements with the ways in which literature has been theorised and organised as a site of political intervention within Marxist critical and literary–theoretical writings. However, if this tradition provides the starting point for my discussion, my aim is *not* to elaborate a Marxist literary theory, nor even a Marxist anti-literary theory. For reasons outlined in the next chapter, it no longer seems to me fruitful to regard Marxism as providing a system of concepts adequate to the theorisation of any and all social phenomena, including literary phenomena. Whatever Marxist thought has to contribute to re-theorising literature must be regarded as just that: a contribution, and one which must be co-ordinated with inputs from other theoretical positions in ways which respect their differences rather than organising them in a relation of subordination to Marxism.

That said, a critical interrogation of Marxist literary theory does provide one of the more productive routes through which a set of theoretical positions might be extricated from the sphere of

7

aesthetic discourse. This is less because Marxist literary theory offers a ready-made alternative and opposition to such discourse than, to the contrary, because many of its preoccupations and procedures have become all too clearly ensnared within those of aesthetics. Viewed in their wider aspects, of course, many of the concepts which define the Marxist tradition – the concepts of class, of relations of production and social formation, for example – have a history of use and application which has had little bearing on, and been little affected by, the concerns of literary theory.[8] However, in functioning as the point of mediation between this wider body of theory and aesthetic discourse, Marxist literary theory has worked largely to forge points of accommodation between the former and the latter. The result is a corpus of writings characterised by a tension between, on the one hand, sets of concepts and procedures which have an existence independently of aesthetic discourse but which, on the other, have become entangled with aesthetics through the attempt to construe Marxism as capable of providing an alternative theorisation of literature on the terms established by aesthetic discourse. My purpose, in examining some of the ways in which this entanglement of Marxist thought with aesthetic discourse has been effected, is to disentangle it again; to write a way out of aesthetic discourse by means of a critique of the ways in which Marxist categories have been written into that discourse and, in some cases, have formed a part of it from their very inception.

However, this is not to suggest that the task can be limited to one of purifying Marxist categories, scaling away the effects of their ensnarement within the concerns of conventional literary and aesthetic theory, so that, once set free of such encrustations, all will be well. This was the chief contention of an earlier study, *Formalism and Marxism*, where I argued that the idealist concerns of aesthetics sit so uncomfortably with the historical and materialist orientation of Marxist categories that the attempt to align the two should be abandoned. As I put it then:

> The inheritance of the conceptual equipment which goes with the concerns of aesthetics constitutes the single most effective impediment to the development of a consistently historical and materialist approach to the study of literary texts.[9]

I still think this to be so. Yet, while a necessary stage in the argument, it is not a sufficient one. Even when such issues have been addressed, there remains a thicket of difficulties which derive from the analytical topography of Marxist thought whatever the sphere of its application – difficulties which have become more pressing and insistent over the past decade. These questions are explored more fully in the next chapter where, taking my bearings from recent debates between various Marxist and post-Marxist schools of thought, I outline the stance this study adopts in relation to the concerns of Marxist literary and aesthetic theory as well as to those of Marxist thought more generally.

It may therefore be more pertinent, here, to briefly review the main problem areas addressed in this study. Three issues stand at the fore. The first concerns the effects of conventional Marxist concepts of determination on the terms in which the field of literary-social relations is theorised. The limitations of hierarchised conceptions of the flow of determinations between the different levels of a social formation implied by Marx's base/superstructure metaphor are by now familiar. While, in most recent Marxist writings on literature, these are duly noted, many of the terms suggested by that metaphor continue to inform the ways in which literary/social relations are theorised – usually as a set of relations between two terms regarded as referring to entities of different sorts: literature (a specific component of the domain of representations) on the one hand, and society or history (regarded as a somehow ontologically more solid reality) on the other. The chapters comprising part II propose ways of theorising literary/ social relations – precisely by thinking literary relations *as* social relations – which are not impeded by the effects of such dualistic ontologies.

In these chapters, therefore, my concern is with the specific ways in which difficulties associated with the more general characteristics of Marxist thought have been inflected and worked through within Marxist literary and aesthetic theory. In parts III and IV, by contrast, my attention turns to problems which have their provenance within the formulations and procedures peculiar to the literary and aesthetic regions of Marxist thought. Part III is thus principally concerned with the encounter between Marxism and the traditional concerns of philosophical aesthetics. My main contention here is that the deployment of Marxist categories on the terrain constituted by the great aesthetic theories of the eighteenth and nineteenth centuries has proved a largely fruitless undertaking. The most sophisticated Marxist response to idealist and aestheticist understandings of literature's specificity has consisted in the argument, variously formulated, that literature, viewed as a special kind of writing, is the product of historically specific relations of literary production. In countering this, I suggest that literature is more appropriately regarded as a historically specific, institutionally organised field of textual uses and effects. This is not, to be clear, an argument which seeks to spirit literature away, to dissolve its existence. As Stephen Heath remarks, the historicisation of literature 'does not make it any less real, any less specific (on the contrary)'.[10] Indeed, to theorise literature historically and institutionally is to imbue it with a far more concrete existence than is available from any aesthetic conception of 'literature' and, accordingly, allows questions of literary politics to be posed in a more concrete and specific manner.

These matters are turned to in part IV where the relations between Marxism and criticism are examined in the light of the perspectives developed in the earlier parts of the study. Marxist critics have tended to define the goals and tasks of practices of textual commentary in terms derived from the generalised conceptions of criticism's function associated with nineteenth-century Romanticism. My general argument here resists the appropriative logic of claiming the mantle of that tradition for Marxism in favour of more specific and localised assessments of the effects of practices of textual commentary conducted in the light of the institutionally circumscribed fields of their social deployment.

In sum, then, what follows seeks to delineate a set of concepts, methods and procedures whereby the field of literary/social relations might be theorised non-aesthetically and in whose light the practical issues of critical politics might be rethought. Yet I doubt I have entirely succeeded in this. This is, in part, to note the limited scope of my concerns. For what I have aimed for is a series of extrications – and ones which are only loosely co-ordinated rather than forming parts of a cumulative argument – in which the process of getting out of 'literature' predominates. But it is also a way of noting that, as Althusser observed, the process by which a science emerges from what it comes to name as its ideological prehistory is never finally completed. 'Every recognised science,' as Althusser puts it, 'not only has emerged from its own prehistory, but continues endlessly to do so (its prehistory remains always contemporary: something like its *Alter Ego*) by *rejecting* what it considers to be *error* . . . .'[11] In doing so, moreover, it usually 'operates blindly in the dark, because "it" never knows where it is headed, nor, if it ever arrives, where it is going to surface'.[12] Whether what is offered here succeeds in groping toward a more adequate theoretical framework for the analysis of literary/social relations is not for me to say. As a description of what writing this book has felt like, however, Althusser's formulation could hardly be improved.

2

IN THE CRACKS OF HISTORICAL
MATERIALISM

MARXISM/LITERATURE

In his introduction to *Marxism and Literature*, Raymond
Williams notes the respects in which, since the late 1950s,
questions concerning the relations between Marxism and literature
have had to be posed in new ways:

> Even twenty years ago, and especially in the English-
> speaking countries, it would have been possible to assume,
> on the one hand, that Marxism is a settled body of theory or
> doctrine, and, on the other hand, that Literature is a settled
> body of work, or kinds of work, with known general qualities
> and properties. A book of this kind might then reasonably
> have explored problems of the relations between them or,
> assuming a certain relationship, passed quickly to specific
> applications. The situation is now very different. Marxism, in
> many fields, and perhaps especially in cultural theory, has
> experienced at once a significant revival and a related
> openness and flexibility of theoretical development. Litera-
> ture, meanwhile, for related reasons, has become problematic
> in quite new ways.[1]

While mindful of the difficulties this situation produces,
Williams is primarily concerned to mark its positive influence on
his own intellectual biography. The translation into English of an
increasingly wide and diverse body of continental Marxist theory in
the 1960s and 1970s, he argues, significantly altered what had
previously been the dominant tone of English Marxist argument, a
tone governed by 'the model of fixed and known Marxist positions,
which in general had only to be applied, and the corresponding

dismissal of all other kinds of thinking as non-Marxist, revisionist, neo-Hegelian, or bourgeois'.[2] The availability of the highly variable, and even contradictory, formulations of European Marxism, Williams tells us, considerably increased his respect for the Marxist tradition seen, now, in a new light as an 'active, developing, unfinished, and persistently contentious' body of thinking.[3] Two decades earlier, Williams had been careful to distinguish his own work from the forms of Marxist cultural theory then available to him. Surveying the dispute as to whether or not Christopher Caudwell's work should be regarded as authentically Marxist, he remarked that it was a quarrel 'which one who is not a Marxist will not attempt to resolve'.[4] In *Marxism and Literature*, by contrast, and for the first time in so many words, Williams locates his work unequivocally within the Marxist tradition. The position of cultural materialism developed in the book, he pointedly stresses, is one which he regards as 'a Marxist theory, and indeed that in its specific fields it is, in spite of and even because of the relative unfamiliarity of some of its elements, part of what I at least see as the central thinking of Marxism'.[5]

If, in this study, Williams views the Marxist tradition as sufficiently catholic to accommodate his concerns, the proposal that the concept of cultural materialism be regarded as compatible with Marxist thought entails that the elasticity of the latter be increased still further. Reduced to its essentials, the notion of cultural materialism holds that cultural practices should be regarded as forms of material production. As such, it is advanced as a corrective to the tendency of classical Marxism to view culture as consisting of so many forms of consciousness which, although viewed as dependent on the material processes of economic production, are themselves conceived as subjective and idealist in their constitution and, equally, are deprived of any autonomous sphere of determinancy or effectivity that is distinctively their own.

There can be little doubt that the corrective was called for or that it has proved productive. Even so, it is not entirely clear why the position should be aligned with Marxist thought in particular, or how it might serve to distinguish the claims of Marxism from those of other bodies of theory. For the view that cultural practices should be regarded as forms of material production is, to a large degree, theoretically neutral. It does not itself amount to an articulated body of theory but consists rather of a general

13

proposition (culture is material) which can, in principle, be aligned with widely discrepant traditions of thought and, indeed, in practice has been so aligned. Williams has subsequently argued that, unless cultural forms are regarded as themselves material and as the products of materially organised processes of production, 'it is impossible to think about them in their real social relations'.[6] While this may be so, it is equally true that the mere insistence on the materiality of cultural forms and processes does not itself offer any guidance as to how, then, their social articulations might best be analysed. The thesis of cultural materialism, for example, is equally compatible with, and equally necessary to, the concerns of feminist cultural theory. However, the theoretical consequences that follow from its implementation in this framework are significantly different from, and not necessarily reconcilable with, those associated with its use in Marxist thought.

These remarks are not intended as a critique of Williams's arguments on the subject of cultural materialism. Nor am I concerned to query whether or not the encompassing theoretical framework into which the concept of cultural materialism is integrated in Williams's writings on literature is appropriately regarded as Marxist. At one level, there is no alternative, when writing about Marxism and literature, but to recognise that this involves taking up a position in relation to a contested body of thought which embraces widely diverging forms of analysis exhibiting often sharply contrasting principles of reasoning and method. At the extremes – Plekhanov and Benjamin, say – these positions may have little in common beyond the fact that they locate their concerns within the Marxist tradition, albeit often interpreting that tradition differently and – as is the case with Raymond Williams's work, and his avowed intention – not infrequently redefining it as a consequence. In this sense, Marxism is as thinkers who call themselves Marxists do. So long as the discussion remains at this level, it must accept the full range of variable theoretical practices which the tradition encompasses while also, of course, marking out preferred positions and trajectories from others.

Even so, while it is entirely fitting to welcome the openness and flexibility of Marxism's recent theoretical development, this has tended to exacerbate the difficulties associated with developing Marxist approaches to the study of literature. For it has meant that the precise identity of the body of theory which is thus to be related to the study of literary phenomena in their social connectedness has become somewhat indeterminate. Hence, as Williams notes, the tendency for debate to concern itself with problematic theoretical questions rather than passing 'quickly to specific applications'. Add to this the fact that the concept of literature has also increasingly come to be viewed as problematic and these difficulties begin to assume formidable proportions. Not only do we encounter different Marxisms but these, in turn, produce their differing concepts of 'the literary' or, more recently, deconstruct such concepts and propose alternative ones in their place. When both terms of the equation 'Marxism and literature' are uncertain, this does not augur well for the prospects of examining and developing their interrelations. Indeed, it might be argued that when an uncertain theory encounters an uncertain object – or is unable or unwilling to sustain that object – the time might be right for a paradigm shift.

This possibility presents itself more strongly today than in 1977, when *Marxism and Literature* was first published. The concept of literature, understood as a special kind of writing, has been rendered virtually untenable by the varied and extensive criticisms to which it has since been subjected. Remarking that the term 'literature' usually refers to practices of writing which are *judged* to be valuable, Terry Eagleton notes that, as such judgemental practices may vary, this has the 'fairly devastating consequence' that the concept of literature as a permanent and objective mode of writing cannot then be sustained. 'Literature, in the sense of a set of works of assured and unalterable value, distinguished by certain shared inherent properties,' he argues, 'does not exist.'[7] If this is so, Eagleton concludes, it also means that there cannot be a theory of literature, Marxist or otherwise. For how can there be a theory which fails, discursively, to secure the object it addresses? If the idea of literature is a chimera, then so also, it would seem (although we shall have occasion to question this view), is the prospect of a Marxist theory of literature. Equally, recent debates have resulted in the formulations of classical Marxism being significantly qualified – partly as a result of a series of internal revisions and corrections designed, while preserving certain 'basic principles' intact, to accommodate the criticisms advanced from such alternative theoretical traditions as structuralism, deconstruction and the work of Michel Foucault, and partly in response to changing political circumstances, pressures and alignments. Whatever their causes, however, these revisions are now so many and so far-reaching in their implications as to call into question both the theoretical and political use-value of characterising arguments and positions as Marxist.

It's now more than fifty years since Lukács first introduced a degree of open-endedness into the definition of Marxism:

> Let us assume for the sake of argument that recent research had disproved once and for all every one of Marx's individual theses. Even if this were to be proved, every serious 'orthodox' Marxist would still be able to accept all such modern findings without reservation and hence dismiss all of Marx's theses *in toto* − without having to renounce his orthodoxy for a single moment. Orthodox Marxism, therefore does not imply the uncritical acceptance of the results of Marx's investigations. It is not the 'belief' in this or that thesis, nor the exegesis of a 'sacred' book. On the contrary, orthodoxy refers exclusively to *method*.[8]

This passage has prompted many sociologists to observe, and rightly so, that to place such reliance on a method that is deemed capable, even if only in principle, of producing such shaky results is a peculiar way of proceeding.[9] However, it is what Lukács goes on to say next that is cause for deeper concern as it brings down the shutters on debate just as effectively as if they had never been opened. Marxist orthodoxy, Lukács continues:

> is the scientific conviction that dialectical materialism is the road to truth and that its methods can be developed, expanded and deepened only along the lines laid down by its founders. It is the conviction, moreover, that all attempts to surpass or 'improve' it have led and must lead to over-simplification, triviality and eclecticism.[10]

A science which seeks thus to ordain that the path of its future development shall contain no ruptures or surprises which might qualitatively transform or displace its founding theoretical suppositions and procedures is, of course, no science at all. Although conspicuously invalid, the argument has had deep and long-lasting consequences for the ways in which Marxists have related to alternative arguments. The conception of Marxism as an 'untranscendable horizon', to use the Sartreian term cited by Jameson in *The Political Unconscious*, has been responsible, in the very generosity of its openness, for severely limiting the verve and imagination of Marxist thought.[11] For it requires that whatever new theoretical developments may occur must ultimately find some accommodation with the arguments of Marxism's founders, no matter how tenuous or remote, in order to claim a respectable theoretical and political pedigree. To resist this line of argument is not necessarily to suggest that the moment of Marxism's passage has arrived; but it is to suggest that it might be worth considering whether, assessed in terms of its practical use-value, it might have. The difficulties currently in evidence regarding the prospect of defining a coherent body of theory which might be both successfully defended against its contemporary adversaries and meaningfully affiliated to a Marxist tradition are considerable. So much so that the investment of further effort in this enterprise might be counted a positive impediment to the future development of socialist thought in leading to too much stress being placed on the need to align new arguments with old positions at the expense of engaging productively with socialist issues in a changed constellation of theoretical and political circumstances.

If this is so, then it may be necessary, in order to write productively about the relations between Marxism and literature, to place not merely the concept of literature but also Marxism itself under erasure. It may also be necessary to have in view, as the outcome of an interrogation of Marxist writings on literature, something that will be neither a theory of literature, at least as conventionally understood, nor Marxist but which, equally, will be marked by the process of such an engagement.

POST-MARXISM

To entertain this possibility entails considering the wider question of post-Marxism. Broadly understood, post-Marxism encompasses a heterogeneous assembly of theoretical and political positions which, although socialist in aspiration, have registered a definite break with Marxist thought while also remaining substantially indebted to and affected by the Marxist tradition. In brief, it comprises a theoretical formation which, while announcing a trajectory of its own, none the less remains strongly subject to the gravitational pull of Marxism and consequently describes a close, if also critical, orbit around it. The result of this dual orientation, Stuart Hall has argued, is that post-Marxism is marked by a crucial ambiguity in its continued dependence on the body of theory it criticises and claims to have surpassed. To the degree that Marxist categories continue to dog the steps of their would-be gravediggers, the post-Marxist project of constituting a conceptual space that would be clearly distinct from Marxism remains, as yet, unachieved. All of which, Hall argues, 'gives Marxism a curious life-after-death quality. It is constantly being "transcended" *and* "preserved"'.[12]

Hall goes on to remark that this process is most instructively observed in the contemporary debates which characterise the theory of ideology. Certainly, it is true that the term ideology continues to be widely and extensively used in spite of the undeniably damaging criticisms to which it has been subjected. Moreover, its usage retains many of the aspects associated with its initial formulations in classical Marxism: the perception that the organisation of systems of ideas and the mode of their social operation can be satisfactorily understood only if primary consideration is given to their connections to the prevailing system of class relations, for example. Much the same could be said of many other, equally pivotal Marxist categories. The concepts of mode of production, stages of development, contradiction, the dialectic, materialism and the crucially central concept of class: all of these, although they have been tellingly criticised, continue to be pressed into service, albeit hedged around with qualifications, even by theorists who have queried their viability. Whether, as Hall suggests, this is because the project of post-Marxism is premature – or whether, as another reading might suggest, it is an instance of the fairly common process whereby, as a condition of their emergence, new theoretical paradigms are obliged to make use of inherited vocabularies prior to developing their own – is a moot point. Certainly, it might be argued that it is simply too early to tell whether post-Marxism is destined to remain pinioned on a conceptual threshold it cannot cross or whether what is called for is merely a series of terminological adjustments in order to enable a genuinely new field of concepts to emerge more clearly.

However, this way of posing the matter may be misleading if taken to imply that post-Marxism should be regarded as a potential heir to Marxism, capable of supplying a unified and unifying body of theory which offers a more satisfactory way of accounting for the organisation, make-up and development of historical societies and the relations between them. This is not merely to say that no such body of theory is as yet even remotely visible. Rather, such an expectation is forestalled by some of the more searching criticisms to which Marxist thought has been subjected in the process of post-Marxism's emergence. Although his purpose is to check and limit their potentially disruptive effects, Hall is right to argue that criticisms of the concept of ideology have played a particularly important role in this regard. For these have supplied the main route through which perspectives derived from linguistics, semiology, discourse theory and deconstruction have been brought into critical contact with Marxist thought. Spilling over and beyond the theory of ideology, the knock-on effects of such theoretical encounters have been considerable. For they have not merely queried specific Marxist formulations or concepts but have seriously unsettled the very analytical topography of Marxist thought, raising awkward questions for the kind of theoretical enterprise it embodies, particularly in its holistic variants.

The most obvious casualty of these critical engagements has been the collapse of the hierarchy of determinations implied by the base/superstructure conception of the relations between economic conditions and ideological forms and processes. However, this has been less important in itself than for the repercussions which have followed from it. For the uncoupling of such associated dichotomies of Marxist thought as that between being and consciousness, or between the real and its representations, has had the further consequence of challenging the conventional Marxist allocation of analytical priorities within the space produced by these dichotomies. According to classical Marxist formulations, being is regarded as existing prior to and as determining the forms in which it is consciously reflected. Or, in the more recent terminological recasting of this problematic, the real is posited as existing independently of and as determining the ideological forms in which it is represented. Criticisms of the dichotomous structure of this analytical space have placed the explanatory logic of Marxist thought under considerable duress. The view that ideological practices should be conceived as actively organising social relations in their own right – a view suggested by the increased emphasis placed on their autonomous properties and effects – has thus called into question the contention that economic and social relations can be posited as existing independently of representational or discursive forms as well as the assumption that the former might be invoked as the determining ground of the latter.

The attempts to revise Marxist concepts and formulations in order to accommodate such arguments, and yet not stretch those concepts and formulations so far as to transform the integrity of Marxist thought beyond recognition, have been many and varied: Louis Althusser's concept of determination in the last instance, for example, or Nicos Poulantzas's attempt to theorise class relations as being constituted in and by a complexly interacting weave of economic, political and ideological relationships.[13] None, however, has been entirely successful. Indeed, to be blunt, most are visibly flawed by the kind of insupportable tension which results from any theoretical enterprise which seeks to negotiate a *modus vivendi* between logically contradictory propositions. None the less, the reasons for this kind of activity, which can be expected to persist, are clear: unless they can be contained by means of some such accommodation, the difficulties I have pointed to multiply and proliferate with even more disruptive consequences. For example, if it is conceded that ideological or discursive relations partially constitute and form an integral component of social relations, the notion that discourse and society might be differentiated as distinct spheres of activity becomes problematic. Acceptance of this is obviously difficult within the framework of Marxist thought in the respect that its analytical procedures have usually been predicated on the assumption that it is possible, at least conceptually, to clearly distinguish between different spheres of human activity in order that their interrelations might then be examined.

It is in allowing such arguments to run their course that post-Marxism has most clearly distinguished itself from critical or revisionist forms of Marxism in their attempts either to restrain contradictory theoretical developments or to adjust Marxist categories in order to make some room for them. Two such aspects of post-Marxism may usefully be commented on here, particularly as they illustrate the respects in which, in arguing the need to go beyond Marxism, post-Marxists are also committed to a more general project in arguing the need for a transcendence of other systems of thought inherited from the nineteenth century which, although distinct from Marxism in their particularities, are none the less committed to similar forms of theorising. The first, in which Marxism is grouped with sociology, concerns the criticisms that have been advanced against a foundational conception common to both traditions: namely, that society – or a social formation in Marxist parlance – can be constituted as an intelligible object of knowledge.[14] If, the argument goes, social relations are, in part, discursive relations then, since discursive relations are, in their turn, partly relations of meaning and, owing to the diacritical structure of all signification, are therefore characterised by a degree of fluidity and indeterminacy, it becomes difficult to see how the idea of society can be regarded as supplying a conceptually 'fixed' or stabilised object of which there might be a systematic and accumulating knowledge.

The terms of this argument have been most forcibly and succinctly developed by Ernesto Laclau and Chantal Mouffe. Rejecting the possibility of any distinction between discursive and non-discursive practices, Laclau and Mouffe argue that it is consequently necessary 'to abandon, as a terrain of analysis, the premise of "*society*" as a sutured and self-defined totality'.[15] The discursivity inherent in social relations, they argue, means that it is impossible to locate a unifying principle, such as that traditionally supplied by the concept of mode of production, capable of serving as the organising centre for a concept of society as a rationally ordered whole which might reveal its nature to a rationally ordered intelligence. They therefore reject the view that society can be conceived as an integrated whole within which every part is fixed in its position and functioning in relation to every other part by virtue of its relations to a central principle (or contradiction) which underlies the structure of social relationships. Instead, they envisage the field of the social as a network of dispersed differences caught up in a mobile and incessantly changing set of articulatory (and therefore contingent and provisional) relations to one another. Such a disunified set of moving relations, they argue, cannot be stabilised for analysis in the forms required by the unifying theoretical projects of either Marxism or sociology. Nor can they be constituted as an object for a totalising political transformation whereby, in consequence of the effects of a transformation of the relations of production, society will be restructured in its entirety.

It is in this sense, to recall the terms of Lukács's discussion of orthodox Marxism, that post-Marxism has queried not merely this or that thesis of Marxism, nor merely its methods, but has additionally called into question the very kind of theoretical attention it embodies. The claim is not the familiar one that Marxist categories, while adequate to the analysis of nineteenth-century capitalism, need to be updated and revised in order to come to terms with the more complex structure of advanced capitalist societies. Rather, it is argued that, in certain crucial respects, those categories were *always* misconceived and, consequently, that the erroneous predictions to which they gave rise should be regarded as the product of a theoretical apparatus that was flawed from the outset rather than as mere contingencies.

Post-Marxism has also, and just as crucially, registered a departure from the terrain and concerns of epistemology. This has a considerable bearing on what have proved to be the central and enduring preoccupations of Marxist literary theory. Had there not been a Marxist epistemology, there could not have been – and perhaps would have been no need for – a Marxist aesthetic either. As one of my purposes in this book is to argue that this would have been no bad thing, I shall postpone a fuller consideration of these questions for a later chapter. Suffice it to note, for present purposes, that an insistence on the discursivity of social relations dismantles the thought/reality opposition which, as Richard Rorty has argued, supplies the surface of emergence for, and conditions of intelligibility of, the central question of epistemology: how can a relationship of correspondence between thought and reality be established in order that the truth claims of the former might be vindicated.[16] The maintenance of such a thought/reality distinction has often been regarded as politically crucial for Marxist thought. As Paul Patton has noted, the desire for a normative epistemology by means of which Marxism's truth claims – and, thereby, its political credentials – might be privileged above those of competing bodies of theory has usually been accompanied by a concept of materialism according to which reality is conceived as existing prior to and independently of thought in order that it might supply a fixed point of truth in relation to which competing claims to knowledge might be adjudicated: usually, in the Marxist lexicon, by the acid test of practice. The major exception is Althusser's conception of knowledge as a property entirely internal to scientific discourses which, as Patton observes, says 'nothing about the capacity of such "scientific" discourse to provide a useful guide to practice in the real world'.[17]

However, it has been largely via a sustained critique of Althusser's work that the anti-epistemological thrust of post-Marxism has been developed. The work of Barry Hindess and Paul Hirst has been perhaps the most influential – and certainly the most contentious – in this respect. Insisting that 'discourse is

22

interminable' in the sense that 'the forms of closure of discourse promised in epistemological criteria of validity do not work'[18] – that is, do not provide an adequate means of deciding between the contradictory truth claims of different discourses – they argue '*that there can be no "knowledge" in political practice*'.[19] In place of an epistemological conception of knowledge as a relation of correspondence between the thought of a subject and an independently existing object, Hindess and Hirst substitute the notion of *calculation* as the regulative orientation governing all forms of social practice. In the case of political practice, this involves political agents (such as political parties) in 'the *calculation* of effect, of the possibilities and results of political action',[20] with such calculations being affected by the discursive and political relations prevailing during the circumstances in which they are made. In brief, what is offered in place of the foundational certainties of Marxist epistemologies is 'political calculation as a practice with political conditions and without privilege of epistemological guarantees . . .'.[21]

Theoretically, then, post-Marxism is most distinctively characterised by the respects in which it has criticised, sought to distance itself from and to develop alternatives to the view of Marxism as a unifying body of theory committed to developing a totalising knowledge of the laws governing the constitution and development of historical societies, whose validity is to be assessed in terms of its correspondence to the independently existing realities of those societies. 'Just as the era of normative epistemologies has come to an end, so too has the era of universal discourses': it is this conspectus, as Laclau and Mouffe put it, that characterises the distinctive theoretical impetus of post-Marxism.[22]

However, this argument is not merely theoretical either in character or its consequences. The anti-unifying theoretical impetus of post-Marxism has been accompanied by a retreat from, and disavowal of, the traditional Marxist claim that the class struggle between the proletariat and the bourgeoisie constitutes a central political contradiction around which all oppositional struggles can, one day and even just for a day, be expected to unify in a moment of revolutionary rupture. Indeed, it has been the emergence of such oppositional forces as feminism and the peace movement which, in contesting Marxism's ordering of political priorities, has led also to a questioning of its theoretical priorities. The effect of such movements, as Paul Patton argues, 'has been to challenge the pretension of marxism to unify the field of oppositional politics' just as the related emergence of 'quite different concepts and forms of discourse' has challenged its position as 'the "master discourse" on the left'.[23] It is thus not merely the form of theorising which Marxism embodies but, as Laclau and Mouffe argue, the kind of political imaginary associated with that form of theorising that has fallen into disrepute:

> What is now in crisis is a whole conception of socialism which rests upon the ontological centrality of the working class, upon the role of Revolution, with a capital 'r', as the founding moment in the transition from one type of society to another, and upon the illusory prospect of a perfectly unitary and homogeneous collective will that will render pointless the moment of politics. The plural and multifarious character of contemporary social struggles has finally dissolved the last foundation for that political imaginary. Peopled with 'universal' subjects and conceptually built around History in the singular, it has postulated 'society' as an intelligible structure that could be intellectually mastered on the basis of certain class positions and reconstituted, as a rational, transparent order, through a founding act of a political character. Today, the Left is witnessing the final act of the dissolution of that Jacobin imaginary.[24]

In summary, then, post-Marxism constitutes a theoretical and political space which 'goes beyond' Marxism in terms both of the forms of politics and of the modes of theorising to which it is committed. However, rather than simply abandoning Marxist thought, it remains strongly orientated to it as an intellectual tradition which, if its concerns and formulations are reworked, may still contribute powerfully to the formation of a new theory and politics. Marxism is to be preserved but only, so to speak, as the site for a critical salvage operation.

Reactions to such criticisms from within Marxism have been varied. Two, however, may usefully be distinguished. According to the first, the appropriate response is one of 'business as usual', or nearly so. This stance has received its most succinct expression in Perry Anderson's – to use his own phrase – 'cadastral survey of the present state of Marxist theory': *In the Tracks of Historical Materialism*.[25] Offering a 'Marxism of Marxism' in which Marxism is viewed as 'a *self*-critical theory capable of explaining its own

24

genesis and metamorphoses',[26] Anderson thus accords Marxism a unique status as a body of theory that is able to account for its transformations in terms of its own concepts. Given such a starting point, serious criticisms of Marxism scarcely get a look-in. While the specific contours of Marxism's development may be full of surprises, these always turn out to be merely the workings of the ruse of history whose necessities can be confidently predicted after they have happened. The so-called 'crisis of Marxism' thus transpires to have been limited to Latin Europe and – in the broad perspective of cadastral surveys – to have been more than compensated for by, of all things, the rise of British Marxist historiography. This, in showing that 'theory is now history' just as 'history is equally theory',[27] is said to have transformed what, from a lowlier vantage point, looked like a period of severe difficulty for Marxist thought into a period of theoretical self-enrichment.

And so it goes. Crises turn into hiccups just as unexpected reversals of theoretical fortune pave the way for subsequent triumphs: all a part of the twists and turns of Marxism's dialectical advance. To be sure, there are problems. The 'immemorial oppression of women' is a bit of a poser, leading Anderson to express some caution regarding the limits of Marxism's totalising ambit. But not much. Marxism may be characterised by problems and lacunae just as it is confronted with opposing theoretical enterprises and political imaginaries which it has not yet succeeded in aligning to, or subsuming within, itself. For all that, though, it is still the best bet around and for much the same reasons Lukács advanced in the 1920s in construing Marxism as the self-consciousness of History. Anderson's terminology is slightly different, but little else has changed:

> For historical materialism remains the only intellectual paradigm capacious enough to be able to link the ideal horizon of a socialism to come with the practical contradictions and movements of the present, and their descent from structures of the past, in a theory of the distinctive dynamics of social development as a whole . . . it will not be replaced so long as there is no superior candidate for comparable overall advance in knowledge.[28]

In brief, as Ronald Aronson succinctly puts it, Anderson 'produces a breathtaking sketch in which Marxism ends where it began, as *the* theory and practice of our world'.[29] If, Aronson goes on to remark, Anderson succeeds in staving off the crisis of

Marxism, it is only by denying that it ever existed in the first place.

Where the claims of post-Marxism are accorded due weight and engaged with theoretically, an altogether different assessment is appropriate. This is particularly true of the work of Stuart Hall who, over the past decade, has engaged in a series of running theoretical skirmishes with structuralism, Hindess and Hirstism, Foucaultianism and, latterly, the currency of post-Marxism itself. These engagements have consistently been characterised by a willingness, so to speak, to give the devil his due. Hall, that is, acknowledges the difficulties raised by such intellectual traditions and, accordingly, accepts that many Marxist formulations may need to be corrected and revised in order to remain both theoretically credible and politically usable. This orientation has been most conspicuously manifest in his writings on ideology. These have exhibited a preparedness to override Marx's formulations on the subject in the light of more recent debates, to the extent of conceding that the real does not determine, at least not in any simple or direct way, the forms in which it is ideologically represented. An understanding of the latter, Hall has always contended, requires that proper attention be paid to the autonomous properties of ideological discourses, the institutions that circulate them and so on. His sticking point, though, and it's a crucial one, is to insist that, none the less, the real *does* exist prior to the ideological forms in which it is represented.

The difficulties to which this gives rise are clearly visible in the essay cited at the beginning of this section. Hall's stated purpose in this is to retain many of the insights of Marx's writings on ideology while also expanding and qualifying them in the light of more recent theories. Proceeding via a discussion of Marx's argument that the appearances of market exchange under capitalism generate the ideological categories – such as those of freedom and equality – through which those relations are represented in thought, Hall queries the view that this ordains 'a fixed, determinate and unalterable relationship between market exchange and how it is appropriated in thought'.[30] Recognition of the autonomous properties of language, discourse and the whole terrain of signification also entails recognising that the same real relations may be available to thought via different systems of ideological representation. The problem here concerns the sense that is to be attached to the notion of 'real relations' and the means by which access to such an extra-discursive terrain is to be acquired. The difficulties this occasions become acute as Hall proceeds to elaborate his argument:

> The same process – capitalist production and exchange – can be expressed within a different ideological framework, by the use of different 'systems of representation'. There is the discourse of 'the market', the discourse of 'production', the discourse of 'the circuits': each produces a different definition of the system. Each also locates us differently – as worker, capitalist, wage worker, wage slave, producer, consumer, etc. Each thus *situates us* as social actors or as a member of a social group in a particular relation to the process and prescribes certain social identities for us. The ideological categories in use, in other words, *position us* in relation to the account of the process as depicted in the discourse. The worker who relates to his or her condition of existence in the capitalist process as 'consumer' – who enters the system, so to speak, through that gateway – participates in the process by way of a different practice from those who are inscribed in the system as 'skilled labourer' – or not inscribed in it at all, as 'housewife'. All these inscriptions have effects which are real. They make a material difference, since how we act in certain situations depends on what our definitions of the situation are.[31]

The crucial slippage here occurs between the fourth and fifth sentences. In the first of these, Hall's contention is that ideological discourses situate social actors by inscribing them in differing and particular relations to the *same real process of capitalist production and exchange*. The following sentence, however, although seeming to elaborate the same point, advances a quite different argument: that ideological discourses produce positions for social actors by inscribing them in a relationship *not* to the real process of capitalist exchange and production but to an *'account of the process as depicted in discourse'*. There's a world of difference between these two formulations, and one which affects the conclusion Hall goes on to draw: that is, that ideological discourses 'have effects which are real' in the sense that, by inscribing social actors in different relations to the same real processes with consequent implications for their actions, they have repercussions on and for those processes. It is clear, here, that we are to understand ideologies as having effects on a set of real relations and processes conceived as existing independently of discourse. The second formulation, however, undercuts this conclusion. It suggests that ideologies are to be understood not as *acting upon* a set of real economic processes external to them, but as *partially constituting* such processes through the inscriptions they effect. In brief, ideological discourses do not impinge upon economic processes as a set of secondary modifications to them but help make up those processes. Since, correspondingly, economic processes are thus conceived as being partially constituted by and through the variable ideological inscriptions of social actors, such processes cannot be granted the 'fixity' that would allow them to be regarded as identical to themselves such that they might serve as a common ground giving rise to variable ideological expressions. Clearly, in this passage, Hall tries both to have his realist cake and eat it too, reverting to realist formulations which his own analysis undercuts in order – to recall the sticking point of Hall's revisionism – to retain a ground of the real upon which Marxism's claims to truth might be validated.

THE CURRENCY OF MARXIST CRITICISM

The stances toward post-Marxism adopted by Anderson and Hall have their equivalents in Marxist literary theory. Anderson's position is most closely approximated by Fredric Jameson. Indeed, in its more thoroughgoing and philosophically self-conscious totalising impetus, Jameson's work foregrounds and accentuates the Hegelianised conception of Marxism as an unsurpassable horizon which underlies many of Anderson's formulations in spite of the stress he places on the empirical temper of historical inquiry. This is particularly true of *The Political Unconscious* in its vision of a 'pac-man Marxism' capable of gobbling up everything in its path, ingesting structuralism, post-structuralism and deconstruction, correcting their errors while preserving their valuable insights in a seemingly unstoppable, ever-onward dialectical movement of synthesis and transcendence.

By contrast, Terry Eagleton has entered into a more open-ended and, consequently, more productive dialogue with the now burgeoning industry of literary theory. He has thus been punctilious, in his numerous skirmishes with deconstruction, to distinguish Derrida's position from that of the Yale school. Moreover, although sharply critical of the overall direction of Derrida's project, Eagleton has unequivocally conceded both its theoretical significance and its political import. Rather than aiming, Jameson-like, at a pre-emptive closure of debate by seeking to integrate elements of deconstruction into Marxism's unending self-regenerative advance, Eagleton has been more disposed to let Derrida's concepts off the leash in order to provide some grit in the machinery of Marxist thought which might prompt some realignment of the relations between its component parts. Even so, there are limits to Eagleton's revisionism. As with Hall, certain issues are not negotiable, including the question of the priority of the real over the modes of its representation. Wherever the discursivity of the real is insisted upon, Eagleton argues, the consequence is a dilettantist intellectualism serving as an accomplice to political quietism.[32]

Similarly, except for *Criticism and Ideology* – something of a detour, although a consequential one, in the trajectory of Eagleton's work – Eagleton has remained committed to a traditional conception of the political role and vocation of Marxist criticism. 'The primary task of the "Marxist critic",' he writes in his study of Walter Benjamin, 'is to actively participate in and help direct the cultural emancipation of the masses.'[33] As he has subsequently affirmed, this means that, ultimately, the function of Marxist criticism is predicated on the construction of a revolutionary party.[34] Of course, Eagleton is under no illusions that such a role for criticism is currently in prospect. Indeed, in his recent pronouncements on the subject, Eagleton tends to veer between two poles. On the one hand, a good deal is invested in what a Marxist criticism might accomplish under more propitious circumstances. Its role, in the formulations of *The Function of Criticism*, is to assist in the process of revolutionary will formation; that is, to contribute, via a reformation of the consciousness of social actors, to the development of a revolutionary social force ranged against the bourgeois state. On the other hand, in the here and now, nothing of great consequence seems to hinge on how it is conducted.

I shall return, in a later chapter, to argue more fully my reasons for doubting the usefulness of this way of posing the question of criticism's contemporary political vocation. In brief, though, as one given rather more to the utilitarian than to the utopian aspects

29

of the Marxist tradition, it seems likely that a criticism which regards itself as having missed its opportunity once (in the 1920s and 1930s) and which awaits its recurrence is unlikely, in thus preparing itself for a re-match with history, to relate itself productively to the fields of activity that are concretely and practicably available to it in the meantime. For there are other ways of thinking about the role of criticism from within a Marxist framework than that which sees its ultimate vindication in the degree to which it succeeds in establishing contact with the working masses and contributing to the formation of their revolutionary consciousness.

And this bears on my reasons for raising these considerations here: namely, to suggest that what is invested in the currency of Marxism – and, consequently, the practical issues at stake in either preserving that currency or jettisoning it – varies from one institutional site of its discursive application to another. For it is misleading to proceed as if the Marxist tradition possessed a singular currency such that intellectual work needs to be aligned either with or against it across all the surfaces of its operation. As Paul Patton argues:

> As an effective political operator, marxism functions on a variety of diverse social surfaces throughout the world. Accordingly, there can be no single crisis of marxism. It must be asked: which marxism, and for whom is there crisis?[35]

This is a helpful formulation in suggesting a need to estimate the varying kinds of effectivity and presence that can be claimed for Marxist discourses across the diverse social surfaces on which they have been politically operative. It is thus important to recognise that, with the exception of brief periods – the aftermath of the October revolution in Russia and the 1920s in Germany, for example – Marxist writings on literature and, more generally, aesthetics have impinged only marginally on the concerns of labour movements. For better or worse, the primary social surface on which Marxist literary and aesthetic discourses have functioned as 'effective political operators' has been that constituted by educational institutions – and the university systems in particular – of advanced capitalist societies. It is equally clear that such discourses have been deeply marked by this situation, as is evident in their characteristic concerns, orientations and modes of address.

Michel Foucault has argued that French Marxist intellectuals who followed the line of the French Communist Party in the 1950s sought to align their work with the interests and problems of the universities in order to acquire their recognition and, thereby, increase the status accorded to Marxism within French culture. The consequence, he argues, was that Marxists sought 'to take up the "noblest", most academic problems in the history of the sciences', focusing on mathematics and physics rather than psychiatry and medicine which, since they did not 'stand on the same level as the great forms of classical rationalism', hardly seemed to merit the same attention. 'We may be Marxists,' Foucault writes in parody of this orientation, 'but for all that we are not strangers to your preoccupations, rather we are the only ones able to provide new solutions for your old concerns.'[36]

A more apt characterisation of the central, almost constitutive, orientation of Marxist literary and aesthetic theory would be hard to come by. The specificities of art and literature; the determination of the peculiarity of the aesthetic as a cognitive mode; the problem of aesthetic value: these have been enduringly to the forefront of Marxist theoretical attention, as if to say to the literary intelligentsia: 'We may be materialists, but for all that we appreciate art too and, moreover, can elaborate and account for its unique and transcendent properties better than you can.' At least until recently, the tradition has produced conspicuously few attempts to displace the central problems and concerns of bourgeois literary and aesthetic theory. Instead, the primary orientation has been to forge some kind of accommodation between the historical and materialist bent of Marxist categories and the universalising disposition of bourgeois concepts of art, literature and the aesthetic. The result has been a tortuously skewed discourse in which Marxist principles of social and historical determination have been pressed into service largely in order to account for a pre-given conception of art and literature as practices transcendent to their determinations.

This is not to imply that the tradition is lacking in positive achievements. It is possible, however, to arrive at different assessments of these achievements. Perry Anderson has argued of western Marxism – a tradition which, as Anderson defines it, begins with Lukács, runs through the Frankfurt School and comes to a close in the work of Althusser and Colletti – that the inquiries into aesthetics produced in this period 'may in the end prove to be the most permanent collective gain of this tradition'.[37] My own view is somewhat different. For the aesthetic theories which proliferate and mark the trajectory of western Marxism are more meaningfully viewed in a positive light if assessed for their conjunctural ideological yield rather than for their long-term theoretical consequences. Indeed, to sharpen the point, I would argue that such gains were made at the price of *closing off* the tradition's longer-term theoretical and political potential. To the degree that the writings of Lukács, Benjamin, Marcuse, Adorno, Della Volpe and Althusser locate their concerns mainly within or in relation to those of the tradition of philosophical aesthetics developed in the course of the eighteenth and nineteenth centuries, their primary achievement was that of appropriating bourgeois aesthetic discourse for Marxism. The consequence and theoretical price of this achievement, however, was a bourgeoisification of Marxist discourse in so far as an inherited sense of the aesthetic was thus made to comprise one of the surfaces of its operation. As a result, the texts comprising this tradition are systemically ambiguous. In effect, by installing a Marxist aesthetic in the place previously occupied by bourgeois aesthetics, they constitute the swan song of bourgeois aesthetic discourse, both potentially nullifying that discourse while at the same time perpetuating it.

On the one hand, the deployment of the socialising and historicising impetus of Marxist categories within the discursive field of aesthetic theory has seriously disabled bourgeois aesthetics by revealing the class discourses which lie behind its universalising tendencies, unmasking its universality as a pseudo-universality. In further harnessing those universalising tendencies to the cause of a generalised human emancipation as represented by Marxism (in its humanist and historicist variants), Marxist aesthetic theory has constituted an undoubted impediment to the continued use of philosophical aesthetics as a discursive site for the development and legitimation of bourgeois cultural hegemony. On the other hand, though, in thus presenting itself as the legitimate heir to, and logical outcome of, bourgeois philosophical aesthetics, Marxist aesthetic theory remains a move *within* that problematic albeit the *last* move and, indeed, the *last possible* move – but one which is secured merely rhetorically by the invocation of an ideal futurity in which both the subject and object of aesthetic judgement will be genuinely universalised. The effect of this, however, is largely to limit the socialising and historicising impetus of Marxist categories in subordinating them – and, in the meantime, concrete questions of cultural politics also – to the movement of a historically produced, but yet-to-be-achieved unity.

If, then, as I am suggesting, the history of Marxist aesthetics is best regarded as comprising the course through which bourgeois philosophical aesthetics has been worked out and brought to grief against insurmountable obstacles, this is by no means a negligible achievement. It is, however, one that needs to be placed in historical perspective, for the accomplishment is not one that needs to be or can be never-endingly repeated – as some contemporary Marxists are wont to do – except at the price of boomeranging on itself, and quite badly. For the productivity of developing a Marxist alternative to bourgeois aesthetics on the terrain of philosophical aesthetics must now surely be questioned given that this terrain has largely been abandoned. It no longer furnishes the privileged or even a major site for the elaboration of bourgeois claims to cultural hegemony. Of course, older variants of the problematic – particularly the Kantian aesthetic – continue to be pressed into service, hence the need to subject them to a continuing critique. But philosophical aesthetics has not produced any active or developing contemporary heirs except – and the paradox must be faced – for Marxist aesthetics. In this circumstance, an entirely different set of calculations pertains. While it may be appropriate to assess the achievements of western Marxism postively for having pushed the discourse of philosophical aesthetics to its internal breaking point, the continued rehearsal of a customised Marxist aesthetics must be counted as deeply regressive in furnishing what is now virtually the only avenue through which the idealist concerns of bourgeois aesthetics retain a contemporary currency.

BEING HISTORICAL AND MATERIALIST

I can now, in the light of these considerations, return to my opening discussion regarding the position that can most produc- tively be taken up, today, in writing about the relations between Marxism and literature. The tradition of theorising about literature bequeathed to us by western Marxism, I have argued, no longer provides a satisfactory basis for the study of the relations between literary phenomena and social processes. The difficulties associated with the tradition are such that they cannot be overcome by working on the theoretical terrain established by its founding assumptions and procedures, correcting and refining these through a process of extension and revision. Rather, it is necessary to have in view a more radical re-working of the tradition, one which will proceed by querying the assumptions governing the terms in which questions are put and answers sought so as to establish a significantly different terrain on which to interrogate the relations between literary and social processes.

This is partly because, within this tradition, the socialising and historicising impetus of Marxist categories has been held in check or deflected from what might have been more productive avenues of inquiry by dint of its susceptibility to the idealist categories of bourgeois aesthetic discourse. However, as I suggested in the previous chapter, it would be misleading to imply that such problems are of an accidental or contingent kind, the product of alien and external theoretical accretions which have merely to be scaled away in order to reveal an underlying bedrock of concepts which, once available in their pure form, have merely to be applied. Such idealist deformations are constitutive of Marxist aesthetic discourse; they *define* the tradition rather than comprising its incidental and, therefore, easily corrigible by-products.

Many of these difficulties are indissolubly associated with the broader problems which are now evident in the structure and analytical topography of Marxist thought as a whole. Of the problems discussed thus far, those which call into question the totalising ambit of Marxist thought and its related tendency to secure for itself an epistemological privilege over contending discourses are especially relevant. For such arguments have been crucial to the formation of Marxist aesthetics, particularly in supporting its own totalising claims and privileging procedures. To call these more general characteristics of Marxist thought into question, therefore, unsettles many of the more particular concepts, formulations and procedures of Marxist aesthetics. These difficulties are particularly acute in relation to the tactical and strategic questions that are posed by the practical conduct of Marxist criticism. Too often, the practical tasks of Marxist criticism are simply mortgaged to totalising conceptions of criticism's function which, in their turn, derive their cogency from totalising theories of knowledge whose objectives and methods can no longer be supported. Finally, account must also be taken of the difficulties which Marxist aesthetic theory shares with Marxist approaches to other spheres of ideological activity, particularly in their tendency toward a dualistic ontology of the social: being and consciousness, the real and its representations.

It is for these reasons, then, that, rather than following its tracks, my aim is to work in the cracks of historical materialism, to probe the deficiencies of its legacy in the aesthetic realm in order to facilitate what I hope will prove to be more productive and politically pertinent lines of inquiry. In doing so, I shall draw on non-Marxist theories (principally those of Foucault and deconstruction). I do so, however, not with a view to effecting some higher-level synthesis between their concerns and those of Marxism. Rather, my purpose is to use elements of these traditions to identify more clearly the problems which need to be addressed in order to develop a historical sociology of literary forms, functions and effects – a sociology which, while it will recognise a host of problems of a *particular* kind concerning the relations between literary and social processes, will not argue for the existence of any problems of a *special* kind, occasioned by the peculiarities of an aesthetic mode, which require that historical and sociological modes of reasoning be transcended. But – and equally – it is also my purpose to argue for a sociology which, unlike classical Marxism or classical sociology, will not construe literary and other texts as the epiphenomenal manifestations of underlying social 'realities' but will rather insist on their status as directly active components in the organisation of social relations themselves.

In brief, what I have in view is the development of a theoretical framework that will enable the investigation of literary/social relations to proceed from historical and materialist premises, albeit not always those – and not only those – of historical materialism. The distinction is necessary because of the ambiguous currency of the term 'historical materialism' and the nature of its association with Marxism. On the one hand, it refers to the distinctive particularities of Marxist thought in its founding of all social conflicts in the capitalist mode of production. Yet, as Mark Poster argues, it also refers to the broader impetus of Marxist thought which 'takes all social practices as transitory and all intellectual formations as indissociably connected with power and social relations'.[38] Yet however true it may be that this perspective originated with Marxism, it is now by no means limited to it. Nor can the two be connected in the form of a privileged relation. Foucaultians, feminists and even some schools of deconstruction all say the same thing, and often with better credentials – at least in literary studies – for practising what they preach.

As we have seen, Lukács introduced a degree of openness into his definition of Marxism, but only to close it down again in decreeing that the path of its future development could contain no surprises or fundamental transformations. Derrida, never one to close things down, proposes an alternative conception of Marxism's openness:

> Marxism presents itself, has presented itself from the beginning with Marx, as an open theory which was continually to transform itself. . . . It is one which does not refuse *a priori* developments of problematics which it does not believe to have itself engendered, which appear to have come from outside.[39]

In his attempt critically to articulate Marxism and deconstruction, Michael Ryan endorses this view. Its merit, he argues, is that it accepts the necessary indeterminacy and incessant mobility of the object (history) to which Marxism must open itself:

> Marxism, as a historical mode of theory and practice, is from the outset undecidable, that is, open to extension according to what history proffers. To constitute marxism as an axiomatic system immune to the historical opening of undecidability (the revelation of incompleteness) and the necessity of extension is both antimarxist and un-scientific. . . . From the moment at which its axioms are established, it opens itself to extension according to the movement of history. Its axioms are always provisional, because history is a domain of change, modification and extension – open-ended.[40]

The argument is attractive in that it neither denies nor guarantees Marxism a future but suggests, instead, that its claims to continuing relevance will depend on how it is practised. If, as Ryan suggests, Marxism is best regarded as a co-ordinated set of theoretical strategies which take their cue from a specific body of theoretical writings and share its political affiliations, then the question of its future is not resolvable by appeals to epistemology or to the inviolable status of this or that axiom. Rather, it depends on how effectively Marxist thought opens itself to engage with new systems of thought – and not with a view to absorbing them but accepting the need to learn from, and be complemented by, them – in order to influence the conduct of socialist politics in constantly changing circumstances.

Yet, if Marxism's identity is forever undecidable, it becomes merely a blank cheque which can never be cashed; a theory destined always to be around even though no one knows quite what it is or might yet be. This merely fetishises Marxism, as if it were important to keep it alive at any price and, seemingly, just for the sake of it. For, ultimately, it is not Marxism's openness that is in question but our own, and that openness will prove an empty gesture unless we can say of Marxism as we would of any other body of theory – for Marxism has no claim to be special in this regard – that it is characterised by specific forms of reasoning whose capacity for adjustment in response to new developments is subject to definite limitations. It is only a nervous concern for political credentials that converts such a programme of theoretical and practical assessment into a commitment to a body of theory which has a name but no definable substance. Nothing is served by making Marxism undecidable in this way. To the contrary, its particularity and historical determinateness have become progressively clearer the more its claims to constitute *the* theory of our times have been shown to be insupportable – not by anti-Marxist idealisms but by traditions of thought sharing the socialising and historicising impetus Marxism inaugurated. What *is* undecidable – or, at least, undecided – are the new forms of theoretical reasoning and political practice that will emerge from a continuing open and critical engagement within and between the now many and varied traditions of thought concerned with the historicality and sociality of forms of human conduct, subjectivity and inter-relation. If there is to be produced an overarching theoretical apparatus capable of co-ordinating the results of such inquiries, it has not yet emerged and we may safely defer worrying what to call it until it does.

Part II

3

LITERATURE/HISTORY

Early in *Criticism and Objectivity* Raman Selden states that his
purpose is 'to regain the footing which has been denied to the
historical critic by the incisive acid of deconstruction'.[1] Spurning
the feckless pursuit of the infinite play of signifiers which results
once the quest for their foundations has been abandoned, Selden
contends that:

> From the point of view of a Marxist criticism, there is no
> pleasure in the prospect of never hitting bottom; as a theory
> of history, Marxism discovers its ultimate footing beneath the
> level of the textual in the socio-economic.[2]

All this talk of footings and bottoms leaves us in little doubt
that Selden's discussion is to be governed by the metaphorics of
base and superstructure. Yet, at various points in the ensuing
analysis, the terms of that opposition are transposed to another
couplet: literature and history, where the latter stands in the place
of the base and the former figures as a specific ideological
superstructure. This rhetorical shift is fairly common within
Marxist literary theory where, indeed, rival positions are often
most clearly distinguished by their conceptions of the relations
between literature and history. Within the hermeneutic project of
a Lukács or a Jameson, for example, history functions as an
interpretative device for deciphering the meaning of literary texts –
individually, and in the order of their succession. In being
conceived as a set of real (i.e. extra-discursive) developmental
tendencies of which literary texts are regarded as the mediated
expressions, history here safeguards the critic's interpretations from
the charge of subjective arbitrariness in supplying them with an
objective foundation. In the Althusserian tradition, by contrast,

41

history functions as a set of real conditions and relations invoked to account for the specific forms in which the real (i.e. history itself) is signified or alluded to within literary texts.

Important though such differences are, they are less so than the ground which these positions have in common. For they share the view that literature and history belong to different realms of being, history being regarded as a somehow more basic and 'more real' reality than the domain of textual representations and, moreover, as knowable independently of the latter. The effect of this dualistic ontology is to privilege history as both literature's source and its ultimate referent. As the former, history supplies the means through which, to use Selden's terms, literary analysis hits bottom. Where literature and history are brought together on these terms, literature always constitutes the phenomenon to be explained just as surely as history provides the means of explanation; no other ordering of their relations is imaginable. If this conception of history is thus crucial to Marxism's claims to scientific objectivity in literary scholarship, the conception of history as literature's ultimate referent is no less central to the need to secure a basis on which the political effects of literary texts might be calculated with, apparently, equal objectivity. It matters little in this regard whether the terms proposed for such calculations are those of reflection theory or whether, as in Althusserian formulations, literary texts are regarded as subjecting history to a distinctive semiotic transformation via their work on the intermediate categories of ideology. In both cases, the political effects and value of literary texts are assessed on the basis of the position accorded them in relation to the independently known history which is assigned the status of their ultimate referent.

A brief consideration of Eagleton's construal of the relations between literature and history in *Criticism and Ideology* will serve to illustrate the difficulties to which these conceptions give rise. Eagleton's central contention in this study is that works of literature signify history indirectly via the ways in which they signify the ideologies which mediate their relations to history. In organising specific lived relations to history for the subjects they produce, ideologies supply literary practices with their raw materials. In subjecting these raw materials to a process of transformation, the literary work gives rise to a distinctive semiotic effect in which the text '*puts* the ideology into contradiction, discloses the limits and absences which mark its relations to

42

history'.[3] Eagleton summarises this conception in which literature is regarded as a specific signification of ideological significations of history in the following diagram:

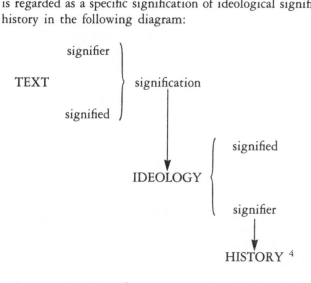

At no point here do we escape the circuit of significations between literary text, ideology and history. While supplying the ultimate terminus of the relay of significations from ideology to literature and back again, history, as it figures here, is conceived as *the effect* of that process of signification. Yet, as Geoff Bennington has argued, Eagleton wants history to function not merely as literature's signified but as its ultimate source and referent too.[5] This is made clear a few pages earlier where Eagleton argues:

> The text is a tissue of meanings, perceptions and responses which inhere in the first place in that imaginary production of the real which is ideology. The 'textual real' is related to the historical real, not as an imaginary transposition of it, but as the product of certain signifying practices whose source and referent is, in the last instance, history itself.[6]

As literature's ultimate source, history thus, in the last instance, determines the properties of the literary forms in which it itself is signified. As its ultimate referent, it also serves as the measure of those literary significations of itself. However, since history is additionally literature's ultimate signified — and, indeed, as Eagleton suggests a couple of pages earlier, its ultimate signifier also[7] — what history measures in assessing the relations of literary significations to itself are the relations of itself to itself. The position is nonsensical, a mere play with words whereby history's magical ability to double as literature's source and referent, its signifier and signified, depends entirely on Eagleton's failure to distinguish two different senses in which he uses the term. When he speaks of history as literature's signified, he clearly has in mind a set of meanings which – for such is the nature of signifieds – are internal to and the product of processes of signification. Yet when he speaks of history as literature's source and referent, he draws upon another meaning of the term in which history figures as an extra-discursive origin of discourse. If this jumbling is undone – a jumbling which is the consequence of Eagleton's trying to operate in both the space of discourse theory and that of classical Marxism at the same time – the incoherence of the position is manifest. Were the functions Eagleton accords history to be represented diagrammatically, the result would be something like that suggested below. To be capable of fulfilling the multiple tasks Eagleton assigns it, the history from which the process of signification is initiated (the bottom left of the diagram) and that at which it ends up need to be conceived as identical, whereas in fact they are antithetical. Moreover, were they to be translated

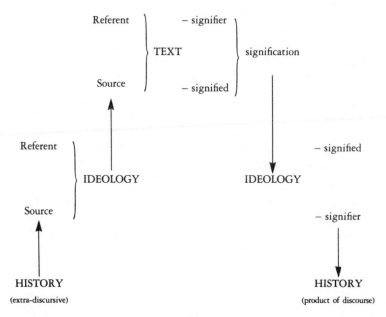

back into the metaphorics of base and superstructure, they would have to be allocated to different realms: whereas we start off with history as base, we end up with history as superstructure.

Clearly, then, relatively little is gained by displacing the metaphorics of base and superstructure on to the literature/history couplet. To the contrary, this move merely brings a series of added difficulties in tow. For the most part, these derive from the semantic ambiguity of the term 'history' which, in most discussions on the subject – as in Eagleton's – functions as a double-dealing rascal, generating pseudo-solutions in relation to pseudo-problems. Very little of any theoretical consequence hinges upon the outcomes of such debates whenever they aim at a general theory of the relations between literature and history where these are conceived as general categories relating to different orders of being whose interrelations are held to require some distinctive kind of specification. In what follows, I shall resist the suggestion that the terms literature and history pose a *general* problem of a *special* kind. The questions raised by such debates, I shall argue, can be cogently pursued only if they are dispersed into a series of discrete and particular problems which are either of an empirical kind or, where theoretical, are so because of their similarities with difficulties in related fields of inquiry rather than for any special reasons.

In brief, I shall suggest that there can be no general solution to the question of the relations between literature and history because there is no general problem to be addressed. The historical study of literature is neither dependent on nor served by the development of general theories of the relations between literature and history. To study literary forms and functions 'historically', I shall argue, means neither more nor less than to study them in their own particularity, contingency and variability in the context of their variable and mutable relations to the other social practices with which they are temporally co-existent. While such concerns produce innumerable problems of a detailed nature regarding the imbrication of literary forms and institutions with other forms of social activity and their institutional articulations, such problems are not *different in kind* from those affecting other areas of historical inquiry – the history of law or of politics, for example. The supposition that they are derives from a unique amalgam of aesthetic conceptions of the literary and empiricist conceptions of history which has held Marxist literary theory in its thrall for too long.

LITERATURE/HISTORY: PAST/PRESENT

A good example of the terminological slipperiness of the literature/history couplet is provided by Peter Widdowson's discussion on the occasion of the tenth anniversary of the journal *Literature and History*. In outlining the varying senses in which the terms literature and history have been related to one another, Widdowson suggests that two have predominated and poses these as options to be considered in the development of future work:

> *One*: do we wish to place literary works in the historical context of their moment of production in order to understand them better? In this case we are, of course, privileging literature – history is little more than an auxiliary in a study of literature. . . . So, *two*: do we wish to read literature as a form of historical knowledge, as a particular mode of access to the past? In this second case, we are privileging history – literature merely assists in the understanding of past societies.[8]

Two ways in which literature and history may be combined, then, each of which seems arbitrarily to privilege one term of the couplet over the other. A part of the difficulty here is that the logic of these evaluations could easily be reversed. In the first case, literature is privileged above history in comprising the object of study. Yet it could equally be argued that, from the point of view of method, history constitutes the privileged term here in view of the explanatory role accorded it in relation to literature. Similarly, whereas the second case privileges history as the object of study, it can also be associated with a privileging of literature where, as Widdowson's earlier formulation of this position suggests, literature is regarded as 'offering a unique access to history'.[9] In effect, all that happens between these two options is that literature and history exchange places with regard to the functions assigned them of supplying either the object of analysis or the method of study.

Practically speaking, all this amounts to is a different ordering of the relations between the evidential procedures of two disciplines. This, to be sure, occasions difficulties, but particular ones which, depending on the purpose of the inquiry, are susceptible to particular resolutions without the need for any overarching theory of the relations between literature and history understood as generalities. While Widdowson acknowledges the different evidential procedures and problems implied by his two formulations, what is of interest here is the way he then proceeds to reduce these to a common general problem: the problematic nature of our access to the past. Thus, where history is to serve as an auxiliary to the study of literature, Widdowson asks:

> can we, in any event, expect to get any closer to the original meaning of past literature – to its effect, let us say, on its own contemporary audience; can we really slough off the thick skin of our own historical positioning in relation to that hypothetical 'original' meaning; and even if, theoretically, we could enter a critical time-machine, what would be the point of it?[10]

Similarly, when discussing the study of literature as a form of historical knowledge, the same problem crops up again:

> leaving aside the overwhelming question of whether, in any case, we can ever discover with true historical veracity the reality of the past (doesn't the past, now and always, only reside within discourse?), leaving this aside, what information about the past does literature give us if we accept that we cannot know its original historical meaning, that its meaning is only ever the product of its transmission through history to the ever-changing historical present?[11]

In brief, the problem of the relations between literature and history is re-cast here as part of a more widespread and endemic problem of a hermeneutic kind concerning how the horizons of past and present might be merged so as to recover the meanings lived and experienced by subjects in epochs remote from our own. Owing to the degree to which the pursuit of knowledge is itself historically situated so that 'present determinations constitute the frame in which "the past", or the "meaning" and "value" of literature, are set',[12] Widdowson concludes that such a merging of time horizons is unachievable. In its place, therefore, he suggests a reformulation of the concerns of literary-historical scholarship in which the problem of the relations between past and present is overcome by denying the alterity of the past from the present. The aim, he suggests, should be:

> to shift the ground from a study of 'the past' and 'past meanings' to an analysis of the processes and institutions of reproduction in which those impalpable essences are given a material form in the present. The meaning of *King Lear*, its use and its value, are what it means now, how it is 'read' now or 'produced' now in late twentieth-century culture; what the Gordon Riots *were* is what they *are* now in relation to contemporary discourses of power and resistance.[13]

This is, indeed, a violent solution, but not an incoherent one. The work of Patrick Wright and others has demonstrated both the cogency and value of treating the past as a currently existing social reality: a set of meanings produced and circulated by a range of institutions – television, museums, state ceremonies, heritage organisations – comprising a 'public historical sphere' which effects 'a publicly instituted structuring of consciousness'.[14] Literature is undoubtedly implicated in such processes, and the examination of the part played by literary institutions in producing and circulating specific meanings of the past – along the lines of Graham Holderness's work on Shakespeare,[15] or Widdowson's own work on Hardy[16] – contributes significantly to our understanding of one of the more important aspects of the contemporary social deployment of literary texts. Yet it is clear that such investigations do not pose problems of a special sort inasmuch as literature and history here refer to realities of a similar kind – the functioning of specific, presently existing institutionalised sites of representation.

Nor, moreover, do such examinations pose any epistemological problems of a general kind concerning the relations between past and present. For it is clear that the functioning of the past, conceived as a currently existing social reality, can be examined without any reference to the past in its more conventional sense – that is, the past 'as it really was'. One can, in other words, assess how representations of the Gordon Riots function in relation to contemporary discourses of power and resistance without having to resolve, or even address, the question as to the 'real nature' of the Gordon Riots conceived as a set of past events. For the political effects of such socially constructed pasts do not depend on their authenticity – on their fidelity to or distortion of the past 'as it really was' – but on their differential value: that is, on the position they take up in relation to the rival socially constructed pasts with which they compete or earlier ones which they seek to displace.

Yet it is a far cry from this to closing down any gap between these two different senses of the past by contending that 'what the Gordon Riots *were* is what they *are* now'. This would entail that the only conceivable role for historical scholarship would be with the synchronic functioning of a set of contemporary social institutions – which, of course, is no role at all. Moreover, as I have intimated above, even such analysis must presuppose some differential relation between contemporary constructions of the past and those discourses of the past put into circulation in earlier periods, even though the question of the relations of either or both of these to 'the real past' may be infinitely deferred. To reverse Widdowson's formulation, the significance of how the Gordon Riots are now represented within discourses of power and resistance depends on how they were earlier represented within such discourses; without some such set of relations, either of rupture or continuity, an analysis of the current placement and functioning of representations of the Gordon Riots within 'the contemporary past' would lack political pertinence.

This is not to venture a return to the view, now surely archaic, of history as a discipline committed to the recovery of the past in some elementary, pre-discursive state. For what is at issue in historical scholarship – and it's all that *can be* at issue – is what can be derived from the historical record or archive. This is not to suggest that this might be fetishised in being abstracted from the social processes through which 'the past', conceived as a specific social zone of representation, is organised. To the contrary, historical records are only too clearly highly volatile and mutable products of a complex of social processes. Apart from the considerable amount of organised social labour (of archivists, librarians, archaeologists) which goes into their production, the composition of such records may vary considerably from one period to another – witness the influence of feminist historiography in expanding the range of what now counts as the historical record. None the less, this area of 'the past' (still conceived as a specific social zone of representation) occupies a relatively distinct position in relation to the representations produced and circulated within the public historical sphere. In effect, it functions, not as their referent in the sense of an extra-discursive real, but *as if it were* such a referent in the sense that it constitutes the last court of appeal for historical disputes, the point at which, so to speak, they hit base – but a base within discourse.

What I'm suggesting here is that, once 'the past' is conceived as a social product, it is necessary to go one step further and recognise that, as such, it is a highly differentiated one. For this then allows that the issues involved in the nature of historical scholarship may be rethought in a manner which allows a break with the ways in which they have traditionally been posed as part of a general epistemological problem concerning the nature of our access to the past *as such*. That is not the point at issue in historical inquiry, and never has been. History, as a discipline, constitutes the locus through which the representations of the past circulated by the institutions comprising the public historical sphere are brought into contact with the historical record in order to be either corrected by it or allowed to change with it. As such, it consists of a specific set of rules and precepts governing the discursive moves which may be made in relation to this record, including those regulating the reorganisation of that record itself in periods of marked historiographical controversy. It is these rules, which historians are right to insist on as constitutive of their discipline, which limit the arbitrariness of 'the past' (still in the sense of a currently existing social reality) in the sense that either its maintenance as it is, or its transformation, depend on certain conditions being met – even though, of course, these may themselves be bones for contention.

My suggestion, then, is that history (as a discipline) is most appropriately regarded as a specific discursive regime, governed by distinctive procedures, through which the maintenance/transformation of the past as a set of currently existing realities is regulated.[17] It constitutes a disciplined means for the production of a 'historical past' which exercises a regulatory function in relation to the 'public past'. Its role in this regard is enormously important. While their effects may not be immediately apparent in the short term, the conduct of historical debates and their (always provisional) resolution decisively influence the public face of the past over the long term. Yet such debates require, as a condition of their intelligibility, the sense of a distinction between past and present and an orientation to historical records *as if* they comprised a referent. That this referent proves to be intra-discursive and so mutable does not disable the historical enterprise. To the contrary: the discipline's social productivity consists precisely in its capacity to reorganise its referent and thus transform 'the past' – not as it was but as it is. Understood in this way, the cogency and productivity of historical inquiry may be admitted without the question of its relations to 'the real past' ever arising. This is not to doubt that such a past existed but is merely to say that, from the point of view of what is at issue in historical debates and the manner in which they are actually conducted, it may be allowed to go its own way – as it surely has. The productivity of historical inquiry is produced by the tension between the pasts it organises and those enjoying a broader circulation. It is this tension that guarantees its nature as a revisionist discipline as it brings pressure to bear on the public past to conform to the past that is the fruit of its own labours – and all this without the 'real past' ever entering into the matter except rhetorically.

The violence of Widdowson's solution, then, stems from the fact that he falls short of following his arguments through to their conclusion. The problem consists not in his perception of the sociality of the past but in holding to that view while also not entirely letting go of an empiricist conception of the past. It is this that makes his denial of the alterity of the past ('what the Gordon Riots *were* is what they *are* now') problematic. For it rests on a mismatch between an empiricist conception of the past and a view of the past as a discursive construct. The position I have argued, while allowing a tension between two different pasts (that produced by disciplined examinations of the historical record or archive and the representations and institutions constituting the public historical sphere), does not conceive of these as entities of different sorts or as belonging to different times but merely as relatively distinct components of a specific, complexly structured social zone of representation. While I shall return shortly to the implications of these considerations for the question of the relations between literature and history, their general import may be briefly summarised: namely, that rather than involving epistemological problems of a general kind concerning our access to the past they have to do with the place accorded literary texts in relation to other components of the historical record within, on the one hand, the procedures of literary scholarship and, on the other, those of historical inquiry. Or, more precisely: it concerns the ground on which these are to be brought together.

However, in order to relate this argument to my earlier discussion of the effects of transposing the metaphorics of base and superstructure on to the literature/history couplet, it will be necessary to consider the implications of deconstructionist criticisms of this couplet. These provide both Selden and Widdowson with their bearings: Selden by way of opposing them, or at least seeking to mute their effects, and Widdowson by way of ruefully admitting that 'logically the deconstructionists are right: if we cannot know the "real" meaning of the past or of past literary works, then why not treat them as solely the possession of the present with infinitely diverse possibilities of meaning?'[18] In both cases, however, what tends to be emphasised is the weaker aspect of the deconstructionist case, which leads merely into an impasse, at the expense of its stronger arguments which, while seemingly more destructive, can contribute positively to reformulating our sense of the issues posed by the literary/history couplet.

NARRATIVE, HISTORY, POLITICS

'The history invoked as ultimate reality and source of truth', Jonathan Culler argues, 'manifests itself in narrative constructs, stories designed to yield meaning through narrative ordering.'[19] Although, properly speaking, a structuralist argument given its major statements by Barthes and Lévi-Strauss,[20] this view has since come to be associated with deconstruction in a number of secondary commentaries.[21] It is also the aspect of deconstruction which has most exercised the attention of Marxist literary theorists.[22] What does the argument amount to? In brief, it constitutes a rebuttal of those systems of explanation in which history is assigned the status of a metalanguage capable of furnishing the means for the explanation of social and textual phenomena. The history which is assigned such a role, it is argued, can never fulfil its obligations to the degree that it always turns out to be the product of a series of narrative and rhetorical devices. An effect of discourse itself, it is unable to function as an extra-discursive source of anything else. Historical explanation thus turns out to be a way of telling stories without any particularly convincing means, where such stories differ, of deciding between them. Of course, the objection is not limited to history but applies to any system of explanation in which a signified is granted an existence independently of the signifiers which produce it. In this sense, the argument undermines the pretensions of all would-be metalanguages in contending, as I have summarised its import elsewhere, that there is 'no language which can claim an absolute or transcendental validity for its ways of "fixing" other languages, discourses or texts as objects within itself or which can efface the traces of writing or language within itself'.[23]

So far as the literature/history couplet is concerned, this means that the latter cannot figure as an extra-discursive real in relation to which the former might find its footing. The consequences of this are particularly telling where history, conceived as a set of developmental processes with an inherent direction, is supposed to provide an objective anchorage for the meanings of literary texts – in their own time and, through a continuity of interpretative horizons guaranteed by history's inherent direction, in the present also. All that such arguments amount to, it is objected, is a narrative ordering of the relations between two series – a series of literary texts and a series of extra-literary events or structures – which cannot secure any warrant except for that provided by its own discursive manoeuvres. To paraphrase Lévi-Strauss, we might say that literary texts have their meanings vouchsafed by history only on the condition that, within the limits of a particular interpretative paradigm, we view them so. But it is then necessary to add, as Lévi-Strauss does, that *this meaning is never the right one*: superstructures are *faulty acts* which have "made it" socially'.[24]

The argument, it seems to me, is unassailable and it is notable that Marxist responses have been less concerned to refute it *per se* than to find some way of curtailing its implications. Usually, this leads to an attempt to negotiate some leeway between the irreconcilable views that, one, history is an effect of discourse and, two, that it is an extra-discursive real. This results in formulations such as those suggested by Jameson in *The Political Unconscious*: history (sense one) is a narrative construct but it is history (sense two) which, in the last instance, determines the narrative orderings to which history (still sense two) subjects itself. The chief difficulty with such arguments, as Geoff Bennington and Robert Young have noted, is that they are ultimately pressed to take their stand on precisely that conception of history which post-structuralists have called into question.[25] The consequence of the various equivoca-tions and circumlocutions which masquerade as dialectical reasoning is that the history that is shown the front door in concession to post-structuralism is ushered in through the back door where its re-entry is legitimated in the name of the nitty-gritties of last instances and the like.

What is it that motivates and sustains such counter-arguments in spite of the desperate circularities to which they are driven? Two concerns predominate – one which Marxists share with other critics of post-structuralism, and a second which is more specific to Marxist thought, and particularly to the way in which, in its classical formulations, it conceives the relations between epistemological questions and the conduct of politics.

Within the first concern, what is resisted is the threat to the very possibility of rationality which seems to be embodied in the argument that there are no metanarratives or, more generally, no metalanguages capable of resolving the differences between contending narrative and linguistic orderings of reality. If narratives are all that we can have and if all narratives are, in principle, of equal value – as it seems they must be if there is no touchstone of 'reality' to which they can be referred for the adjudication of their truth claims – then rational debate would seem to be pointless. If the non-accessibility of a referent means that the theorist is 'drawn into labyrinths of textual "undecidability" where any kind of systematic truth-claim could only tell the story of its own undoing'[26] – then why bother? The political consequence of such a radical relativism, Norris suggests, can only be quietism:

> The upshot in political terms would be a 'liberal' consensus forswearing the idea of social improvement through rational critique and relying instead on the free circulation of communal myths and values.[27]

The danger is real enough. While Derrida's own work may be exempted from the charge, its annexation to the intellectual currents of postmodernism often results in a *jouissance*-like exultation in the pleasures of a free-wheeling relativism. However, as the painstaking argument of Norris's *Contest of Faculties* testifies, the prospect of a relativism without limits can be successfully resisted without resurrecting the concept of an extra-discursive referent as the final arbiter of competing truth claims, and certainly without seeking to reinstate history as such a referent. Ultimately, the weakness of such arguments consists in the fact that they concede too much from the outset in accepting the polar opposites proposed by the positions they oppose: truth claims must be able, under some specifiable set of conditions, to be established absolutely or they cannot be established at all; or, if there is no way of escaping the constraints of narrative and language, then all narrative and linguistic orderings of reality must be regarded as equally valid.

These are non-sequiturs. It by no means follows, because we cannot establish certain propositions as absolutely true, that we have no means of establishing their provisional truth – of determining that they meet conditions which justify our regarding them as true and so as capable of serving as a basis for both further thought and action. Nor does it follow, if we accept that there can be no escaping the constraints of language and narrative, that anything goes – that all possible narrative systems or language games are to be ranked equally with regard to their propositional content. The violent 'all or nothing' logic of such polarities need hold us in its thrall only so long as we subscribe to the tenets of traditional epistemology in supposing that what is at issue in competing truth claims is the demonstration of a correspondence between thought and reality, conceived as separate realms, and, should that prove to be impossible, of accepting that all we can demonstrate is the correspondence of thought (regarded as a property of the subject) to itself.

I've already suggested why such conceptions can contribute little to our understanding of the manner in which historical knowledge is produced and validated – and in ways which allow for reasoned debate as well as for the empirical regulation of propositional statements – without the question of our access to an extra-discursive past ever arising. Mark Cousins has argued a broadly similar position. Addressing himself not to 'History in the upper case' but to history 'as a "craft" with skills and rules, as a definite technique of discovery',[28] he likens its procedures to those embodied in the law, contending that both address themselves to two primary questions: Did a specific event occur or not? If so, into what class of event does it fall? These, once answered, give rise to a similar series of further questions: Who was responsible for the event? What links of causality can be established in relation to the event and to other pertinent events? In a court of law, Cousins argues, such questions are pursued by means of definite rules governing the admissibility of, and relative credence to be given to, different types of evidence which, for an event to be legally recognised, 'must be assembled into an edifice which is to be accepted as a representation of the event which is beyond all reasonable doubt'.[29] The key phrase here is 'representation of the event' rather than 'the event itself'. As Cousins elaborates:

> It might appear that the legal process attempts to establish what really happened in the past, but 'really' is used in a specialised sense. 'Really' is what is relevant to the law, what is definable by law, what may be argued in terms of law and evidence, what may be judged and what may be subject to appeal. 'Reality' as far as the law is concerned is a set of representations of the past, ordered in accordance with legal categories and rules of evidence into a decision which claims to rest upon the truth. But this truth of the past, the representations of events, is a strictly legal truth.[30]

Similarly, the past, in so far as the historian is concerned with it, is never the past as such – not everything that may be said of it – but only the past as a product of the specific protocols of investigation which characterise the discipline of history in its concern to establish, classify and order the relations between events pertinent to the inquiry in hand. In this way, Cousins argues, the practice of history may be said 'to produce (uncover) events, whose representations are called historical facts'.[31] In this conception, the reality of those events – and thereby, so to speak, of the 'historical past' – consists in nothing but, and certainly nothing beyond, the status of historical facts that is accorded those representations whose evidential standing has passed the test of disciplined scrutiny. Although this knowledge cannot claim to rest on any foundations other than its own procedures or to know anything other than the historical facts which those procedures produce and validate, Cousins does not see this as an occasion for any general scepticism:

> But to reject any general foundation to historical truth or any general truth of History does itself not undermine a notion of historical truth as such. There is no need to enter a form of scepticism about statements about the past. It is enough to recognise that the justification for truth claims about the past are [sic] part of the particular practice of historical investigation. Historical facts are not illusions; we may as well say they are true.[32]

Indeed, it is these truths, the truths comprising the 'historical past', which serve as a check, and as the only possible check, on the forms in which earlier epochs are represented. Of course, it is not an absolute check. Nor could it be to the degree that the 'historical past' is characterised, and necessarily so, by areas of marked uncertainty and instability in consequence of the historiographical disputes concerning the forms of evidence pertinent to particular inquiries and the rules of reasoning to be applied to them. The effect of such disputes – and it is such disputes which *constitute* the discipline rather than being its accidental by-products – is to introduce a degree of indeterminacy into the 'historical past'. But only a degree, for this indeterminacy is located against a bedrock of what are taken to be determinate historical truths. It is true that this bedrock may be shifted in the sense that some truths may be added to it while others are subtracted as specific historiographical disputes are worked out. Yet such disputes never throw the totality of the 'historical past' into question. Indeed, it is a condition of its intelligibility that historical debate should take place within a horizon of both determinacy and indeterminacy: it requires both – the former to supply conditions of resolution, the latter to be purposive.

Imperfect though it is, it is only to this unstable, always provisional and forever changing 'historical past' that propositional statements about the past can be referred for the adjudication of their truth claims. The degree to which this enables the 'historical past' to serve also as a check on the broader terrain of historical representations constituted by the public historical sphere, however, is not given by this past itself. Rather, it depends on the relations which obtain between the practice of history and the other institutional contexts and discursive regimes within which representations of the past are produced and circulated. There is nothing within the protocols of historical inquiry that can prevent historical representations which violently traduce the 'historical past' from gaining an effective currency and so becoming a major social force. In such circumstances – the ascendancy of fascist myth, for example – it is not a general crisis of reason that is at issue but the failure of the specific form of reasoning embodied in the procedures of history to establish their pertinence or carry much weight in the general political arena.

It is, then, the ratio of determinacy/indeterminacy within the 'historical past' and the degree of weight accorded this past in relation to other spheres of historical representation which effectively limits what can be said about the past with any degree of warrantability in a particular set of circumstances. And if this is not an absolute check, neither is it one which can be imposed on the future. As the past which is produced by the social labour of historians may change in unforeseeable ways, it must be allowed that it may one day furnish a support for statements which it currently provides no warrant for.

This is a far cry from any transcendental guarantees. It amounts to neither more nor less than saying that the discipline of history – like a court of law – constitutes a particular institutionalised form for the social regulation of statements about the past. As such, it never goes beyond referring such statements to those representations comprising the 'historical past' which function as history's truths. But what other kind of regulation could be applied to such statements? A higher order of certainty could only be obtained by reaching back beyond the past produced by historical inquiry to the notional referent of the past as it really was and as revealed to some ideally situated observer. It is only where the demand for such transcendental certainties prevails that when it is disappointed – as inevitably it must be – its all-or-nothing logic asserts itself. Since the practical forms that are available to us for the regulation of historical truths cannot satisfy this demand, the only alternative seems to be a radical relativism in which, since nothing can be absolutely secured, anything must be allowed to go. The paradox here is that the only condition which could stop this slide – that is, knowledge of the past *as such* – would, at the same time, put an end to history conceived as a specific type of inquiry governed by definite protocols of reasoning. One might say that historical inquiry is kept open because the gap between what functions as if it were its referent (records, primary sources, etc.) and, so to speak, that referent's referent (the past 'as it really was') is never closed down.

It is this demand for transcendental certainties that is present in 'History in the upper case': that is, philosophies of history which purport to assign events their objective significance by identifying their place and function within a general schema of historical development. It is clear, of course, that the boundary line between history, thus understood, and 'the historian's craft' is not a rigorous one. In practice, the procedures of historical inquiry are often too visibly governed by the assumptions of some general theory of history. Yet, as it is equally clear that this need not be so, the distinction – understood as a theoretical one – remains useful. It is thus primarily the philosophical sense of the term that Derrida has in mind when he argues that 'if the word "history" did not carry with it the theme of a final repression of différance, we could say that differences alone could be "historical" through and through and from the start'.[33] For philosophies of history must reduce all differences to the identity of History as an objectively known process which, since it assigns all events their significance, closes off – or promises to close off – that infinite deferment of ultimate meanings which Derrida intends by the concept of *différance*.

It is usually conceptions of history of this kind that Marxist critics have been concerned to defend in resisting the 'incisive acid of deconstruction'. The actual procedures of historical inquiry seem scarcely to have entered into the matter.[34] This is regrettable for, as I have tried to show, an argument which takes these as its point of departure can arrive at a means of specifying how historical truths are produced and socially deployed which satisfies many of the requirements of Marxist thought. The adjudication of statements about the past effected by the disciplined procedures of history consists in a particular institutionalised set of social processes whose relations with other social practices are historically variable and contingent. This may not be what Marx meant when he said that men make their own history, but on the basis of determined conditions. None the less, the phrase will serve nicely as a summary of the position I have been arguing.

This neglect of historiographical concerns and procedures has the further consequence that there rarely seems to be any specific content at issue in Marxist critics' advocacy of history. The question of how to order the relations between literary texts and other evidential sources in the context of specific historical inquiries, that is to say, rarely arises. Nor is much attention paid to showing how and why Marxist accounts of the functioning of literary forms within past social relations might claim sounder historiographical credentials than their principal contenders. Rather, what seems to be at issue is the defence of history as a generality – and as a very abstract generality at that. There has thus been a marked disinclination to elaborate any specific narrative account of history conceived as a definite process, driven by particular mechanisms, whose past course is known just as surely as its future trajectory is already determined. Certainly, there has been little support for the verities of old-style historical materialism where history is understood as a process which, from its very beginnings, has been propelled by an unstoppable momentum toward communism by virtue of the tension between the forces and relations of production. Instead, what is insisted on is merely the *possibility* that history will generate – if not now, then one day – a position from which its story might eventually and truthfully be told.

Why should so much energy have been spent in defending such an abstract possibility? The reasons have less to do with epistemological issues *per se* than with the specific ordering of the relations between epistemological and political concerns within classical Marxist thought: namely, that theory becomes a material force when it gains a hold of the consciousness of the masses and that, to do so, it must be true, must correspond to the real processes of historical development. In this conception, the advance to communism is held to be dependent on communist society both *being* the culmination of the objective processes of historical development, and *being known* to be such. For it is only when a knowledge of history's objective course informs the practice of a subject capable of effecting a revolutionary transformation of society that the objective developmental tendency of the historical process will be actually realised. If the historical process were not objectively one of progress toward communism, then there would be no basis for its representation as such and, accordingly, no possibility of such a representation enlisting sufficient support to become, through the activity of a revolutionary subject, a part of history's objective tendency. History, so to speak, cannot be duped into progress by tricking its subjects into believing that it has an objective progressive tendency. Its course must *be* one of progress in order to *be known* as such, and it must *be known* as such in order to realise itself.

It is this nexus of relations specifying the conditions which must be met in order for there to be produced a political subject capable of playing its allotted historical role which produces the requirement that, at least in principle, all events might be ordered into a history conceived as a progressive totality which, in enfolding its representations into itself as a part of its own movement, comes to know itself. The logic of this coupling of epistemological and political concerns is nowhere more clearly discernible than in Lukács's writings. In considering the basis on which claims to the intellectual leadership of society might be justified, Lukács thus converts this question into an epistemological question which he breaks down into two parts:

First, we have to ask: what must be the nature of the forces moving society and the laws which govern them so that consciousness can grasp them and human will and human objectives can intervene in them significantly? And secondly: what must be the direction and the composition of human consciousness so that it can intervene significantly and authoritatively in social development?[35]

Contending that only Marxism has been able to answer this 'epistemological question of the leadership of society', Lukács expresses that answer in a number of theses:

The first such thesis is: that the development of society is determined exclusively by forces present within that society (in the Marxist view, by the class struggle and the transformation of the relations of production). The second: that the direction of this development can be clearly determined, even if it is not yet fully understood. The third: that this direction has to be related in a certain, albeit still not fully understood fashion, to human objectives; such a relationship can be perceived and made conscious, and the process of making it conscious exerts a positive influence on the development itself.[36]

The most interesting aspect of this argument, taken from Lukács's 1919 essay 'Tactics and Ethics', derives from the context in which it is made: a consideration of the problems of socialist ethics where the question of 'morally correct action' is held to be a function of 'the correct perception of the given historico-philosophical situation'.[37] Where ethical questions are understood as concerning the relations between knowledge and action, where morally correct action can only flow from a correct understanding of objective historical tendencies, then it is easy to see how the question of intellectual leadership comes to be reformulated as a problem concerning the relations between truth and morality.

It is, I think, this particular ordering of the relations between epistemology, ethics and politics – between the questions of truth, morality and action – which accounts for the reluctance to abandon the view that, at least in principle, history might be objectively knowable. For, if it is not, how might the attempt to acquire intellectual leadership over society be justified? If there neither is nor can be an absolute warrant for Marxist accounts of history, then how does Marxist historical interpretation differ from fascist myth? Isn't a similar degree and type of duplicity involved in both practices? While Lukács's specific formulations would no longer recruit much general support, there is little doubt of the continuing influence of the concerns which motivated them. Take Terry Eagleton again. In contrast to his position in *Criticism and Ideology*, Eagleton has subsequently proved more receptive to structuralist and post-structuralist criticisms of history. In his study of Walter Benjamin, he thus accepts that historical narratives function primarily as devices which organise the individual's insertion into the ideological formations which define the terms in which, as historical subjects, men and women live, move, act and are acted upon:

> The insertion of the subject into an ideological formation is, simultaneously, its access to a repertoire of narrative devices and conventions that help to provide it with a stable self-identity through time. . . . But this is not to argue that narrative is merely 'illusory', any more than we should chide the working-class movement for nurturing its mighty dramas of universal solidarity overcoming the evils of capitalism. Such motifs are the necessary inflections by which the theory of historical materialism 'lives itself out' in the practice of class struggle. And just as the individual subject is permitted to construct for itself a coherent biography, so a revolutionary or potentially revolutionary class creates, across the structurally discontinuous social formations identified by Marxism, that 'fiction' of a coherent, continuous struggle which is Benjamin's 'tradition'.[38]

Yet the fictionality of such narratives is immediately qualified:

> But that fiction is not a *lie*. Narrative continuities do not merely orchestrate into momentary cohesion a cacophony of historical noises. For there *are* real historical continuities. . . .[39]

Fictions but not lies; imaginary continuities but also real ones: in formulations such as these, the question of history spills over into the broader one concerning the problematic status of the concept of ideology in Marxist thought. For, no matter how it is expressed – whether as 'false consciousness' or as a lived relation to the subject's conditions of existence which induces a misrecognition of his/her real relations to those conditions – the concept usually implies some form of truth/falsehood distinction. It suggests that knowledge or science on the one hand and ideology on the other are to be differentiated as fundamentally distinct modes of the subject's mental relations to reality. The crucial difficulty this then occasions for Marxist conceptions of history is that of somehow negotiating a transaction between the two different relations to history which Marxism posits – the knowledge relation it claims for itself and the lived relation of ideology which, as Gramsci put it, organises 'the terrain on which men move, acquire consciousness of their position, struggle, etc.'.[40]

In historicist formulations, this problem is met by anticipating that the gap between ideological representations of history and historical knowledge will be closed as the impedimenta which obscure the subject's relations to reality are overcome, thus producing a subject which, knowing history, can take its appointed place within it. Althusser, insisting on the universality and necessity of ideology, denies this solution; in theorising ideology as an invariant structure, it becomes impossible to argue that the subject might undergo a general historical transition from a state of ideology to one of knowledge. Yet, in theorising both science and ideology as atemporal essences, Althusser is unable to specify any convincing mechanisms through which Marxism, as a science of history, might become influential on the plane of presently existing ideologies of history. The problem which motivated the formulations of historicist Marxism remains; only now there is no possible means of resolving it. For if ideology represents history to the subject as a continuous process, a grand narrative, in which s/he can find a place, science – that is, Marxism – represents it as a set of dispersed, discontinuous and subjectless processes which, precisely because it lacks a subject, cannot interpellate one either. It is no use, given this conception, to argue, as Eagleton does, that the ideologies developed by socialist forces in the midst of class struggle constitute the specific forms in which the categories of historical materialism 'live out' their relations to history, as if those categories were themselves phantom subjects. For how can a system of thought whose structure eschews a subject relation to history come to inform the terms in which relations to conditions of existence are concretely lived? And how can a system of thought whose structure is non-interpellative provide an epistemological warrant for any particular set of interpellations?

The fracture remains – a split between *Capital* and *The Communist Manifesto*, or between intellectuals (theory) and workers (practice) whose interpellations are subjected to a 'knowing' regulation by the former. The difficulty with this, apart from its elitism, is that the worlds of theory and practice cannot be so clearly separated. Where it is a requirement of the theory that interpellations be rooted in the real tendencies of historical development, interpellations which cannot be so legitimated lose that condition of credibility which is essential to their becoming effective organisers of the consciousness and action of social agents. Under these circumstances, the requirement for narratives capable of interpellating subjects into relations of solidarity and action within a conception of history as a subject-centred process which can claim some epistemological foundation in the structure of reality seems both pressing yet impossible to meet.

But is the requirement a real one? Is the political need for grand and universalist narratives established? Is the conduct of socialist political struggles in the present dependent on the production of subjects who will represent their actions to themselves as moments in the unfolding of a continuist historical narrative? And one whose superiority over contending narratives of a similar type can be demonstrated? If this is the key question, it is important to understand that it is a *historical question*. It refers not to whether such a narrative can secure an epistemological validation but to whether only such narratives are able to fulfil the practical social function of enlisting subjects – a question which refers to the actual organisation of the field of discourses which regulate the relations between thought and political action and, thus, to how political action is itself conceived.

'Many people', Lyotard has argued, 'have lost the nostalgia for the lost narrative.' But, he continues, it 'in no way follows that they are reduced to barbarity'.[41] Nor does it follow that they are reduced to inaction. As Silverman and Torode have argued, there is no reason to assume that the doer of a practice must take the form of a subject of ideology.[42] But even if this objection is placed to one side and the assumption that political action is dependent on the subject's insertion in an ideology allowed, the decline of grand narratives still need not be thought of as disabling socialist forms of politics. To suppose that it does is to mistake a particular historical system for the formation of subjectivities for a universal one. The fact that, in the initial terms of their practical deployment, Marxist categories were translated into a narrative of history as a total and continuist process was not a necessary outcome dictated by the requirements of narrative conceived as a universal mode of consciousness. Rather, it was a particular requirement occasioned by the eschatological theodicies of meaning developed by Christianity and secular progressivist philosophies of history. To the degree that these supplied the dominant systems for subject formation in nineteenth-century Europe, they constituted the field of discourses regulating the relations between thought and action with which Marxist thought had to engage in order to become an effective social force. Poulantzas once touched on this question. While upholding Althusser's distinction between Marxism as a science of history (conceived as a set of subjectless processes) and nineteenth-century ideological conceptions of history (as a unified and subject-centred process), he also insisted that, in practice, the line between the two could not always be so clearly drawn as Althusser had suggested:

> But we are also now aware of the fact that the *break between science and ideology is far from possessing the radical character that we ascribed to it some years ago*. The theory of history of Marx's 'maturity' even shares certain elements with the ideological-philosophical representation of History current in his age. The penetration of the capitalist social matrix by eschatological evolutionism, rationalistic progressivism, universal linearity, humanist historicism and I know not what else does not affect merely the fringes of the 'kernel' of Marx's theory, and nor is it a simple deviation or deformation introduced by the epigones of the Second and Third Internationals. It is present in Marx's theory of history itself.[43]

But this is to speak of an effect induced by the organisation of a particular field of discourses; that is, of a contingent rather than a necessary pressure and one which, therefore, it would be sheer folly to translate into a transcendent virtue. And particularly so as that same pressure no longer exists, at least to nowhere near the same degree, in what is now, quite clearly, a radically altered field of ideological relations. The problem with 'History in the upper

65

case', Hayden White has suggested, is not whether grand narratives of historical development might be represented as true but whether they any longer have, or can have, any 'sticking power'.[44] Or, one might say that such narratives can no longer function as true because they no longer have any sticking power; they cannot take hold of subjectivities because subjectivities are no longer where they once were, already 'in the groove', so to speak, of grand narrative systems.

This is not to embrace the rhetoric of postmodernism which, as Stuart Hall has argued, there are good reasons for resisting.[45] Rather, it is merely to register the effects of those changes for which the tag of postmodernism serves as a convenient shorthand: the proliferation of sites of political struggle and of the issues which are regarded as political, but without there being any unifying centre around which those struggles cohere; the shortening of time perspectives as the long pasts and long futures projected by nineteenth-century teleologies have collapsed into more abbreviated (and usually nationalised) conceptions of historical time;[46] the refusal of the times relevant to different areas of political struggle to form a single, unified time. It is customary to register such changes in the language of crisis: a crisis of meaning, a crisis of identity, a crisis of narrative, a crisis of rationality and so forth. Yet it is difficult to see why, and even more so to fathom why Marxists should seek either to underwrite this language of crisis or, *per contra*, to nurse the subject through its rocky passages by offering the consolation of a narrative system which, one day, just you wait and see, will prove to be true. To the contrary, these effects of 'the postmodern' ought to be welcomed as comprising, in their rejection of man-centred myths of history, an event as significant as Copernicus's challenge to the Ptolemaic system.

Wasn't this precisely the significance Althusser attributed to Marxism when pressing its claims to be considered a science of history: that, in its tendency if not as an accomplished fact, it embodied a break with those closed truths of philosophies of history which could only ever find in the real their own mirror reflections, in favour of an open-ended orientation to the production of new truths which did not require the figure of man as their organising centre?[47] In a word: yes. But if this is to be welcomed as a heroic achievement at the level of theory, why should its manifestations at the level of everyday life and culture be any the less welcome? Why should it be a problem that we live decreasingly under the miasmic weight of unifying, subject-centred narratives of history? Lynn Hunt has argued that the French Revolution witnessed the development of a thousand new 'political "microtechniques"' which, in investing costume, ceremonies, speech and behaviour with political significance, 'opened up undreamt-of fields for the play of power'.[48] Similarly, we are currently in the midst of a process in which the emergence of spheres of political struggle separated from the unifying influence of class struggle has led to an enormous increase in the politicisation of social and cultural life. The only proper response to this situation is not one of grudging and provisional tolerance, of granting a temporary autonomy to racial, sexual, familial politics, etc., with the rider that, eventually, these must be re-articulated to a unifying centre (class struggle) if any 'real changes' in social relations are to occur. Rather, it is one of recognising its irreversibility and responding positively – that is, non-appropriatively – to the rapid augmentation and rapid proliferation of the political which it produces.

From this perspective, to return to the concerns of literary history, there is no longer any political point to be served by the attempt to organise and validate continuist and unifying narratives of history through the constitution of literary texts as privileged representations through which the developmental course of the real might be deciphered. The production of such narratives is not necessary to the organisation of political subjects who are quite able to vote, strike, campaign for peace or for abortion law reform without imagining their activities as contributing to the realisation of a process governed by a phantom subject. Nor is it helpful in a field of ideological relations whose disposition increasingly gives such narratives little hold on the terms in which, to paraphrase Gramsci, subjects acquire a consciousness of their situation and act within it. We are all capable of acting as political agents within different histories without needing to believe that those different histories will be dovetailed and their different periodicities finally squared in some meta-History. And of acting as socialists. Socialism, as a set of political values representing the betterment of specific types of human relations, is perfectly capable of functioning as a regulative norm for political activity and of enlisting subject support without there being any need to represent its attainment as historically guaranteed or promoting the illusion that it will lead to the betterment of all types of human relations in the fulfilment of some historical prophecy. Indeed, the localisation and more precise specification of what is, and what is not, at stake in the conduct of socialist politics, the more precise delineation of what is to be gained, and lost, in the pursuit of socialist objectives, and the framing of such questions within more limited time frames: all of these – the prosaicisation of socialism – may well be necessary if it is to remain a significant political ideology.

In endorsing Nietzsche's concept of 'effective history', Foucault argues that 'knowledge is not made for understanding; it is made for cutting'.[49] If we adapt the terms of this argument to the concerns of literary history, it suggests that the question to be posed in relation to literary texts is not how to *understand* them but what to *do* with them – that is, how to modify their forms of deployment within contemporary social relations. And this requires a literary history that will seek not to distil the meaning of literary texts by referring them to a history which is conceived as providing an interpretative key to their meaning. Rather, it requires a literary history which, in producing a knowledge of the specific and differentiated ways in which literary texts have been deployed within past social relations, as parts of strategies of power and its contestation, will function as a cutting edge within the present, opening up the theoretical and political spaces in which literary texts might be detached from their current modes of social deployment and attached to new ones. It suggests a literary history that is less concerned with the hermeneutic interlacing of past and present within an overarching horizon of meaning than with establishing the discontinuities and differences which have characterised the forms of deployment and uses of literary texts in different historical circumstances.

Such a history is possible, however, only if the metaphysical associations of the literature/history couplet are abandoned.

LITERATURE, HISTORY, METAPHYSICS

In one of the more expansive formulations of the theoretical orientations informing his work, Stephen Greenblatt pins his colours to a conception of theory which will allow an understanding of literary works in the contingent and particular forms of their historical embeddedness. In doing so, he acknowledges his debt to deconstruction which he argues has contributed, alongside Marxism, to subverting 'the tendency to think of aesthetic representation as ultimately autonomous, separable from its cultural context and hence divorced from the social, ideological, and material matrix in which all art is produced and consumed'.[50] How so? Since the connections between deconstruction and the concerns of the 'new historicism' Greenblatt represents are not immediately apparent, it is worth looking closely at Greenblatt's answer to this question:

> For the undecidability that deconstruction repeatedly discovers in literary signification also calls into question the boundaries between the literary and the nonliterary. The intention to produce a work of literature does not guarantee an autonomous text, since the signifiers always exceed and thus undermine intention. This constant exceeding (which is the paradoxical expression of an endless deferral of meaning) forces the collapse of all stable oppositions, or rather compels interpretation to acknowledge that one position is always infected with traces of its radical antithesis. Insofar as the absolute disjunction of the literary and the nonliterary had been the root assumption of mainstream Anglo-American criticism in the mid-twentieth century, deconstruction emerged as a liberating challenge, a salutary return of the literary text to the condition of all other texts and a simultaneous assault on the positivist certitude of the nonliterary, the privileged realm of historical fact. History cannot be divorced from textuality, and all texts can be compelled to confront the crisis of undecidability revealed in the literary text. Hence history loses its epistemological innocence, while literature loses an isolation that had come to seem more a prison than a privilege.[51]

If deconstruction thus helps to return literature to 'the slime of history', it also helps us to rethink the nature of the history to which it is returned. No longer a domain of solid extra-textual realities, history is rather thought of as a complex of relations between different regions of textuality, including the literary. Consequently, since this embroils history within the endless play of *différance* – that is, the constitution of identities and meanings within the inherently unstable relations of their differing from and deferring to other identities and meanings – the question as to what history is and what it signifies becomes forever undecidable. Yet, while not disputing that this is so, Greenblatt is quick to note the limitations of the position:

> The problem with this theoretical liberation, in my view, is that it is forced, by definition, to discount the specific, institutional interests served both by local episodes of undecidability and contradiction and by the powerful if conceptually imperfect differentiation between the literary and the nonliterary.[52]

Two rather different points are being made here. The first is that to disqualify history from performing the role of a context or background in relation to which the meaning or effects of literary texts might be stabilised need not result in a perspective of radical indeterminacy. The gist of Greenblatt's argument here is that questions which may be undecidable in principle are frequently subjected to specific practical resolutions, albeit ones which may subsequently be undone so that those questions become undecided again. Thus, to take the question which concerns him – how to read Shakespeare historically – the fact that the history of the Elizabethan and Jacobean periods can no longer be regarded as providing an extra-textual anchor for 'the meaning' of Shakespeare's plays need occasion no major impediment to the continued pursuit of historical questions in the field of literary scholarship. Rather, he suggests it should prompt a re-alignment of literary and historiographical concerns. In place of the use of history as a means of deciding 'the meaning' of literary texts, Greenblatt proposes that historical inquiry should aim to recover the specific institutional strategies within which, at particular moments, literary texts are circumstantially embedded and from which – not forever and not for everyone, but for specific audiences and publics – they can be said to have functioned as the bearers of specific meanings and effects.

The argument is partly Wittgensteinian ('meaning' equals 'use') and partly Foucaultian ('use' refers to a text's placement within institutional strategies and power relations rather than its functioning in inter-individual communication). In both respects, it involves a displacement of the front/back, surface/depth model of the relations between literature and history. Consequently, to recall the alternatives posited by Widdowson, history no more serves as a means for the study of literature than literature serves as a means for the study of history. For the terms which allow these to be posed as opposites have been undercut. History does not supply a key with which to unlock the meaning of the literary text, nor does the latter function merely as a particular route into the study of a history conceived as a set of realities outside its own boundaries. Rather, the analysis of the literary text is incorporated within a project of historical recovery where the history that is to be recovered — that of literature's deployment within and as a part of institutionalised strategies of power — includes the literary as one of its integral components.

Yet this by no means denies the concept of the literary its specificity by simply flattening it out into a general, undifferentiated concept of history. This brings me to the second strand of Greenblatt's argument. For while admitting that the boundary line between the literary and the nonliterary is 'conceptually imperfect', Greenblatt none the less insists that analysis must take account of the particular terms in which this line is drawn and secured in specific circumstances. Although lacking any rigorous theoretical coherence, Greenblatt argues, the 'impure terms that mark the difference between the literary and the nonliterary are the currency in crucial institutional negotiations and exchanges'.[53] To discount this currency, therefore, would be to neglect one of the crucial institutional operators governing the terms in which, depending on how and where this boundary line is drawn, texts classified as literary are socially deployed.

It is possible, taking one's bearings from these arguments, to make use of those aspects of deconstruction which most radically unhinge the literature/history couplet, and yet do so without succumbing to their thrall. For the couplet is clearly vulnerable to the terms of Derrida's critique of the metaphysics of presence. This, as Michael Ryan summarises it, consists in the binary structure of thought, discernible throughout the history of western reason, which 'posits first and final causes or grounds . . . from which the multiplicity of existence can be deduced and through which it can be accounted for and given meaning'.[54] This structure of thought, in which one term of the polarity (history) is assumed to be prior and superior to the second (literature), inevitably means that the latter is 'made out to be external, derivative, and accidental in relation to the first'.[55] Deconstruction replies by upending such systems of opposition in showing that what is posited as an originary ground or foundation — and

71

thus as an identity complete in and of itself – can always be shown to be affected by, and thus dependent upon, what is posited as secondary and derivative in relation to that foundation. There can thus never be established that absolutely pure set of first causes, or unmoved movers, which metaphysical reasoning requires in order, so to speak, to get off the ground – for it can never secure the ground it needs from which to set itself in motion. In consequence, as Derrida summarises the argument:

> What is produced in the current trembling is a reevaluation of the relationship between the general text and what was believed to be, in the form of reality (history, politics, economics, sexuality, etc.), the simple, referable exterior of language or writing, the belief that this exterior could operate from the simple position of cause or accident.[56]

This, then, is the strong argument of deconstruction and where, to recall Selden's terms, its acid is most incisive. For it calls into question the very analytical topography of classical Marxism, refuting that dualistic ontology of the social whereby the economy or history is posited as an originary ground in relation to what are then construed as its secondary and derivative manifestations in ideology and literature. Yet, while unassailable on its own terms, difficulties accumulate rapidly if this aspect of deconstruction is allowed to run its own course untrammelled. For the result is then often a radical indeterminacy in which usable analytical distinctions of any kind are difficult to secure. Yet this need not be so if account is taken of those practices Greenblatt points to whereby conceptually imperfect distinctions (between the literary and the nonliterary, for example) are none the less secured as analytically focusable distinctions within the organisation of the social through the forms in which their distinctness is institutionally embedded.

It is by means of considerations of this kind that John Frow is able both to use and moderate the insights of deconstruction. The difficulty with the literature/history couplet and its analogues, Frow argues, consists in their subscription to a 'substantialist ontology' in which reality is conceived as divided 'into two parts, one of which is more real than the other'.[57] As an alternative, Frow proposes a conception of the social as consisting in the intricate interplay between institutionally zoned regions of practices whose make-ups are always integrally semiotic but which also, since signification always requires a material sign-vehicle, are equally material. In their combination of material and semiotic components, such practices thus constitute and occupy the same plane of an ontologically undifferentiated real in which all semiotic/material realities are allowed the same ontological force and presence:

> There can therefore be no absolute ontological distinction (of the order material/immaterial or real/symbolic) between the systems whose complex intrication constitutes the social structure. Rather, social structure can be thought in terms of a play of constraints, determinations, and restrictions exercised upon each other by a range of semiotic practices and institutions. This play will result in particular states of balanced tension which will shift as the complex convergence of forces at any one point shifts; there are no necessary outcomes or stages of struggle, and there can be no *general* model of the relation between components of social structure.[58]

Frow thus allows that the organisation of, and relations between, different institutionally zoned regions of practice are likely to vary with both time and place. Yet he also stresses the systematising mechanisms which work to secure those practices in particular positions and particular sets of inter-relations. It is in this light that Frow, resisting the deconstructionist temptation to smudge the boundary between the literary and the nonliterary, argues the need to retain a category of the literary – not for aesthetic reasons, but for the purposes of a refined and differentiated historical analysis. Arguing that 'the essentialist concept of "literature"' should be 'replaced by the concept of its particular historical occasions',[59] Frow both relativises the concept while also institutionalising it. If the former move avoids the sense of any transcendent and necessary distinction between the literary and the nonliterary, the latter prevents a slide into total indeterminacy; a literary/nonliterary distinction is maintained, but only at the level of the institutional mechanisms which work to secure it in different ways in different circumstances. A specialising function for the category of the literary is retained, but one whose effects are regarded as liable to variation in consequence of the institutional ordering of the relations between the literary and the nonliterary associated with different 'literary formations'.

I shall consider the details of this argument in a later chapter.

For now, I want merely to note the respects in which, in by-passing the effects of the literature/history couplet, it suggests an alternative approach to the tasks of literary history. For once this couplet is detached from a dualistic ontology, the logic which binds its terms into a relationship of connection-yet-separation falls apart. There are no longer any relations between different types of being to be fathomed. History becomes merely a catch-all word for the study of past social relations which, since those relations are now theorised as partly constituted through the imbrication of literary with other social systems, includes literature in its concept. The tasks of literary history thus cease to be the ones of a *special* kind previously enjoined by the need to theorise the connections between different types of phenomena. Instead, they become historiographic questions of a specific type in which the key issues concern the appropriate means of reading literary texts to examine the modes of their functioning within a specific literary formation and thus, through the specific modes of their imbrication with other social systems which result from the organisation of that formation, to reconstruct their place within the wider economy of the social.

At the same time, the nature of these particular tasks and their associated difficulties is significantly transformed. Foucault, in discussing the terms in which the history of thought is usually written, resists what he calls its interpretative or allegorical mode. The primary question in such inquiries, he argues, is: 'what was being said in what was said?'[60] Such analysis seeks to reach back behind the surface level of statements to discover, in the history which backgrounds them, another, deeper level of meaning, their unsaid, which allegorical analysis then claims as their real meaning, their truth. Foucault's concept of archaeology refuses this temptation: 'it does not question things said as to what they are hiding, what they were "really" saying, in spite of themselves'.[61] Instead, it examines statements at the level of what they say and, through what they say, what they do when viewed in terms of the conditions of existence which mark their relations to other statements within the same discursive field. Frow's contentions point in a similar direction. For their implication is that literary texts should be examined not to reveal what they say about past social relations but, through what they say, what they do within them where that doing is conditioned by the particular organisation and social placement of the literary formations which regulate the concrete forms of the social deployment and functioning of literary texts.

Expressed in this way the problems of literary history cease to be posable as general problems of a special kind to which there might be a general solution. Instead, analysis devolves upon the decipherment of the practical social functions performed by literary practices in the light of the ordering of their relations to other semiotic practices and institutions effected by the literary formations of which they form a part. The focus of such analysis might be, as in Greenblatt's study of Renaissance self-fashioning, on the part played by institutionalised literary practices as parts of more extended social systems bearing upon the formation of the structure of the self.[62] Or it may fall, as in Leonard Tennenhouse's work, on the part played by theatrical practices within the public staging of power.[63] Whatever the case, such lines of inquiry can only emerge from a close and detailed examination of the relevant literary and historiographic sources conducted with specific theoretical ends in view. Such analysis is not dependent on, nor is it aided by, any general theory of the relations between literature and history conceived as different orders of being which are then required to exhibit identical relations to one another in all possible circumstances.[64]

THE PAST IN THE PRESENT

In the mid 1970s, Barry Hindess and Paul Hirst caused something of a furore in Marxist circles when they sought to disentangle the concerns of Marxist theory from those of historical scholarship. The contention that all Marxist theory, however abstract and however general the field of its application, 'exists to make possible the analysis of the current situation'[65] drew down enough fire on their heads. Yet this was nothing compared with the flurry of objections created by their argument that history, conceived as the study of the past, was both incoherent and scientifically and politically valueless. Incoherent, they argued, because, as a matter of definition, the past does not exist and cannot therefore be conceived as a possible object of investigation. For if the past does not exist, how can it be studied? How can there be a disciplined study of what is acknowledged to be non-existent? And, if this objection is granted, then it follows that historical inquiry must be politically valueless. For if its object, the past, refers to that which

75

no longer exists, how can the study of such a non-existent affect the analysis of, and the conduct of politics within, the current situation? 'Historical events', as Hindess and Hirst put it, 'do not exist and can have no material effectivity in the present.'[66] The only way round this objection, they argued, was to conceive of social relations as essentially spiritual relations so that 'the past, although it has no material existence, has a spiritual effectivity, that is, it exists through its influence on the minds and souls of currently existing subjects'.[67]

It is small wonder that this set the cat among the pigeons. For if, in face of these objections, Marxism were to insist on conceiving itself as a historical discipline, it was implied that it could not then claim to be materialist too. And if it wished to be materialist, then it must abandon its pretensions to offering a science of history. A little hard to take for a tradition which had always suggested the necessary coupling of these two terms in insisting that analysis must always be historical *and* materialist, and that it could not be the one without the other. Yet most of the responses to Hindess's and Hirst's argument missed their mark, mainly because of their reluctance to concede the force of their critique of traditional conceptions of historical reasoning. For the logic of their position is unassailable. 'History's object, the hitherto existing,' as they put it, 'does not exist except in the modality of its current existence, as representations.'[68] As the argument is definitionally true, there is no point in employing the subtleties of dialectical reasoning in an attempt to circumambulate it. Yet the conclusions Hindess and Hirst draw from it by no means follow. Indeed, in manoeuvring history into an empiricist conception of its relations to its object (the past) and demonstrating the untenability of such a conception (owing to the non-existence of the past defined as the hitherto existing), Hindess and Hirst betray the iconoclastic impetus of their argument when they then go on to assert that historical inquiry cannot define its cogency or purpose in any other way.

While concurring with the logic of Hindess's and Hirst's critique, I have tried to show why this need by no means result in historical inquiry being driven into the corner in which they try to trap it. Rather than seeing history as aiming at a knowledge of the past, in the sense of the hitherto existing, I have suggested that it is more appropriately viewed as *producing knowledges which surface and have their effects within the past*, where the past is conceived as a complexly laminated social zone of representation. Viewed in this way historical inquiry may be allowed both a cogency and a political pertinence in the sense of having a direct and compelling influence on the present without that influence needing to be thought of as in any way dependent on the idealist mechanisms of spiritual effectivity. In subjecting representations of the past to a disciplined regulation, in its elaboration of rules and procedures for the disciplined interrogation of evidences which allow new knowledges to emerge and transform the face of the past, history does indeed make a material difference to and within the present. So, too, does literary history. But not in any special way. Its particularity consists merely in the types of evidences with which it deals and the particular zones of the past within which its knowledges surface.

4

THE SOCIOLOGY OF GENRES: A CRITIQUE

The development of a historical sociology of literary forms and functions – understood, here, as comprising both uses and effects – requires that answers be found to at least two questions. First: how are the relations between literary forms and functions to be viewed? And second: how are the tasks of synchronic and diachronic analysis to be conceived? It also requires that the answers to these questions should be co-ordinated so as to produce a coherent articulation of the relations between the formal and the functional and the synchronic and diachronic components of analysis.

For the most part, Marxist literary theory has premised its answers to these questions on the assumptions of the sociology of genres. According to these, the orders of the historical appearance, development, transformation and succession of genres – understood as 'kinds of writing' – are held to be socio-genetically accountable. Analysis thus focuses on the common social conditions obtaining whenever and wherever genres make their first and subsequent appearances, seeking in these their real foundations and supports. Or it accounts for the processes of generic transformation, whereby new genres develop out of and replace old ones, by relating these to underlying processes of social transformation which are held to constitute the propelling mechanisms responsible for the timing and direction of genre change. An identity, or relatedness, of form is thus attributed to an identity, or relatedness, of underlying social conditions. And, so long as this is so, then an identity, or relatedness, of function is held to flow from the similarities of form shared by writings belonging to the same genre. As Lukács once summarised the position:

> The forms of the artistic genres are not arbitrary. On the

contrary, they grow out of the concrete determinacy of the particular social and historical conditions. Their character, their peculiarity is determined by their capacity to give expression to the essential features of the given socio-historical phase. Hence the different genres arise at particular stages of historical development, they change their character rapidly (the epic is transformed into the novel), sometimes they disappear completely, and sometimes in the course of history they rise to the surface again with certain modifications.[1]

The argument is, at first sight, persuasive. It specifies a clear and convenient relation between formal and functional analysis – convenient because, since function, understood here as an expressive capacity, flows from form, the analysis of form and the analysis of function are identical. Moreover, it suggests a clear-cut and easily operational distinction between the tasks of synchronic and diachronic analysis. Synchronic analysis focuses on the form and function of temporally co-existent instances of a genre in the context of their shared conditions of production, whereas diachronic analysis claims the mechanisms of genre development – whether within a genre or from one genre to another – as its proper object of study.

Perhaps the most important aspect of the argument, however, has consisted in its strategic value as a vehicle for Marxist claims to found the study of literature on historical and materialist premises. For it has proved a useful and influential means of pressing such claims in rebuttal of the concerns of formalist literary analysis. In the purview of the latter, as Thomas Kent summarises it, genre theory is concerned 'to codify the objective, unchanging, formal literary conventions that remain inert or fixed throughout history'.[2] René Wellek and Austin Warren offer a forthright summary of this view. 'Theory of genres', they maintain, 'is a principle of order: it classifies literature and literary history not by time or place (period or national language) but by specifically literary types of organisation or structure.'[3] A socio-genetic conspectus on the orders of appearance and succession of genres thus brings literary forms down from the world of atemporal essences and archetypes to the mundane ground of variable social and historical realities. Yet, in doing so, it seems simultaneously to avoid the charge of reducing literature to a socially determined content. For, since it is insisted that it is at the level of form that the influence of social relations is registered within literature, such an approach to genre seems harmoniously to combine the tasks of formal analysis and those of social and historical analysis in suggesting that these should be regarded as integrally related. For since the form of a genre is regarded both as the bearer of social relations within the text and as the route through which the text re-enters social relations via its influence on the reader, the analysis of form, conditions, functions and effects can all proceed together and by the same means for they are all there, condensed in the same place, in the form.

It is small wonder, therefore, that many of the major applications of Marxist literary theory have been exercises in the sociology of genres – Lukács on the novel, Goldmann on tragedy, and Jameson on romance, for example.[4] Yet the logic of the relations which are posited, within such approaches, between social conditions, literary forms and their functions or effects can easily be unpicked. Here's Peter Bürger, also a Marxist, writing of periods in which similar kinds of writing can be found and warning against what might be called the 'sociological fallacy' underlying the sociology of genres:

> To turn this question into an occasion for a search after common historical and social characteristics of the two periods would surely be a mistake, for it would imply that identical art forms necessarily have an identical social base, which is certainly not the case. Instead, one will have to recognise that whereas art forms owe their birth to a specific social context, they are not tied to the context of their origin or to a social situation that is analogous to it, for the truth is that they can take on different functions in varying social contexts.[5]

Yet, if this is so, as it patently is, the series of equations on which the sociology of genres depends – commonality of conditions equals commonality of form which supports commonality of function – is called into question. And in its place there emerges a more complex set of possibilities for articulating the relations between form and function, between synchronic and diachronic analysis. Forms of analysis, for instance, in which the question of function is not tied to the analysis of originating conditions but may instead be related to the weave of determinations structuring particular relations of reception.

There are, then, grounds for reservation regarding the degree to which socio-genetic conceptions of genre are adequate to the requirements of a historical sociology of literary forms and functions. However, this is not to suggest either that the concept of genre might be dispensed with or that it should not be used and interpreted sociologically. Rather, my purpose here is to rethink the concept of genre and, in so doing, to redefine the nature of the historical and sociological enterprise within which it may be most productively and pertinently used. To anticipate my line of argument, it will be suggested that the concept of genre is more usefully interpreted when used as a means for analysing historically and culturally variable systems for the regulation of reading and writing practices than as a kind of writing amenable to a socio-genetic explanation. First, though, a fuller exposition of the logic of the sociology of genres is called for in order to identify its requirements and to show why these cannot be met.

THE SOCIOLOGY OF GENRES

In grouping Marxist approaches to genre under this heading, I do not mean to imply a relationship of complete identity between such approaches and those derived from the various strands of thought which define the tradition of classical sociology. To the contrary, the differences between these are readily apparent, consisting mainly in the way the social relations which are held to provide the underpinnings of literary genres are conceived. If, in the case of Marxist accounts, the prevailing structure of class relationships is typically called on to perform this role, Durkheimian sociologists look to the system of norms regulating social conduct, and especially to the ratio or balance between such norms, in order to provide genres with their social supports and rationales. Or, where Weberian assumptions predominate, the accent more typically falls on the mechanisms through which specific ideas and values – such as those of individualism and rationalism – come to suffuse the structure of the social relations from and within which genres emerge and develop. Yet, once such differences are allowed, the *type* of relations which these approaches posit between genres and social structure are substantially the same as are the various stages in the analysis through which such relations are organised. In brief, they differ at the level of the particularities of their arguments but not at that of the form of reasoning involved.

At the price of some over-simplification, this form of reasoning can be reduced to three moments: the moment of definition, the identification of the historical location of the genre in question, and the moment of socio-genetic explanation. I say 'moments', although 'components' would be more accurate since, in practice, each of these operations is conducted simultaneously in the sense that definitional criteria are often advanced in the light of prior decisions regarding where and when particular genres can be said to make their appearance and why they do so in those circumstances and not others. None the less, it will be convenient, for purposes of presentation, to proceed as if these three operations do constitute separated moments of analysis.

The first operation, the moment of definition, is essentially concerned to police the boundaries of the genre under investigation. It consists in the identification of formal criteria which can be used to distinguish the genre in question from other kinds of writing – both those which co-exist with it in the synchronic constitution of a given literary field and those which precede or succeed it in the historical evolution of genres. The requirement that there be such criteria is one imposed by what Derrida (subversively) calls 'the law of genre' where genres are conceived as taxonomic classes:

> There should be a trait upon which one could rely in order to decide that a given textual event, a given 'work,' corresponds to a given class (genre, type, mode, form, etc.). And there should be a code enabling one to decide questions of class-membership on the basis of this trait. For example – a very humble axiom, but, by the same token, hardly contestable – if a genre exists (let us say the novel, since no one seems to contest its generic quality), then a code should provide an identifiable trait and one which is identical to itself, authorising us to determine, to adjudicate whether a given text belongs to this genre or perhaps to that genre.[6]

The traits held to define a genre may be arrived at in a number of different ways. Very commonly, genres are defined and constituted in accordance with a logic of the lowest common formal denominator, thus grouping under the same genre writings which, although often markedly distinct in other respects, share at least one formal characteristic – and usually a fairly minimalistic one. Where this is the case, genres tend to be conceived as large classes with extended and usually fairly elastic boundaries. B. E. Perry, for example, defines the novel as an 'extended narrative' relating a story for the purposes of entertainment rather than edification, and is consequently able to include in the novel not merely all modern prose forms but those of classical Greece and Rome too.[7] Occasionally, genres are conceived as ideal-types defined in terms of a cluster of attributes which, while derived from specific instances of the genre in question, are rarely all present in their fully developed form in any one of these instances. When this is the case, the process of genre definition is essentially one of compiling an inventory of generic characteristics and, occasionally, of identifying key texts in which the resulting ideal-type of the genre is closely approximated. Howard Haycroft relies on this approach in proposing a check-list of the distinguishing generic traits of detective fiction – the convention of the locked room, the solution by surprise, and so on – and attributing both their innovation and their ideal-typical use to Poe.[8]

The more influential sociological studies of genre, however, have usually distinguished genres in terms of what the Russian Formalists called their dominants. As Jakobson defines it, the dominant is conceived as 'the focusing component of a work of art: it rules, determines, and transforms the remaining components'.[9] Where this is the case, genres are comprised of texts in which the same formal trait performs the structuring and organising role of the dominant, subordinating all other traits to its ruling influence. The mere occurrence of this trait is not a sufficient criterion for a text's inclusion in a genre. That trait must both be present and perform the function of the dominant if genre membership is to be granted. Equally, it matters little what other formal traits might co-exist with the generic dominant since this 'overdetermines' their functioning. Cervantes' *Don Quixote* and Kafka's *The Trial* may thus have little else in common, but they would both fall under Lukács's definition of the novel as a narrative form dominated by the function accorded the quest of a problematic hero for a set of authentic values in a world from which God, as the guarantor of life's meaningfulness, has withdrawn. For in both cases, it is this quest for a principle of transcendence – seemingly lacking but powerfully desired – which motivates the narrative.

The method used to define a genre clearly has significant consequences for the ways in which the remaining components of the analysis are conceived and conducted. Defining genres in terms of their lowest common formal denominators, for example, tends to result in genres being conceived as very broad categories including writings derived from societies which are historically distant from one another and often manifestly contrastive in their principles of social organisation. This then obliges the socio-genetic component of the analysis to focus on those minimally common aspects of social structure which might be looked to in order to provide the genre with a common social foundation in all of the social and historical contexts in which it occurs. Thus, when Perry asks why the novel, defined as an extended prose narrative aiming to entertain, should be found in both second-century Rome (*The Golden Ass*) and eighteenth-century England, he finds his answer in the rise of individualism.

If the procedure of defining genres in terms of their dominants has proved most influential within the sociology of genres, this is because it offers the most highly focused means of locating genres historically and of accounting for the orders of their historical appearance, repetition and/or succession. In so far as genres, so viewed, are defined in terms of their highest common formal denominators, they tend to emerge as more delimited and more precisely delineated classes with correspondingly sharper, less diffuse patterns of social and historical distribution. This tends both to limit the range of the inquiry as well as enjoining a more focused direction on the socio-genetic component of the analysis, since what has to be accounted for is not a spread of generic traits but the nature and functioning of the generic dominant. Since this is defined as essential to the constitution of the genre, the socio-genetic task is to identify an aspect of social structure which occurs wherever instances of the genre occur and which can be construed as equally essential in providing the generic dominant with its necessary social support.

Two types of such analysis might usefully be distinguished. The first concerns genres exhibiting an episodic or interrupted pattern of social and historical occurrence – appearing in one context, subsequently disappearing from the repertoire of culturally active genres, to reappear in later contexts. In such cases, analysis seeks to identify a distinctive principle of social organisation capable of supporting the generic dominant in all of the historically dispersed contexts of its distribution. Thus, Jean Duvignaud, interpreting the dominant of tragedy as consisting in the contradiction between the hero's/heroine's aspirations and the limitations imposed on their realisation by social restraint and tradition, argues that:

> tragedy and, more widely, theatrical creation in general, thus appear linked to the disequilibrium between social structure and spontaneity, between archaic restraints and appurtenances and liberty, between the systems of traditional values becoming a-typical in relation to individuals who revere them and the dynamism of modern life.[10]

Thus, both Greek and Shakespearean tragedy are said to be rooted in the common social condition of *anomie* (understood in the Durkheimian sense of an absence of clear and binding normative constraints on the limits of human aspiration) characterising the two periods. Moreover, this common condition is viewed as the effect of similar underlying social processes as fifth-century Athens and Elizabethan England are held to have been subject to similar forms of social transition – from relatively closed and traditional societies based on the principles of status ascription to the more open-ended and pluralistic structures of achievement-oriented societies. The distinguishing formal characteristic of tragedy is thus accounted for in terms of what are construed as the most important distinguishing social characteristics of the two periods: the highest common formal denominator meets and finds its support in the highest common social denominator. A commonality of form based upon a commonality of social conditions which, finally, has a commonality of function: that of facilitating an adjustment to the social and psychic strains occasioned by the condition of relative normlessless which accompanies the transition from one type of society to another.

A somewhat different logic of analysis is applied where a genre, regarded as having a distinctive moment of origin, is conceived as having subsequently been uninterruptedly present within a given historical repertoire of culturally active genres. This is most obviously true of definitions of the novel which construe the genre as a modern form and treat its origins and development as coincident with the origins and development of capitalism. In this case, the generic dominant finds its social support in social relations which are held to be constitutive of a particular type of society, thus enabling the continuing presence of the genre to be accounted for in terms of the continuing presence of the social relations which characterise that society. However, this often introduces a further dimension into the analysis in so far as the generic dominant may then be conceived as subject to a process of *progressive realisation* which proceeds alongside, and is conditioned by, the progressive development of the social relations which furnish its supports.

While this teleological conception of genre is not limited to the novel, its logic has been most fully and consistently developed in relation to theories of the novel. As this is also the genre which has attracted most sociological attention, it will be convenient, having identified the conditions required by the sociology of genres, to turn, now, to sociological accounts of the novel's origins and development in order to show why these conditions cannot be secured.

THEORIES OF THE NOVEL

Accounts of the novel which define the genre in terms of formal attributes accorded the role of a generic dominant share a number of general characteristics. First, they are largely agreed in viewing the novel as a distinctively modern genre whose origins and evolution are held to be coincident with the rise and development of capitalism. Second, they theorise the relationship between the novel and capitalism in terms of a 'master-text' of capitalism which specifies those aspects of social organisation which most clearly distinguish capitalism from other economic and social systems. Just as the definition of the generic dominant enables novels to be distinguished from other forms of writing with which they may share subordinate traits, so this component of the analysis enables capitalism to be distinguished from other social systems – with which it may otherwise share similar features – in terms of its 'social dominant'.

The result of these two procedures is the organisation of two diachronic series, each conceived in terms of a dominant – the origins and development of the generic dominant of the novel, and the origins and development of the social dominant of capitalism. The greater part of the analysis proper then consists in tracing a set of correspondences between these two series, but of correspondences subjected to a hierarchical organisation in that the social dominant nominated by the 'master-text' of capitalism is interpreted as providing the determining conditions for the novel's dominant and its evolution. The relations between these series, that is to say, are interpreted allegorically in the construction of the social dominant of capitalism as the previously hidden, but now revealed, support of the novel's dominant. As this social dominant is usually construed as a set of real social relations which exist prior to and independently of the novel, this has the further consequence that the latter's dominant is viewed as a secondary effect of social relations whose primary determinations are located outside of the literary sphere. This therefore gives rise to the need to identify mechanisms of connection through which the influence of the social dominant within the literary sphere can be accounted for.

We can differentiate such approaches, then, in terms of (a) their characterisations of the generic and social dominants, (b) their interpretation of the relations between them, and (c) the mechanisms of connection they posit in order to account for the influences of the latter on the former. However, this does not allow us, where such approaches differ significantly, to adjudicate their competing perspectives on the relations between the rise of capitalism and the development of the novel. This would require that such differences be conceived as contrasting accounts of the same set of literary and social phenomena, and their inter-relations, in order that they might then be regarded as susceptible to an empirical resolution. This is not the case. More typically, we confront theories which work with different empirical materials – that is, which accord their attention to different texts within different historical circumstances – as a consequence of the ways in which the generic dominant of the novel and the social dominant of capitalism are respectively defined. The main points at issue between competing sociologies of the novel thus centrally concern definitional decisions and their effects and, for this reason, often prove insoluble, driven into a discursive deadlock.

The consequences of this can be illustrated by considering two of the more influential accounts of the novel/capitalism relation that we have: Ian Watt's and Lucien Goldmann's. While identical in their explanatory logic, these differ significantly in all other respects. Their conceptions of the novel's dominant differ, so do their conceptions of the social dominant of capitalism. So, too, do the 'master-texts' of capitalism which govern their analyses and order their conceptions of the relations between the diachronic

87

series constituted by these two dominants: Weber's *The Protestant Ethic and the Spirit of Capitalism* for Watt, Marx's *Capital* for Goldmann. And they differ also in their conceptions of the mechanisms of connection which link these two series.

Let us consider Watt's account first. Watt identifies the first requirement for a theory of the novel as consisting in the need for 'a working definition of the characteristics of the novel – a definition sufficiently narrow to exclude previous types of narrative and yet broad enough to apply to whatever is usually put in the novel category'.[11] Watt meets this requirement by proposing that the novel be defined in terms of what he calls its formal realism, a distinctive narrative mode oriented toward an individualising, particularising and 'circumstantial view of life':

> The narrative method whereby the novel embodies this circumstantial view of life may be called its formal realism; formal, because the term realism does not here refer to any special literary doctrine or purpose, but only to a set of narrative procedures which are so commonly found together in the novel, and so rarely in other literary genres, that they may be regarded as typical of the form itself. Formal realism, in fact, is the narrative embodiment of a premise that Defoe and Richardson accepted very literally, but which is implicit in the novel form in general: the premise, or primary convention, that the novel is a full and authentic report of human experience, and is therefore under an obligation to satisfy its reader with such details of the story as the individuality of the actors concerned, the particulars of the times and places of their actions, details which are presented through a more largely referential use of language than is common in other literary forms.[12]

In the course of the discussion leading to this definition, Watt several times sounds a note of caution regarding the possibility of arriving at a clear-cut definition of the novel and, accordingly, of locating its genesis at any particular point in time. He thus points to the differences between the works of Defoe, Richardson and Fielding and the lack of mutual influence between them, noting also that the very term novel was not in current usage until the end of the eighteenth century. And no sooner is the definition advanced than Watt considers the further objection that many of the attributes of formal realism were not entirely new but had their analogues and forerunners in earlier forms of writing: Homer, Chaucer and Bunyan are among the cases he cites. Watt deals with this difficulty as follows:

> But there is an important difference: in Homer and in earlier prose fiction these passages are relatively rare, and tend to stand out from the surrounding narrative; the total literary structure was not consistently oriented in the direction of formal realism, and the plot especially, which was usually traditional and often highly improbable, was in direct conflict with its premises.[13]

This effects a reassessment of the significance accorded the attributes of formal realism. For they now appear not merely as 'so commonly found together in the novel, and so rarely in other literary genres', but as the novel's dominant, governing its total literary structure rather than, as was the case with their earlier use, being merely incidental features within genres governed by other dominants. It is this step that then enables Watt to specify the moment of the genre's origins more confidently and forthrightly than he had earlier been prepared to. Eighteenth-century England is justifiably regarded as the cradle of the novel to the degree that it marks a moment of mutation in the history of prose fiction, one in which attributes having a marginal existence in earlier prose forms are crystallised into a new combination which supplies the governing principle of a new literary structure.

Through these means, then, Watt is able (a) to mark off the novel as qualitatively distinct from earlier forms of prose fiction, (b) to produce a precise social and historical location for the genre's origins, and (c) to identify, in those origins, the defining attribute of the genre as a whole. This last step is critical. For if the first novels can be regarded as paradigmatic of the novel as such – as it seems they must be in order to be counted as the genre's origins – then all subsequent instances of the genre, since they are governed by the same dominant, can be regarded as exhibiting essentially the same type of relation to their supporting social contexts as those discernible in the relations between form and social structure which mark the moment of the genre's origins. This is a fortunate argument, for it means that the socio-genetic analysis of the genre's originary paradigm suffices also – allowing for the differing particularities of time and place – for the analysis of its subsequent instances.

It is thus that Watt's discussion of the paradigmatic instances of the eighteenth-century novel allows him to identify the social conditions required by the novel form *as such*:

> The novel's serious concern with the daily lives of ordinary people seems to depend upon two important general conditions: the society must value every individual highly enough to consider him the proper subject of its serious literature; and there must be enough variety of belief and action among ordinary people for a detailed account of them to be of interest to other ordinary people, the readers of novels.[14]

And, sure enough, Watt looks and finds the necessary supports for such a literary orientation in the 'uniquely individualist' orientation of modern societies which he attributes to two interacting causes: the rise of modern capitalism, understood in its Weberian sense as governed by an ethic of individualism and rationalism, and the spread of Protestantism. It is clear, moreover, that the forms and manifestations of individualism in societies in which such economic and religious ethics are implanted differ qualitatively from individualist forms of behaviour in earlier societies owing to the new role accorded values of individualism in constituting the governing principle of the social structure:

> In all ages, no doubt, and in all societies, some people have been 'individualists' in the sense that they were egocentric, unique or conspicuously independent of current opinions and habits; but the concept of individualism involves much more than this. It posits a whole society mainly governed by the idea of every individual's intrinsic independence both from other individuals and from that multifarious allegiance to past modes of thought and action denoted by the word 'tradition' – a force that is always social, not individual.[15]

If this suggests a relationship of correspondence between the generic dominant of the novel and the social dominant of capitalism, it does not provide a mechanism of connection capable of explaining how the latter came to furnish the former with its social underpinnings and support. This is supplied by Watt's account of the changes in the organisation of literary production and the composition of the reading public which enabled the social relations of capitalist individualism to become concretely influential within the literary sphere. The rise of an extended reading public, and of a new market-based system of literary production, thus enabled the novel to develop in response to the tastes and interests of middle-class readers (among whom the values of individualism were most deeply rooted) while also weakening the cultural influence of earlier, aristocratic forms of literary patronage and of the traditional literary genres which had been dependent upon them.

Watt's discussion is, of course, limited to the eighteenth-century English novel. However, his final chapter offers a glimpse of his understanding of the degree to which his analysis might be extended to other novels produced in other contexts. Two such forms of generalisation are envisaged. First, so far as the subsequent development of the English novel is concerned, Watt conceives this as a process in which the attributes of formal realism are progressively refined and developed until they achieve their finally perfected form in the novels of Jane Austen. In this account, the originating conditions of the novel are held to give a certain formal impetus to the genre which then develops along the trajectory marked out for it by the circumstances of its birth and in harmony with the subsequent development of the social relations – of middle-class individualism – which supplied its initial supports. The novel/society relation is thus held to be of essentially the same type throughout the different stages of the novel's development within the English tradition. Similarly, in the second extension to his argument, Watt argues that the novel becomes a significant genre outside England only when social conditions similar to those which occasioned its initial appearance come to obtain elsewhere:

> The course of French literature provides confirmation of another kind as to the importance both of the social and the literary factors whose connection with the early development of the novel in England has been presented here. The first great efflorescence of the genre in France which began with Balzac and Stendhal occurred only after the French Revolution had placed the French middle class in a position of social and literary power which their English counterparts had achieved exactly a century before in the Glorious Revolution of 1689.[16]

In summary, then, Watt defines the novel in terms of the role accorded a particular set of formal attributes. These, in being construed as expressive of particular forms of life, are thus connected to a particular structure of social relationships in which they find their support, doubling as both the novel's expressed content and its enabling conditions. The novel thus seems to be defined in positive terms – it consists of a definite set of attributes combined in specific patterns of inter-relation – as does the society which supports it.

Yet this appearance of positivity is misleading. In a recent review of genre theory, Anne Freadman argues that the procedure through which genres are defined and their boundaries delimited consists in a combination of like-statements and not-statements. Within this procedure, moreover, she suggests that, whatever the order of their presentation, not-statements are logically prior to, and govern the functioning of, like-statements. This entails that the attributes held to distinguish a genre cannot be specified as such without a prior delimitation of the space and boundaries of that genre by means of the use of not-statements. There is further, Freadman contends, a tendency for such not-statements to proliferate in view of the requirement that the boundaries of a genre be secured along many fronts at the same time. Establishing even the potential for the existence of a specific genre thus depends on securing a set of attributes whose potential for generic specification is derived from a contrastive analysis of their absence/presence and, if present, their function in what are taken to be the already-known formal fields of other genres.

'This seems to suggest', as Freadman puts it, 'that a genre cannot be defined by a single not-statement, but rather, that a generic definition ("definition" is, literally, "the tracing of boundaries" rather than the discovery of an essence) arises as (or "from") a series of contrasts which position "this" kind in among other adjacent kinds of texts.'[17] As a consequence, what Freadman calls the 'recipe theory of genres' in which genres are held to be definable in terms of a set of inherent characteristics, constituting a definite generic positivity, is called into question. For what are posited as inherent generic characteristics can only be so posited 'because they are correlated with *places in a system of contrasts*'.[18] Constituted as a system of differences (not-statements), genres are inherently relational constructs. Their positivity, once this is admitted, melts into air. It is no more than an appearance-effect which results from the organisation of a set of differences into an inventory.

92

To return to Watt: if formal realism is able to figure as the defining dominant of the novel, this is only because its component attributes have already been disentangled from other kinds of writing. It is, moreover, only the establishment of this system of negative relations which allows the novel's candidacy for generic specificity to be advanced. There is, then, no surprise in noting the profusion of not-statements in the opening chapter of *The Rise of the Novel*. The attribute of individualising characterisation is thus secured, potentially, as an aspect of the novel's constitutive positivity through a series of not-statements: names did not have the function of individualising character in comedy or earlier prose fiction, for example. Similarly, the particularisation of time and place is secured as a defining attribute of the novel through a further series of not-statements which detach this attribute from other kinds of writing: Aeschylus, Shakespeare and Bunyan, for example.

The difficulty is evident. If the positivity of the novel is defined in terms of a cluster of attributes which are arrived at via a process of negative differentiation, that positivity is liable to be differently conceived depending on the generic reference points which govern this process of differentiation. Nor is this merely a theoretical possibility. Theories of the novel abound and, more often than not, they are irreconcilable so far as their characterisation of the genre's positivity is concerned. Yet these incompatibilities are not the result of any procedural or methodological differences. To the contrary, they result from the fact that entirely the same procedural steps are taken but from within contrasting conceptions of the field of generic differences within which the novel is to be inserted and in terms of which its positivity is theorised.

Lucien Goldmann thus defines the novel as 'the story of a search for authentic values in a degraded mode, in a degraded society'.[19] The genre's positivity is thus held to consist in the narrative structure which results from the quest of a central character for a set of authentic values by which to live in a world which seems to lend such values neither sustenance nor support. The inspiration for this theory is drawn largely from Lukács's *Theory of the Novel*. Whereas Watt's not-statements mainly differentiate the novel from sixteenth- and seventeenth-century English literature as well as from earlier forms of prose writing, Lukács's theory of the novel is governed mainly by the statement that the novel is not the epic. As the genre of a world abandoned by God, the positivity of the novel consists not only in its difference from the epic but also in its necessarily thwarted aspiration to restore a sense of epic fullness and proportion to life. In the epic, Lukács argues, the lives of the protagonists are regulated by values whose authenticity, communal power and validity are unquestioned. Epic heroes do not agonise over what to do; their behaviour is prescribed for them by tradition and in this, Lukács contends, the epic reflected a society in which life was regulated by binding and accepted norms grounded in the rhythms of daily life. In the novel, by contrast, the hero has become problematic: the code by which he should live is no longer prescribed, and the novel's course consists in his attempts to discover and adopt such a code – attempts destined either to result in failure or to be realised only imperfectly.

Goldmann seeks a determining social ground for this characterisation of the novel's positivity in the structures of capitalist exchange. This involves an allegorical trans-coding of the novel's narrative structure such that it is read as emblematic of the everyday relations between man (*sic*) and commodities in societies dominated by capitalism. If the novel's structure is governed by the hero's quest for authentic values in a degraded world then so, in capitalism, everyday experience is informed by a tension between the desire for authentic use-values and the mediation of that desire via exchange-values which debase and degrade use-values. There is, Goldmann argues, a '*rigorous homology*' or correspondence between the two structures such that the novel can be read as '*the transposition on the literary plane of everyday life in the individualistic society created by market production*'.[20]

While this suggests that the novel embodies a specific form of social experience generated by capitalist economic relationships, it provides no account of the mechanisms of connection through which the process of this embodying is effected. This is provided by a slightly reworked version of the thesis of the artist's social marginality. Writers and artists, Goldmann argues, experience life as 'essentially *problematic* in so far as their thinking and behaviour remain dominated by qualitative values, even though they are unable to extract themselves entirely from the existence of the degrading mediation whose action permeates the whole of the social structure'.[21] So placed within the social structure that they experience, in a heightened form, a contradiction that is endemic to social life, writers are able to give that experience a formal shape and expression.

While, clearly, methodologically similar, Goldmann's construction of the novel–capitalism relation differs from Watt's in almost every salient particular. In part, as has already been noted, this is because the 'master-text' of capitalism governing the account is provided by Marx's discussion of the fetishism of commodities in *Capital* rather than by Weber's *Protestant Ethic and the Spirit of Capitalism*. Yet we can also now see how the deployment of such 'master-texts' is conditioned by a prior delimitation of the novel's positivity derived from the system of generic contrasts which governs the process of generic definition.

It is difficult to see how the respective strengths and weaknesses of such contrastive accounts of the novel's positivity might ever be adjudicated. In each case, the definition of the novel carries with it a set of already-determined rules for reading the relations between texts and social structure. There is, moreover, relatively little in common between the empirical ground to which these rules for reading are applied. In the Goldmannian view, for example, the founding paradigm of the novel is provided by Cervantes's *Don Quixote* which, as Pierre Vilar suggests, finds its social support in the early sixteenth-century Spanish experience of hyper-inflation.[22] In this reading, Quixote's chivalric illusions are a trans-coding of the money-illusion through which the relationship between desire and its object is mediated, money assuming the aura of a phantasmic value just as, in Quixote's world, everyday objects bask in the glow of chivalric values. Moreover, the trajectory of the genre's subsequent development is also differently conceived. In Goldmann's view, the novel is neither paced and conditioned by the development of bourgeois individualism, nor is its course that of the progressive refinement of realist techniques. Rather, the main staging-points in its development are provided by transformations in the structure of capitalism; it is the shift from one stage of capitalism to another – from liberal through monopoly to advanced capitalism – that accounts for the shift from one novel-type to another, from Balzac through to Robbe-Grillet.

When the deployment of the same method results in irreconcilable theories whose competing claims cannot be meaningfully assessed, there are good grounds for thinking the method is inherently flawed. It was with these difficulties in mind that Bakhtin suggested the concerns of genre theory, and particularly those of the theory of the novel, should be radically revised. Of the various attempts to distinguish the novel 'as an already completed genre from other already completed genres', Bakhtin argues, none has 'managed to isolate a single definite, stable characteristic of the novel – without adding a reservation, which immediately disqualifies it altogether as a generic characteristic'.[23] Either that or, *per contra*, the novel is defined in unduly restrictive terms with the result that one kind of novel is chosen as the privileged exemplar of the form at the price of neglecting other forms of writing commonly viewed as instances of the genre. In brief, no definition can be sufficiently precise to secure the novel's hermetic separation from the seepages of other genres, nor any sufficiently elastic to encompass its proliferation of sub-genres.

Nor, in Bakhtin's view, can the first of these difficulties be avoided by defining the novel in terms of the role of generic dominant assigned to certain formal attributes which, though they may occur elsewhere, are not accorded the same organising function. This move is illegitimate since, in Bakhtin's view, the novel is an unfinished genre and forever destined to remain so. The novel is, he argues, 'the genre of becoming'[24] – but, unlike the teleological structure of Watt's account or of Lukács's Hegelian conception of the novel's tendency to develop toward a restored epic fullness – of a becoming without fixed end or finality. For Bakhtin, the novel *is* not – it has no permanent set of formal characteristics which might define it – but *becomes*, constantly changing and developing, but not in any specified or pre-ordained direction dictated by the organisation of the relations between literary form and social structure which marked the circumstances of its origin. This being so, there can be no question of defining the novel in terms of the formal attributes governing its structure for it has no such structure; it never reaches a point of development at which its attributes congeal into a stable and identifiable pattern.

Instead, Bakhtin suggests, the novel should be conceived less as a definite form than as a set of processes operative within the field of writing. The novel, he argues, exists only as a loosely co-ordinated set of processes through which the 'novelisation' of the field of writing is effected, renewing, extending and enriching its possibilities. As Michael Holquist summarises this aspect of Bakhtin's argument:

'novel' is the name Bakhtin gives to whatever force is at work within a given literary system to reveal the limits, the artificial constraints of that system. Literary systems are comprised of canons, and 'novelisation' is fundamentally anticanonical. It will not permit generic monologue. Always it will insist on the dialogue between what a given system will admit as literature and those texts which are otherwise excluded from such a definition of literature. What is more conventionally thought of as the novel is simply the most complex and distilled expression of this impulse.[25]

While this novelising impulse had existed within the literatures of the classical and medieval periods, it was largely confined to subterranean literary forms. It took the form of a sub-literature which mocked and parodied the official genres of epic and tragedy but which also, when brought into contact with them, renewed and extended their possibilities. The point at which specifically social and historical considerations enter Bakhtin's analysis is the account he offers of the circumstances which allowed these earlier novelising tendencies to assume a position of cultural dominance. He attributes this mainly to the development, in the early modern period, of a heteroglossic literary culture in which many languages (of different nationalities, different dialects and idioms, etc.) interacted with and interanimated one another. This provided a basis not for a new genre characterised by a definite positivity; rather, it produced an expanded field of action for a set of processes which had hitherto impinged only marginally and periodically on literary culture. With the modern period, by contrast, novelisation becomes systemic and all-pervasive, the dominant principle of the modern literary system.

Nor, of course, do other genres remain unaffected by this process. Bakhtin prefaces his discussion of the novel by remarking that the novel is fundamentally distinct from the classical genres of tragedy and epic. Shaped in periods which preceded historical records, Bakhtin argues, these achieved a completed and fully perfected form which allowed them to function as canonical forces in the subsequent history of literature. Yet this is true only historically. When the process of novelisation becomes the literary dominant, it affects all genres, novelising them just as they, in turn, become sources of novelisation. If the novel is characterised by its forever openness and unfinishedness, then so, too, are other genres. In sum, if, as Derrida contends, the law of genre is that genres should not be mixed, yet they always are, Bakhtin socialises and historicises this process of generic mixing by relating it to the perpetual motion of modern literary culture produced by its openness to the endless mixing and mingling of languages, cultures and literary styles.

In summary, then, the conditions required by the logic of the sociology of genres cannot be met. There is no reason to suppose that genres can be constituted as definite literary structures underpinned by similar sets of social conditions. Indeed, if Bakhtin's arguments hold, there is every reason to suppose that what we call novels, for example, are just as distinct from one another as they are from other conventionally recognised genres and, accordingly, that they are related to quite different sets of conditions in different ways in different literary and social and historical circumstances. This being so, the capacity of the concept of genre to serve as a privileged means of organising the concerns of the socio-genetic analysis of literary forms is called into question. If genre is to be accorded a place within the concerns of sociological inquiry, some rethinking is in order regarding the kind of distinction the concept is capable of registering and the purposes for which it can be used.

GENRE AS INSTITUTION

In the early sections of *Philosophical Investigations*, Wittgenstein reviews the many and varied phenomena which, without any apparent sense of incongruity, we call 'games' even though there is no single common feature which they all share: .

> Consider for example the proceedings that we call 'games', I mean board-games, card-games, ball-games, Olympic games, and so on. What is common to them all? — Don't say: 'There *must* be something common, or they would not be called "games"' — but *look and see* whether there is anything common to all. — For if you look at them you will not see something that is common to *all*, but similarities, relationships, and a whole series of them at that. To repeat: don't think, but look! — Look for example at board-games, with their

multifarious relationships. Now pass to card-games; here you may find many correspondences with the first group, but many common features drop out, and others appear. When we pass next to ball-games, much that is common is retained, but much is lost. . . . And we can go through the many, many other groups of games in the same way; can see how similarities crop up and disappear.

And the result of this examination is: we see a complicated network of similarities overlapping and criss-crossing: sometimes overall similarities, sometimes similarities of detail.

I can think of no better expression to characterise these similarities than 'family resemblances'; for the various resemblances between members of a family: build, features, colour of eyes, gait, temperament, etc. etc. overlap and criss-cross in the same way. – And I shall say: 'games' form a family.[26]

There are, in short, no absolute or fixed boundaries which demarcate what may be counted as a game from what may not; not all games are counted as such for the same reasons, nor do they share some uniquely distinguishing property of 'gameishness' because they are so counted. Much the same, Alistair Fowler argues, is true of genres:

Representatives of a genre may then be regarded as making up a family whose septs and individual members are related in various ways, without having any single feature shared in common by all.[27]

Disputing the view that genres comprise taxonomic classes, Fowler's *Kinds of Literature* is an exercise in Wittgensteinian 'looking and seeing'. Reviewing what he calls the 'generic repertoire' – aspects of writing which have, either individually or in clustered combinations, at one time or another acquired specific generic associations – Fowler concludes that none can be regarded as essentially defining a particular genre or as being exclusively associated with it. Take, for example, the organisation of the reader's task, one of the elements of Fowler's 'generic repertoire'. Detective fiction is often defined in terms of the dominant position it accords what Barthes calls the hermeneutic code,[28] in which the reader's interest is made to centre on resolving the mystery which motivates the narrative. Yet there are many detective fictions in which the hermeneutic code does not predominate even though, in other respects, they are much like other detective fictions and would normally be regarded as such. This is true of Poe's 'The Purloined Letter', where any sense of a mystery to be resolved is dispelled from the outset, even though it is regarded as having established one of the founding paradigms of the genre. Equally, the hermeneutic code may play a major role in many narratives which would not normally be regarded as instances of detective fiction. Victor Sklovskij has thus shown how Dickens's *Little Dorrit* criss-crosses and superimposes on to one another a series of mysteries in ways which constantly maintain hermeneutic questions at the forefront of the reader's interests.[29]

In place of the view of genres as taxonomic categories, therefore, Fowler suggests genres are more meaningfully viewed as effecting a much looser organisation of relations of similarity and difference in the field of writing. Rather than being characterised by any definite positivity, they can perhaps best be regarded as comprising a relay structure of resemblances in which x is related to z not because of any shared fundamental characteristics but because both bear resemblances, albeit perhaps different ones, to y. Genres, thus viewed, function as devices of assimilation. One would be hard put, for example, to trace any fundamental similarities between Peter Corris's Cliff Hardy novels and Poe's 'The Murders in the Rue Morgue' or, for that matter, between their supporting social conditions. Yet these novels can be assimilated to Poe's stories via their similarities to/differences from the stories and novels of Chandler and Hammett, which in turn can be related to/ distinguished from the tradition of Sayers and Christie and so on, through Conan-Doyle and back to Poe. This does not, it should be clear, establish a chain of equivalences; to the contrary, the process of generic assimilation depends upon, and results in, the establishment of a set of significant differences within a loosely related textual corpus.

This may suggest, contrary to the logic of the sociology of genres, that the concept of genre is amenable to sociological deployment in highlighting those specific differences between related forms of writing which most stand in need of sociological elucidation. As in a family, so to speak, resemblances are of less interest than the variations between its different septs and branches. The point of locating Conan-Doyle's Sherlock Holmes stories and Chandler's Philip Marlowe novels in the detective fiction genre is thus not to identify a fundamental commonality between them to be accounted for in terms of similarities in their underlying social conditions. Rather, it is to pinpoint those aspects in which they most manifestly differ – their differing representations of the city, for example – as the most pertinent focal points for social and historical inquiry.

While of an evident pragmatic value, this interpretation of genre still courts a theoretical objection in its assumption that the system of family resemblances comprising a genre consists in a set of inherent differences/similarities which are available for observation and description. Here, Wittgenstein's injunction to simply look and see proves misleading. For, in the case of genre as well as that of games, one does not know what to look at or for without some prior delimitation of the field. However, as we have seen, precisely how the potential field of a genre will be delimited depends on the functioning of those not-statements which differentiate the genre concerned from other genres. It is only when the possible existence of a generic field has been cleared in this way that the process of assimilating texts to one another within that field via a system of family resemblances can commence. The evident difficulty here is that, depending on the not-statements deployed in its constitution, the way a genre is conceived – in itself and in its relations to other genres – may prove liable to considerable cultural variation.

Fowler alludes to this consideration when he remarks that genres 'have circumscribed existences culturally'.[30] That this is so, however, is due to cultural and historical fluctuations in the composition of generic systems. If genres are unstable entities, this is because the generic systems, within which their differences from/ similarities to other forms of writing are thematised, are themselves unstable. The genre distinctions which are operative in one society may not be so in another, with the consequence that the same texts may be subject to different generic classifications in different social and historical contexts. Detective fiction provides a convenient case in point. While, in the British context, detective fiction is regarded as generically distinct from the spy thriller, this is not so in America where, in subsuming both spy and crime thrillers, detective fiction functions as a more expansive genre.[31]

The differentiating/assimilating function of a genre, then, depends on the organisation of the system of generic contrasts within which it is deployed. Apart from varying culturally, such generic systems are also mutable, constantly in the process of being transformed as the development of new forms of writing allows new ways of organising relations of similarity and difference in the field of writing. At times, this may result in a violent, kaleidoscopic restructuring of the field of generic contrasts which retrospectively nullifies earlier generic systems in severing particular writings from the genres to which they were earlier assimilated and installing them in new ones. Indeed, this is typically the process involved in the constitution of a new genre. It is only retrospectively, for example, that Poe's 'The Murders in the Rue Morgue' has been viewed as a detective story, since this was not an operative genre category in the period of its initial publication. First published in *Graham's Magazine*, the Philadelphia weekly edited by Poe, the story was subsequently brought out in a collection of Poe's works entitled *Tales of Mystery and Imagination*. Indeed, in some contexts, the story was not even classified as fiction: when first published in Britain, in an 1844 issue of the *Edinburgh Journal*, it was introduced as an 'article' while Poe was described as 'an acute observer of mental phenomena' rather than as an author.[32]

In the light of these considerations, Fowler suggests, genres are best viewed as literary institutions whose primary function is to organise the framework of expectations within which, in specific social and cultural contexts, reading is located. They form a part of what Jurij Lotman calls the 'extra-text': that is, the culturally specific knowledges, associations and assumptions which inform and animate particular reading practices.[33] Anne Freadman reaches a similar conclusion, while also lending it a specific inflection, when she suggests that 'what we do with genres is not to know them inherently but to know – "tell", or enact – the differences *between them*'.[34] A text's genre belongingness, she argues, is determined not by its semiotic properties but by its uptake in particular reading practices. In this sense, a genre consists in nothing but its definition and the particular organisation of reading practices it proposes. Given this, she argues, 'all attempts to correlate a system of generic labels with a system of semiotic properties must therefore fail'.[35] In lieu of the search for a true taxonomy, Freadman suggests, the proper concern of genre theory is with the part played by culturally operative genre distinctions in the social administration of reading practices:

> In these circumstances, the task of a theory of genre might be to provide strategies of analysis of the intrication of a text in the systems deployed to classify it, of the operations of these systems as they determine use, and of their clash, their intersection, or their complicity in the guidance and governance of semiosis.[36]

This formulation usefully avoids many of the difficulties associated with the sociology of genres which, as we have seen, rests on what might be called a 'cultural logic' in that it constitutes its object of analysis on the basis of formal attributes which are posited as intrinsic to the genre under investigation. Freadman's approach, by contrast, is de-essentialising. Genres, in this account, emerge as variable social and historical constructs to the degree that their constitution − which is, in any case, always provisional − is held to be intertextually determined. As the product of culturally specific organisations of the relations of similarity and difference within the sphere of textuality, genres are relationally rather than immanently determined. As such, moreover, their determination is always temporary. Whether a particular genre will be recognised as distinct or not, and if so, the ways in which it will be aligned to/differentiated from other genres is not given once and for all but will depend on the effects of changes taking place elsewhere in the sphere of intertextuality and the forms of inter-generic readjustments to which these give rise.

The chief difficulty with this account, however, consists in the particular kind of de-essentialising analysis it embodies. For it is, at root, a literary one. The deconstruction of the concept of genre as a taxonomic category results in a deconstructive conception of literary history in which the indeterminacy of genres is accounted for in the same way as is the indeterminacy of signification in general. The identity of genres, that is, cannot be positively specified to the degree that genres are held to be caught up within an endless play of *différence* and *différance*. Equally, their provisional fixity is accounted for as merely a culturally arbitrary way of calling this endless play to a halt, of governing semiosis. As a consequence, all of the qualities which deconstruction attributes to the literary text are transferred, via the category of genre, to the sphere of literary history in general. Analysing the uptake of literary texts in reading practices turns out to mean that attention should focus on the specific forms of intertextuality governing the composition of a given inter-generic field and attributing to this the power to determine the circumstantial forms in which literary texts are deployed. The role of genres in the social regulation of reading practices thus turns out to be an invariant one ('the governance of semiosis') whose accomplishment subordinates the role of extra-textual considerations – the particular occasions and uses of reading – to the influence of a generalised form of intertextuality.

The source of these difficulties lies in Freadman's failure to limit the place she accords the perspectives of deconstruction in her argument. These perspectives are of considerable value in two respects: first, in showing how and why the genre taxonomies proposed by traditional (and sociological) literary scholarship cannot be secured; and, second, in stressing the degree to which both the genre-belongingness of individual texts and the systems of relations between genres are historically mutable. They are, however, of little concrete assistance when it comes to examining how and why changes in both a text's genre-belongingness and the constitution of genre systems may change. While, in resisting the closures of essentialising forms of analysis, deconstruction theoretically opens the door to new forms of historical analysis, it offers no means of passing through that door to produce new forms of historical knowledge. All it can accomplish is the transformation of the past into an endless text which can then be subjected to a literary reading which, as it must, promises its own eventual deconstruction.

It is thus quite erroneous to assume that the theoretical instability of genres as taxonomic categories results in a necessary instability in the functioning of the genre categories prevailing in particular circumstances. Indeed, as Bakhtin's perspectives on the novel suggest, such instability might more pertinently be regarded as a distinctively modern phenomenon, an effect of the processes of generic mixing he attributes to the 'novelisation' of literature, rather than as a necessary result of the structure of difference/ deferral attributed to signification in general. For, of course, however true it may be that all systems of signification can be so characterised, it by no means follows that this perspective can serve to analyse the functioning and modes of deployment of historically specific regimes of signification. Indeed, although this is to anticipate the argument of a later chapter, deconstruction can pertinently be regarded as a specific variant of the modern regime of literary reading, whose application to the study of past regimes of reading constitutes an instance of the tendency of ahistorical literary formalisms to extend their sway beyond the sphere of the literary in subsuming all spheres of inquiry within their protocols for reading.

We must, then, look elsewhere for an adequately social and historical alternative to the cultural logic of the sociology of genres. It will therefore be useful to review again the objections to this approach, but this time from a different perspective – one which will locate the boundaries between genres in terms neither of intrinsic formal attributes nor of relational constructions of similarity, *différence* and *différance*, but in the social occasions and technologies which, regulating practices both of writing and of reading, constitute genres as particular, socially circumscribed fields of textual uses and effects. This will entail construing genres not as particular forms of textuality nor as provisional nodal points within specific systems of intertextuality which serve to keep the threat of semiosis at bay – a threat which, practically speaking, has relatively little bearing on the circumstances of literature's deployment outside of the modern literary formation whose effects we have no wish to eternalise.

Rather, it will entail viewing genres as being *inter-textually* constituted – that is, as being constituted in the particular socially organised sets of relations between texts, and between texts and readers, which obtain in particular circumstances in view of the reading formations and reading technologies which govern the relations between texts and readers.[37] It will, that is to say, entail viewing genres as immanently social and historical entities – not in the sense that they are relational constructs but in the sense that they form organised spheres of sociality of which their textual components are but a part. Rather than being literary kinds that are to be accounted for socio-genetically, it will be argued, genres are more appropriately regarded as themselves directly sets of social relations which, in structuring the sphere of reading practices, serve also to condition writing practices. They perform this conditioning role, however, not as a set of social realities 'behind' the text which analysis must therefore read through to uncover but as organised regions of sociality which call forth the practices of writing they require in order to be sustained.

GENRE SYSTEMS: PRODUCTION, READING

In our previous remarks, particularly when comparing historical novel and historical drama, we went to some length to show that every genre was a particular reflection of reality, that genres could only arise as reflections of typical and general facts of life that regularly occur and which could not be adequately reflected in the forms hitherto available.

A specific form, a genre must be based upon a specific truth of life. When drama divides off into tragedy and comedy (we shall disregard the intermediary stages), the cause lies in the facts of life which these forms reflect and *dramatically* reflect.[38]

A more succinct statement of the logic of the sociology of genres could hardly be asked for. It is true that the ambiguity in Lukács's terminology – oscillating between the 'facts of life' and the 'truth of life' – reflects a somewhat uneasy compromise between the Simmelian legacy of his earlier sociology of drama and the Marxist base/superstructure conception.[39] None the less, it is clear that, for Lukács, the central problems of genre theory concern the decipherment of the relations between socially determined forms of life and forms of writing so as to reveal the impress of the former on the latter. Literary form, here, flows on from social conditions as their determined effect. Where such conditions remain relatively constant, then so does the repertoire of genres; where, *per contra*, changing conditions of life cannot be adequately reflected within existing genres, then new literary forms are brought into being to achieve this end. Perhaps most indicative, however, is Lukács's contention that a case for genre specificity can be upheld only if a particular form of writing can be shown to rest on and give expression to distinctive social conditions. He thus disputes the view that the historical novel might be regarded as a genre in its own right on the grounds that the answer to the decisive question here – 'which facts of life underlie the historical novel and how do they differ from those which give rise to the genre of the novel in general' – must be: 'none'.[40]

I have sought to query the rationality of such approaches to genre by subjecting the procedures on which they rest to a (mildly) deconstructive critique. Genres, it has thus been argued, cannot be characterised in terms of a definite positivity in the manner required for them to be pinned down to specific attributes of social structures in a one-on-one relation. At the same time, the limitations of such a purely deconstructive critique were also noted. The mere insistence that genres are indeterminate, it was suggested, does not make amenable to analysis the processes through which, in particular contexts, genres are constituted as particular spheres of social relations which both summon forth particular writing practices and regulate their social uses.

The implications of these considerations, however, are not restricted to the theory of genres. As was noted at the outset, the sociology of genres offers a paradigm case of the logic governing the ways in which socialising and historicising categories of analysis are deployed within classical Marxist and sociological approaches to the study of literature. My criticisms of the sociology of genres have therefore had a broader purpose in view: to identify the presuppositions and lacunae inherent in this specific mode of deployment of socialising and historicising categories of analysis and, in the light of these, to propose an alternative analytical logic that will be better able to account for the intrication of texts and social relations.

Or, more accurately: the intrication of texts *in* social relations. For, at root, the problems inherent in the sociology of genres derive from the antinomial conception of the relations between literature and society which dogs its footsteps at every turn. The problem is not that such conceptions deny literature an active role in social life; the invention of an appropriate optical metaphor − literature as true or distorted reflection, or literature as offering a vision of ideology − always ensures that such a role can be found. Rather, it consists in the fact that literature/society relations are always theorised from a standpoint which posits their initial separateness and from within a hierarchical conception of the relations of determination between them which entails that literature's sociality is held to consist in the ways in which it is shaped by social (= nonliterary) pressures. It is this formulation of the matter, of course, which gives rise to the famous problem of mediations: that is, of how to theorise the connection between, while also retaining the separateness of, literature and society. Yet, no matter how complex and nuanced the role accorded such mediations, this way of posing the problems implies a definite order of priorities in which society always comes first and literature follows on – however indirectly – as its determined effect. As a consequence, the role of literature in the constitution of social relations is always conceived as essentially epiphenomenal and as dependent on an invariant mechanism: the nature of the consciousness of, or mode of adjustment to, society which the subject derives from the structure of the literary text. Thus conceived, literature's role in society is always a reactive one consisting in the modifications to already determined social relations which might be expected to flow on from its effects on the always already-determined subjectivities of social agents.

By contrast, in the view argued here, literature might appropriately be regarded as an institutional site providing a specific set of conditions for the operation of other social relations, just as those relations, in turn, provide the conditions for its own operation. Raymond Williams alludes to such a conception when he argues that the 'changing relationships which are evident in the changing practice of writing . . . are in themselves social and historical relationships', suggesting that the analysis of the practical history of writing should focus on how, 'in this increasingly important practice, people assumed, developed, extended, realised and changed their relationships'.[41] In this view, literature is regarded as itself directly a field of social relationships in its own right and one which interacts with other fields in which social relationships are organised and constituted *in the same way as they interact with it and on the same level*. Thus viewed, it emerges not as a mediated reflection or refraction of society, nor as a distinctive semiotic production of ideology – as if society or ideology had clearly defined existences which could be described independently of the operations of the literary sphere – but as a distinctive sphere of social action that is centrally implicated in and imbricated with the constitution and functioning of political and ideological relations of power and its contestation.

The implications of this for the theory of genre are clear. Its tasks do not devolve upon the decipherment of the impress of socially determined 'forms of life' on the structures of literary forms and the orders of their succession. Rather, its concern is with the ways in which forms of writing which are culturally recognised as generically distinct in the contexts under investigation function within the 'forms of life' – the specific modes of organised sociality

– of which they form a part. Its purpose, moreover, is to examine what genres *do* within and as parts of such modes of sociality rather than to reveal how their determined conditions speak through them.

Stephen Heath's *The Sexual Fix* offers a convenient illustration of the lines of theoretical inquiry which are opened up once this position is adopted. Rather than approaching the novel as a specific form whose peculiarities are to be accounted for in terms of a set of underlying social conditions, Heath views it as forming a part of a wider culture – the culture of 'the novelistic' – which, since the nineteenth century, has effected 'the constant narration of the social relations of individuals, the ordering of meanings for the individual in society'.[42] This is not a question of uncovering the forms of an already-determined individualism which the novel expresses; rather, attention focuses on the role of novels (rather than the novel), alongside related forms of writing and practices, in constituting and organising specific social forms of in-dividuality. Viewed in this light, novels are to be investigated with regard to their functioning as parts of an extended, but none the less historically specific, cultural technology of self-formation.

While not privileging sexuality as the only region of sociality in relation to which novels play this crucial formative role in the organisation of social life, Heath's own interests centre on the part they play in the social regulation of sexual conduct. Within this context, he examines the consequences of a particular change in the functioning of 'the novelistic' associated with the transformation from marriage to orgasm as the typical form of novelistic narrative resolution. This transformation in the 'sexual economy' of novelistic writings is theorised and described in relation to the development and extended social circulation of new discourses of sexuality associated with the twentieth-century rise of sexology. Neither of these developments, however, is construed as the cause or origin of the other. Rather, in Heath's account, they overlap and interact – not just discursively but also at the level of the institutions which produce and circulate them (the blurred boundaries between fictions and sexological reports in soft-porn men's magazines, for example) – as parts of related apparatuses or technologies for the regulation of sexed identities and behaviours. Nor is either viewed as reflecting or being prompted by changes in sexual conduct or in attitudes toward sexuality taking place in some space of society notionally secured as separate from the effects of literary, medical and scientific discourses. Such a view will not wash, Heath argues, because 'life is permeated by and – as "life" – made up of representations, grasping and rendering and ordering all experience'.[43] Novelistic constructions of sexuality, in other words, help to organise the spheres of sociality within which particular sexual capacities and identities are formed; they are among the instruments – the social engines – of particular forms of sexualisation.

What conclusions follow from this regarding the place of genre theory within the concerns of literary history? In so far as such investigations are concerned to recover the field of functions, uses and effects through which literary texts contribute to the formation of specific modes of organised sociality during the period of their initial production/reception, they require a set of procedures which must be precisely the reverse of those of the sociology of genres. For, as we have seen, the processes of genre constitution which characterise this approach require that literary texts be abstracted from the genre systems within which they were initially deployed in order that, on the basis of the shared formal attributes deemed pertinent to the definition of the genre concerned, they can then be lined up with other texts, similarly abstracted from the genre systems pertaining in the contexts of their initial production, so that the quest for shared underlying social conditions can be cogently pursued. Watt's constitution of *Robinson Crusoe* as a founding paradigm of the novel, conceived as a distinctively literary form, Ian Hunter has thus argued, depends on its abstraction from the contemporary genre of puritan conduct manuals and the forms of reading these produced.[44] Contrary to appearances, therefore, the method of the sociology of genres is radically ahistorical; its problematic requires that it overlooks such detailed facts of literary history in order to constitute its object.

If, *per contra*, historical analysis is to uncover the regions and modes of sociality within which forms of writing were operative in the circumstances of their initial production, account must be taken of the organisation of the system of generic differences – conceived as a differentiated field of social uses – prevailing at that time in terms of its influence on both textual strategies and contexts of reception. Furthermore, account must also be taken of the specific institutional frameworks conditioning the deployment of literary texts in order to assess the regions of sociality to which, at the time, they were concretely connected and within which they

THE SOCIOLOGY OF GENRES

operated – as parts of technologies of self-formation, nation-formation or class-formation, for instance, or as combinations of these.

The revised understanding of Shakespeare proposed by the 'new historicists' offers as good an instance as any of the compellingly different kind of socialising and historicising logic which results when such considerations are taken into account. The part Foucault's work has played in prompting the 'new historicists' to read Shakespeare's dramas in terms of the place occupied by the theatre within the strategies for displaying monarchical power characteristic of the Elizabethan and Jacobean polities is well-known. However, it is also clear that their revised estimation of the functioning of Shakespeare's work in the context of these political relations has required a suspension of the assumptions of genre analysis – a requirement anticipated by Foucault[45] – in order to view the strategies of the dramas in terms of their relations to the inter-textual and institutional co-ordinates pertinent to the circumstances of their initial production. Leonard Tennenhouse's *Power on Display* is especially interesting in this respect. Noting the devices he resorts to in order to avoid imposing the terms of modern literary readings on Shakespeare's texts – relating these to royal speeches or proclamations, to ledger reports and parliamentary reports, rather than to earlier or later moments in the evolution of drama – Tennenhouse goes on to argue the respects in which he found it necessary to jettison the assumptions of conventional genre analysis in order to open up a sense of the radical historical otherness of the political relations in which Shakespeare's drama was initially implicated:

> To the degree that the Renaissance theatre performed a political function utterly different from the scene of reading, we may assume Shakespeare's plays, unlike the written Shakespeare, were not enclosed within an aesthetic framework. They opened onto a larger arena of events and observed a transgeneric logic. In my account of Shakespeare's drama, then, stagecraft collaborates with statecraft in producing spectacles of power. The strategies of theatre resembled those of the scaffold, as well as court performance, I am suggesting, in observing a common logic of figuration that both sustained and testified to the monarch's power, a logic

111

which by definition contradicts that inhering in generic study such as Frye's.[46]

Why so? Because, as Tennenhouse puts it earlier, the 'arrangement of plays according to generic categories automatically detaches the work from history and presumes the internal organisation of its meaning'.[47] It allows the attribution of a 'cultural logic intrinsic to a particular form' to be substituted for, and to override, 'the vicissitudes of political conflict' determining the operative forms of inter-textual and institutional relations regulating the concrete, historically varying modes of deployment of literary texts.[48] The sociology of genres constitutes a positive impediment to the development of a theoretical framework appropriate to the pursuit of such concerns. Its socialising and historicising rhetoric turns out, on closer inspection, merely to mask a conventional concept of genre which, in spite of its sociological trimmings, abstracts texts from the historically particular inter-textual, institutional and political relations regulating the modes of their social deployment. In so doing, the sociology of genres constitutes what is, in effect, a purely literary tradition – albeit one which appears to be grounded in the real stuff of social relations. If these difficulties are to be avoided, the procedures through which the sociology of genres constitutes the genres it then seeks to account for socio-genetically must be resisted. Indeed, the proper concern of genre theory is not to define genres – for this can only result in sets of institutionalised prescriptions for the regulation of contemporary reading practices – but to examine the composition and functioning of generic systems. Moreover, as Tennenhouse testifies, this requires that analysis must consciously extricate itself from currently existing genre definitions in order to recover the systems of inter-textual and institutional relations which regulate the spheres of political and ideological relationships in which forms of writing function in the originating circumstances of their production, use and reception – recognising, of course, that these may be diverse and even contradictory.

That said, there is no reason the moment of a text's origins should be privileged within such an enterprise. Forms of writing are not active within history once and once only. To the contrary, their very nature as, precisely, writing guarantees their availability to be re-inscribed within new sets of inter-textual co-ordinates and, correlatively, new sets of ideological and political relations, forms of institutional use and so forth. Tennenhouse alludes to these considerations in his remarks, in the passage cited earlier, concerning the 'scene of reading' and the processes in which 'the modern Shakespeare is implicated'. By the 'scene of reading' Tennenhouse has in mind the new forms for the social deployment of Shakespeare's texts produced, in the nineteenth century, by the development of new codes of reading which transformed those texts into source materials for a set of moralising and psychologising discourses and pedagogies aimed at the production of specific forms of social individuality. However much it may be true that Shakespeare's dramas initially functioned as parts of a political technology of power centred on the court, this does not gainsay their subsequent functioning as parts of cultural technologies of self-formation centred on the school and, in the nineteenth century, the home. Nor can a consideration of the former throw much light on the latter: the two are distinct problems, requiring separate analyses of the varying inter-textual and institutional co-ordinates which have regulated the historically distinct forms in which the Shakespearean corpus has been socially deployed.[49]

Yet, as we have seen, care is needed regarding the manner in which the variability of reading practices is to be understood. The point, John Frow argues, of insisting that meaning and use are not inherent in texts, are not inscribed in their internal relations, is not to celebrate a culture's capacity for unlimited semiosis. For to contend that meaning and use are not textually fixed does not entail that, in practice, they will be limitlessly plural either. What it does do is to allow attention to focus on the mechanisms through which there is organised 'a plurality of determinate and stable meanings for a plurality of contexts'.[50] What does this entail?

> Rather than being thought of as a fixed entity with a definite structure, the text is conceived of as shifting and unstable, a system of relations continuously and variably interrelated with other systems of different orders. Textuality thus becomes a function of an intertextual network and of the institutions (the literary system, the regime of reading, the codes of genre) through which this network is constructed and either maintained or shifted.
>
> The focus of analysis is then turned to the multiplicity of constructions of textuality, both diachronically, as the serial

reinscriptions of the text, and synchronically, as the contradictory modes of its social constitution. 'The text' is not separate from these variant constitutions and their determinants, and its 'meaning' becomes a function not of its origin but of its multiple historicities.[51]

It was argued at the outset of this chapter that the development of a historical sociology of literary forms and functions requires that answers be found to at least two questions: how are the relations between literary forms and functions to be viewed? and how are the tasks of synchronic and diachronic analysis to be conceived and related to one another? In the view of the sociology of genres, we have argued, function is conceived as an effect of form which, in its turn, is the result of specific social conditions. Correlatively, synchronic and diachronic analysis are regarded as concerning, respectively, the relations between temporally co-existent genres viewed in terms of the relations between their respective supporting conditions, and the mechanisms of generic reproduction and/or transformation conceived as deriving from the modes of connection which exist between social relations and literary forms. We have commented already on the inadequacies of the bi-polar conception of literature/society relations which backgrounds these conceptions. Frow's formulation, in providing alternative answers to both questions – function derives from a text's place within a specific constellation of institutional, inter-generic and discursive relations, while synchronic and diachronic analysis concern the analysis of temporally co-existent or successive systems of such relations – has the added advantage of underscoring a related inadequacy in the sociology of genres. For if the considerations to which Frow points cannot be raised from within the sociology of genres – and that they have not is perhaps sufficient evidence that they cannot – this is because its view of textuality (the text as a bearer of meanings derived from a moment of origin) renders them unthinkable.

Part III

5

SEVERING THE AESTHETIC CONNECTION

In introducing a selection of Marx's and Engels's writings on literature and art, Stefan Morawski cautions that 'we should distinguish the writings which explicitly and coherently elaborate a topic from the fragments which contain a thesis about a topic but which leave it undeveloped in part and thus rather unclear, and from the hasty or opaque comments which, as such, don't offer a reliable basis for a thesis'.[1] Morawski goes on to note that, for the greater part, the themes clustered under the first of these categories concern the functional aspects of specific attributes of artistic structures. By contrast, he numbers the following among the themes associated with the second and third categories: the distinguishing traits of aesthetic objects and aesthetic experience; the recurrent attributes and enduring values of art; the distinction between science and art; and the hierarchy of artistic values.

The founding texts of Marxism thus seem to authorise, quite clearly and directly, the concerns of a historical and sociological approach to the analysis of artistic forms and functions. The degree to which they also authorise the concerns of a Marxist aesthetic, understood as a theory of a distinct mode of cognition or experience embodied in works of art is less certain. Marx and Engels undoubtedly had views on such matters and interpolated them into their writings from time to time. Yet it is not clear how much reliance can be placed on these as indicative of the arguments they might have advanced had they given such questions their sustained attention. Moreover, even if this conundrum could be resolved, it would hardly be decisive. The considerable pains Marx devoted to establishing the existence of a separate Asiatic mode of production have had few binding consequences for the subsequent development of Marxist thought which, on balance, has judged this an unhelpful suggestion.

Unfortunately, these fragmentary writings are not always approached so circumspectly. They have rightly attracted a good deal of attention from scholars concerned to deepen and extend our understanding of the various tributary sources of Marx's and Engels's intellectual development. Margaret Rose's *Marx's Lost Aesthetic* is a recent case in point, offering a detailed and persuasive reconstruction of 'what Marx's aesthetic theory might have been' by considering his stated views on art and literature in the context of contemporary aesthetic theories and artistic movements.[2] Difficulties arise, however, when such reconstructed accounts are used to justify the view that Marxist thought should ongoingly engage with the concerns of philosophical aesthetics. For the issues are distinct. The first is a historical matter concerning the biographical fullness of thought of a specific (although exceptionally richly) historically determined individual while the second concerns the current theoretical and political requirements of an intellectual tradition whose very commitment requires some degree of adaptability to changing circumstances.

I put the matter this way because I would hesitate to push too hard the contrary view that a concern with the traditional preoccupations of philosophical aesthetics cannot be reconciled with the analytical logic of Marxist thought. Indeed, empirically, the tradition of Marxist aesthetics is largely definable in terms of its attempts to effect such a reconciliation. Nor can there be much doubt that Marxism's political vision has been profoundly – and often disastrously – affected by the influence of Romantic aesthetics on Marx's conception of communist society as a vehicle for the full realisation of humanity. That said, my own view – argued more fully in the next chapter – is that the concerns of philosophical aesthetics *do* pull in an opposite direction from what is, for me, the most important and most lasting innovation of Marxist thought: its socialising and historicising logic – even though this, its 'rational kernel' so to speak, has often to be won from the particularity of Marx's own formulations. If we compare the procedures governing the formation of objects of thought which Marx deployed in his social and economic analyses with those regulating the formation of objects of thought within philosophical aesthetics, then these do seem incompatible. Marx's argument, in the *Grundrisse*, that the concrete is the concrete because it is the concentration of many determinations whose interaction can only be grasped by the violent abstraction of thought thus embodies a methodological orientation that is precisely the reverse of that of philosophical aesthetics.[3] It suggests, for example, that questions relating to the effects of works of art require that the labour of theoretical abstraction be orientated to examining the modes of interaction of the complex concatenation of factors regulating the reception of such works. Within philosophical aesthetics, by contrast, the process of abstraction pulls in the opposite direction. Here, it embodies a procedure for disengaging works of art from the mundane particularities regulating their reception in different contexts in order to arrive at a conception of their effects as being always subject to the influence of an invariant aesthetic relation, itself rooted in an unchanging faculty of the subject deduced from a transcendental analysis of the constitutive properties of art in general.

Aspects of this tension were recognised by Georg Plekhanov in his insistence that, while Marxist categories could account for the socio-genesis of works of art, they could neither explain nor illuminate the nature of aesthetic experience as such. This is not to endorse Plekhanov's view which left the sphere of aesthetic experience and judgement in a position of untouched transcendence. None the less, the point is worth making if only to recall that the alignment of Marxist approaches to art and literature with the concerns of philosophical aesthetics occurred at a relatively late point in the development of the Marxist tradition. The first work to propose such an alignment was Mikhail Lifshitz's *The Philosophy of Art of Karl Marx*, first published in 1933 coincidentally with the first collection (co-edited by Lifshitz) of Marx's and Engels's writings on art.[4] Lifshitz's work was inspired by the publication, a year earlier, of Marx's *Economic and Philosophical Manuscripts*, just as it, in turn, prompted Lukács to draw on the same source in elaborating his historicised man-centred aesthetics in which art is viewed as affording a specific mode of self-consciousness of the processes of man's historical self-making.[5]

Even then, not everyone subscribed to the commitment, derived from this period, to establish a Marxist aesthetic which could rival – and, of course, surpass – the aesthetic theories of the nineteenth century in its capacity to offer alternative explanations of such enduring problems as the defining attributes of art, the hierarchy of artistic values and so on. As we shall see, Brecht didn't. But most of the theorists comprising Perry Anderson's tradition of western Marxism did, and wholeheartedly in the sense that such questions came to supply the organising centre of their inquiries into the spheres of art and literature. Work of this sort still goes on, of course. The cutting edge of most recent Marxist literary theory, however, has tended in the opposite direction, seeking to sever the aesthetic connection rather than to constrain inquiry within its confines and, in doing so, to bring a more thoroughgoing socialising and historicising logic to bear on questions which had previously been resolved abstractly or philosophically.

It is to furthering this process that this and the following two chapters address themselves, albeit in ways which may seem contradictory. For while, in the next chapter, I argue that the structure of aesthetic discourse is incompatible with the socialising and historicising impetus of Marxist thought, I want first to resist a conclusion which is sometimes drawn from this: that the category of literature should be abandoned. To the contrary, I shall argue that it is vital, both theoretically and politically, that such a category should be secured – but only on the condition that its specificity is conceived non-aesthetically.

As a prelude to this argument, however, it will be useful to identify a number of linked problems which derive from the theoretical alignments the tradition of Marxist aesthetics has sought to effect. I shall focus on two such problems. The first concerns the tendency toward an idealist reductionism which, in spite of their socialising and historicising rhetoric, has characterised Marxist approaches to the question of aesthetic value. The second concerns the related tendency for the concepts and procedures developed to enable Marxism to address the concerns of aesthetics to be carried over into adjacent areas of inquiry – those concerning the social determination of works of art, for example – such that the issues pertinent to such areas of inquiry are subjected to a 'logic of aesthetic overdetermination'. The consequence, in both cases, is that the scope of social and historical categories of analysis tends to be restricted while also, through the way their application is conceived, being subject to an idealist inflection.

AN IDEALIST REDUCTIONISM

We could say then that art, like all autonomous, qualitatively distinct spheres, exists as such to the extent that it
transcends the particularity of its social conditioning. This
transcendence, which in essence resides in the very bowels of
art, is the exact opposite of all sociological reductions.
Consequently, if Marx's theory of aesthetics had no other
objective than to explain art from the perspective of its social
conditioning – expressed, in turn, by its ideological content
– it would never amount to more than a sociology of art.[6]

This argument might have been excerpted from any of the classic
texts comprising the tradition of Marxist aesthetics. Here, it is
Sanchez Vazquez speaking, but it could just as easily have been
Lukács, Lifshitz, Goldmann, Lefebvre, Fischer or Althusser, or,
more recently, Eagleton or Jameson.[7] That Marxism is not a mere
sociology of art is a constantly recurring trope within the tradition.
Marxism respects art's transcendence of its social conditioning.
Yet, at the same time, it is not content merely to register this fact
or to posit, in the spirit of neo-Kantianism, a simple duality
between a socio-genetic approach to art and the question of its
value. Marxism both respects art's transcendence and seeks to
explain it in terms of – and this is the central paradox of the
tradition, a discursive contradiction which it can never entirely
disguise – precisely its social and historical conditioning.

Viewed in this light, the argument forms part of a double
disclaimer through which Marxist aesthetics, in telling us what it
is not, has sought to negotiate a specific position for itself within
the field of available discourses about art and literature. If the
formulation of a Marxist *aesthetic* warns us that its concerns are not
to be confused with those of a 'mere sociology', the fact that it is a
Marxist aesthetic that is on offer also tells us that its concerns will
not be subjective or formalist either. If Marxist aesthetics thus
differs from the sociology of art in the attention it accords
questions of aesthetic value and experience, it also differs from
traditional aesthetics in rebutting the contention that the specific
nature of the aesthetic experience consists in relations of mutual
support between the abstracted form of the art-work and the
constitution of a transcendental subject. In the more sophisticated

121

versions of the argument, these two moments of differentiation are integrated by positing an ideological affinity between the subjective formalism of bourgeois aesthetics and the 'pseudo-objectivism' of sociology. Lukács, seemingly with Plekhanov in mind, thus accuses 'vulgar sociology' of adopting an abstract and entirely external approach to art which relinquishes the question of aesthetic experience to the hold of equally abstract subjectivist formulations:

> And the social insights of 'sociological' literary criticism are on an even lower level and thus even more abstract and schematic than those of general sociology; this approach treats aspects of literature it sets out to illuminate as abstractly and formalistically and as much in aesthetic isolation as the non-sociological approaches to literature. The affinity of vulgar sociology to aesthetic formalism, often remarked upon, is not a speciality of those who distort Marxism. On the contrary, it is from bourgeois literary criticism that this tendency toward aesthetic formalism passes into the labour movement. One can discover this direct, inorganic mixing of abstract, schematic sociological generalisations with the aesthete's subjective approach to literary works in full bloom in such 'classics' of sociology as Taine, Guyau or Nietzsche.[8]

Having defined the field of discourses about art as being governed by an antinomy whose terms are ideologically complicitous, Marxist aesthetics defines its own function as that of overcoming the effects of this opposition. It will return to sociology a concern with aesthetic questions while simultaneously grounding such questions in the analysis of social and historical relations. In the classical statements of the position, this is accomplished by conceiving both aesthetic objects and the subjects of aesthetic judgement as being marked by the processes of their historical formation. While this avoids formalist conceptions of aesthetic transcendence and idealist conceptions of the givenness of the subject, it does so in such a way that subject and object are still regarded as the mutual supports of one another. For, in so far as the aesthetic relation between them is concerned, neither the subject nor the object is regarded as being unduly influenced by the immediate social and historical determinations which condition the forms of their inter-relation in specific contexts. Rather, the historicisation of subject and object takes the form of their being written into a long and continuous history of the humanisation of the senses in which – incompletely at first but, once the alienating effects of the division of labour have been overcome, fully – the value inherent in the art-work which embodies this history is recognised by the subject which that history helps to produce. In this way, no matter what stage has been reached within these mutually supportive histories, the aesthetic relation between subject and object is represented as a relation of fundamentally the same type: one in which the subject recognises itself as the product of the processes of man's historical self-making processes which, in turn, the art-work embodies while also heralding their completion. Any examination of the differential structure of the varying social relations within which works of art are valorised, and of the different functions which their valorisation plays within those relations, is thus pre-empted to the degree that such relations are held to be ultimately elevatable to a general subject–object relation susceptible to a philosophical definition.

This idealist reductionism – a reductionism upwards, so to speak – is a consequence of the statute of limitation placed on socialising and historicising categories which results from their deployment *within the discursive field of aesthetics*. Yet the appearance of idealism which this orientation brings in its tow is avoided by the recurrent use of an argument which seems uncompromising, indeed excessive, in the role it accords history. This consists in the view that if art transcends its social conditioning, it is able to do so only by virtue of that social conditioning – by virtue of the fact that, as genuine art, its relations to history are deeply determined. Marked indelibly by the conditions of its production, the genuine work of art is able to rise above those conditions precisely because its value consists in and derives from its relations to them. It is only where the force of historical determination is weak – where a text is affected by history only shallowly or by its more superficial aspects, as popular fiction is often viewed within the tradition – that it proves also to be a limitation.[9]

There are many versions of this argument. Perhaps the most fully elaborated, however, is Lukács's theory of the vocation for universality which derives from the social typicality of the experience reflected in the art-work and the degree to which this experience represents the progressive tendencies of the historical epoch to which the work in question belongs. Through the application of these two criteria, Lukács is able both to construct a canon and effect discriminations within it. All those works of literature which give a shape and coherence to the experience of significant social classes have a place within world-historical literature. However, the place of literary texts within this most totalising of literary canons varies in accordance with the historical functions of the classes whose world-views they fashion. Where the class which provides a literary text, however indirectly, with its ultimately determining social base is of a limited significance within a particular mode of production and, accordingly, has only a tangential bearing on the central political and cultural tendencies of the epoch, then that text's capacity for universality is assessed as a limited one. The same is true of classes which have passed their prime and which, like the bourgeoisie after 1848, act as a halter on the forces of historical development rather than representing their progressive tendencies. If such classes support the texts which constitute the troughs of realism – still important components of world-historical literature, but not its highest achievements – the peaks are constituted by those texts which embody the world-views of those classes which represent the developmental tendencies of their epoch, with an exception clause (the Balzac clause) which allows declining social classes to enrich realist literature through their ability to supply a critical perspective on the development of capitalist social relations.

The internal consistency and elegance of this theory has often been remarked upon. It rests on a view of history as a continuous process – marked, of course, by the vicissitudes of the dialectic, but still pursuing its ever-onward course – in which literary texts can be assigned a definite relation to one another in terms of their relations to the objective tendencies of historical development. Yet this ordering of relations between texts requires that the process of history can be counted on to produce a subject capable of recognising – fitfully at first, but eventually fully – the respects in which both the troughs and peaks of realist literature offer a mediated reflection of the contradictory processes of that subject's self-making. As a consequence, Lukács's assignation of relative value and meaning to literary texts is dependent on an idealist conception in which their future value and meaning is allowed to overdetermine their past and present ones.[10] In this way, the vocation for universality which derives from a text's relations to its conditions of production is, in the final analysis, subject to a future determination. For the way Lukács construes the relations between a text and the social and ideological conditions of its period is always informed by a prior conception of that text's relations to earlier and subsequent texts as specified by the degree to which its conditions of production enable it both to continue earlier realist tendencies and to anticipate later ones. The objective meaning and value of literary texts is thus determined by the place which their conditions of production produce for them within a meta-text of History which Marxism claims to know but whose final judgements – which can only be delivered once the process of History has been completed – it can only anticipate. Hence Lukács's constant insistence that the meaning of a period and its texts will become clearer to us the more distant we are from it – not just because, with time, perspectives settle, but because, with the unfolding of each stage of historical development, we move a little closer to the post-historical unified subject, Man, to whom the meaning of History and, therefore, that of each text within it will finally become luminously transparent.

Yet this future-structured conception of a text's meaning and value does not negate the fact that its vocation for universality is thought of as deriving from its relations to the conditions of its production. For it is still the history which flows into the text from behind it that, come the day of History's final hermeneutic reckoning with itself, is held to determine its relative value. As a consequence, the yet-to-be fixed past of the text is accorded a priority over the real history of its differential valuation and reception within different valuing communities. Indeed, this latter question is rendered devoid of any possible significance as an area of analysis. Discrepant systems of valuation of the same text simply don't count for much within this scheme. Their ontological weight is weak compared with that of the historical forces which prepare the judgements of empirical subjects for their eventual *rendez-vous* with those of Man. Foucault throws some light on this matter in contrasting the functioning of utopian representations within the classical and the modern *epistemes*. Whereas, in the classical period, utopias functioned as fantasies of origins, the development of historical systems of thought in the nineteenth century effects a transformation in the temporal orientation of utopic thought. Concerned 'with the final decline of time rather than with its morning', Foucault argues, the modern utopia projects a future situation in which 'the slow erosion or violent eruption of History will cause man's anthropological truth to spring forth in its stony immobility; calendar time will be able to continue; but it will be, as it were, void, for historicity will have been superimposed exactly upon the human essence'.[11] Foucault's purpose in this discussion is to draw attention to the structural similarities which underlie Ricardian and Marxist economics in spite of their differing end-of-history scenarios – a confrontation with finitude and scarcity in the one case and a leap beyond it in the other. These similarities are precisely mirrored in the complicity between bourgeois and Marxist aesthetics. For in both the aesthetic sense is projected as a utopian condition that will mark the end of time and which, in so doing, will finally legislate the proper modes for the deployment of the faculty of judgement. To concern oneself overmuch with particular histories of valuation would, in this light, be merely vain labour given their impending engulfment within a general history of the formation of a unified subject of judgement.

THE LOGIC OF AESTHETIC OVERDETERMINATION

In *Criticism and Truth*, Barthes argues that the call to respect the specificity of literature 'seems to be the last will and testament of old criticism, so religiously is it held to'.[12] Its advantage as a slogan, he suggests, consists in its pretension to establish literary studies as an autonomous science 'which would at last consider the literary object "in itself", without ever again owing anything to historical or anthropological sciences'.[13] Yet this ambition, he argues, can only place literary studies on a road to nowhere:

> '*On the subject of the gods*,' recommended Demetrius Phalereus, '*say that they are gods*.' The final imperative of critical verisimilitude is of the same kind: *on the subject of literature, say that it is literature*. This tautology is not gratuitous: at first, they pretend to believe that it is possible to talk of literature and to make it the *object* of discourse; but this

discourse leads nowhere, since it has nothing to say of this object other than that it is itself.[14]

Marxist literary theory has also found a way of saying this in its insistence that literature must be regarded as relatively autonomous: that is, as being characterised by specific formal and organisational properties which, in differentiating literature from other semiotic forms, are also the product of determinants unique to it. It is true, of course, that neither these determinants nor their literary effects are envisaged – as they are in Barthes's 'old criticism' – as operating in isolation from other social and historical relations. To the contrary, when adequately formulated, the problem of relative autonomy in Marxist literary theory concerns precisely how to theorise the modes of interaction which characterise the relations between those determinations which are construed as specific to literature and the more general economic, political and ideological determinations which Marxist thought contends are relevant to the analysis of any practice.[15] Yet, whatever their precise pattern in different circumstances, it is foreordained that such modes of interaction will give rise to the same result in supporting those attributes of texts' formal structures which qualify them as instances of literature.

It is in such formulations of literature's relative autonomy that the logic of aesthetic overdetermination most clearly manifests itself. For literature's relative autonomy – its specificity – can be secured only if all texts counted as literary are deemed to be so in essentially the same way in spite of the manifold differences between them in other respects: whether they are texts produced for performance or for reading; the historical circumstances of their initial production and reception; their placement within particular genre systems, etc. Moreover, to specify and account for literature's relative autonomy, analysis must orientate itself to differing historical relations of literary production precisely with a view to abstracting from these some recurring set of determining relations capable of accounting for the recurrence of an underlying commonality in formal structure which confers on such texts their literariness in spite of their differences in other respects. In thus setting out from the assumption that texts nominated as literary *must* have some underlying set of attributes in common, Marxist analysis is led away from the domain of social and historical particularity which it has always claimed as its own.

In these respects, Marxist concern with the question of literature's relative autonomy constitutes the locus of an attempted (but impossible) reconciliation of, on the one hand, an approach to the analysis of the composition and functioning of forms of writing in the contexts of the historical circumstances of their production and social deployment with, on the other, an immanent analysis of literature understood as a distinctive, trans-historical semiotic system. This tension was evident in one of the earliest, and still most influential, formulations of the problem: that developed by Medvedev and Bakhtin in their critique of Russian Formalism. Taking the Formalists to task for positing a division between the extrinsic (systems of patronage, literary markets, etc.) and intrinsic (formal) 'facts' of literature, and for denying the former any influence on the latter, Medvedev and Bakhtin seek to undercut this duality by insisting on the inherent sociality of any influence which literature exerts on itself. In so doing, they are able to deny any essential distinction between the extrinsic and the intrinsic, the social and the literary, studies of literature:

> From within it [the literary work] is determined by literature itself, and from without by other spheres of social life. But, in being determined from within, the literary work is thereby determined externally also, for the literature which determines it is itself determined from without. And being determined from without, it thereby is determined from within, for internal factors determine it precisely as a literary work in its specificity and in connection with the whole literary situation, and not outside that situation.[16]

What, then, is the nature of this interior determination which allows literature to contribute to its own social determination? For Medvedev and Bakhtin, the answer consists in literature's differentiation from other semiotic systems as determined by the specific forms and devices through which it reflects and refracts reality:

> Literature is one of the independent parts of the surrounding ideological reality, occupying a special place in it in the form of definite, organised philological works which have their own specific structures. The literary structure, like every ideological structure, refracts the generating socio-economic

reality, and does so in its own way. But, at the same time, in its 'content,' literature reflects and refracts the reflections and refractions of other ideological spheres (ethics, epistemology, political doctrines, religion, etc.). That is, in its 'content' literature reflects the whole ideological horizon of which it is itself a part.[17]

When it comes to identifying the exact nature of the specific mode of reflecting and refracting reality which the literary work effects, Medvedev and Bakhtin are somewhat vague. The most they offer is a restatement of the metaphor of the artist as seer in which this capacity is (partially) transferred from the personality of the writer to the impersonality of the literary structure:

Literature is capable of penetrating into the social laboratory where these ideologemes are shaped and formed. The artist has a keen sense for ideological problems in the process of birth and generation.[18]

This penchant for theorising literature's specificity by means of metaphors of sight recurs in Althusserian Marxism, as does Medvedev's and Bakhtin's characterisation of literature as a secondary system of signification whose distinctiveness consists in its relations to other semiotic or ideological systems. For Althusser and Macherey, literature's specificity thus consists in its capacity to help us 'see', 'feel' or 'perceive' the ideologies to which it alludes and which provide the ground upon which it works – and works precisely to transform by rendering the occlusions and contradictions of those ideologies perceptible.

Two preliminary difficulties with this conception may briefly be mentioned. First, as must be the case, the relative autonomy of literature, and thereby its capacity to determine itself, is secured only by attributing to it an invariant function and effect. The argument, as Frow puts it, rests on the assumption 'that literature can be described as a distinct ontological realm with a specific difference from the realm of ideology and an invariant function, the demystification of illusion through its parodic formal reproduction'.[19] If this is so, the nature of the literary function and effect must elude the reach of social and historical analysis. As the 'literariness' of literature is held to consist in its invariant relation to ideology, the most such analysis can do is to identify the contingent factors which condition the specific modes in which such an invariant function/effect is realised in particular circumstances. The result is, indeed, an endless demonstration that literature is literature; or rather, and to propose a correction to Barthes's argument, an endless demonstration that literature isn't something else – in this case, ideology – and so must be itself.

The second difficulty relates to the assumption that literature is a second-order system of signification. Medvedev and Bakhtin thus argue not only that literature refracts social reality in its own way but also that it 'reflects and refracts the reflections and refractions of other ideological spheres'. Since this mechanism is not said to work in reverse – since, that is, literary refractions of reality are not said to be, in turn, subject to a further refraction in other ideological forms – the effect is to install literature as the queen of the superstructures, 'reflecting the whole of the ideological horizon of which it is itself a part'. Similarly, Eagleton, in a sub-variant of the Althusserian argument,[20] contends that literature signifies history indirectly via its signification of ideological significations of history. History enters the literary text not as history but as ideological significations of history, these latter significations being transformed in the work so as to produce the distinctively literary effect: 'the literary text's relation to ideology so constitutes that ideology as to reveal something of its relations to history'.[21] Ideology here is conceived as a first-order system of signification with literature functioning as a second-order system of signification operating upon it within what seems, again, a non-reversible relation between them.[22]

It is clear that the terms of such arguments and, consequently, the implied hierarchy of forms of which they form a part, can easily be deconstructed. There is no reason, for example, why the argument should not be simply up-ended by arguing that, in certain regions (criticism, for instance), history also does not enter into ideology directly as history but only as already signified by literature. In brief, when account is taken of the complex networks of reciprocal signification which characterise the relations between different semiotic systems, the distinction between first- and second-order systems of signification breaks down. All ordered systems of signs involve – and work by and through – their relations to other such systems, all of which, so to speak, are

130

equally close to or distant from god so far as their relations to 'history' are concerned. If, in the Marxist conception, literature and ideology are placed in a hierarchical relation to one another, this is only made possible by the fact that the structure of that hierarchy is secured by the role accorded science. For it is science (= Marxism) which, in knowing history, can also know ideology's relations to history and, thereby, come to show us how literature allows us to 'see' (but not to know) something of ideology's relations to history. In sum, if literature is able to be represented as 'queen of the superstructures', it is because that place is secured for it by science's functioning as the 'king of the superstructures'.[23]

It can be seen from this how both problems coalesce and have their provenance in a broader set of difficulties: the pressure to theorise literature's specificity in terms of its difference from ideology. Or rather, since this is only half of the story, the root difficulty with Marxist theorisations of literature's relative autonomy is that this has to be conceived in relation to the places already occupied by science and ideology within the economy of the superstructure. Typically, then, literature is defined by means of a double differentiation: its specificity consists in the conjunction of those properties which allow it to be differentiated from ideology on the one hand and from science on the other. Nor is this true solely of Althusserian Marxism. While differing in content, the procedures deployed by Lukács and Goldmann to identify literature's specificity are structurally identical — literature has in some way to be defined in relation to what are taken to be the already given and fixed poles of reference of science and ideology. As a consequence, Marxist conceptions of literature's relative autonomy typically result in a proliferation of not-statements: literature is not ideology and it is not science, but it is not entirely not ideology either, since it is in some way connected to it by virtue of its function. Nor is it entirely not science for, depending on the formulation, it is either said to constitute a staging post on the royal road which leads the subject from the illusions of ideology to the truths of science (Althusser) or to offer a form of knowledge which, albeit organised differently, is as objective as that offered by science (Lukács).[24]

It is in regard to this definitional issue that the logic of aesthetic overdetermination has borne most consequentially on the concerns of Marxist literary theory, introducing a quite radical ahistoricity into its most basic procedures. For there are no reasons, apart from those derived from epistemology, to assume that literary texts should stand constantly in the same relation to other texts nominated as ideological or scientific. The concern to so argue clearly derives from, as it can now be seen, a historically and theoretically contingent pressure to install literature in an acceptable niche within Marxist variants of the triadic conceptions of the mental economy of the subject inherited from classical epistemology. Indeed, the history of Marxist aesthetics consists largely of competing attempts to map such triadic conceptions of the economy of the subject onto a triadic conception of the organisation of the superstructure: why else, indeed, should it be thought that the superstructure's economy should necessarily be triadic? In consequence, the possibility of examining historically differing sets of relations between different intellectual practices is radically curtailed: science, ideology and literature – these are always there (at least once art and science have been differentiated from magic),[25] and they always exist in the same relation to one another just as each always induces in the subject an invariant mode of mental relation to reality. Viewed from this perspective, differences within the Marxist tradition – between its Althusserian and Lukácsian components, for example – are of quite minor significance. Indeed, virtually the only point at issue between them concerns which pre-Marxist epistemology and aesthetic (Kantian, Hegelian, Spinozan, etc.) should govern the terms in which the relations between ideology, science and literature are to be conceived.

That aside, the problems inherent in this definitional procedure are apparent. They are, in effect, variants of those generated within the sociology of genres by the attempt to characterise genres in terms of a definite positivity. For, as we have seen, that positivity always turns out to be relationally conceived as a set of differences from the properties of other genres whose defining attributes, while assumed as given for the purposes of defining the genre in question, are similarly theorisable only as sets of differences from other genres. This, in turn, means that such genres cannot function in the manner required of them if they are to serve as stable points of reference in relation to which the specific differences of other genres might be defined. The whole ground of inter-generic relations is too slippery, fluid and mobile to allow the process which this procedure of genre definition requires to be initiated: namely, that a particular genre, definable solely in terms of its self-identity, might be abstracted from these relations and so serve as a fixed point around which a series of negatively defined generic differentiations might rotate. To the degree that Marxist characterisations of literature's positivity are dependent on the series of not-statements which govern the process of literature's definition – literature is not science and it is not ideology – then so, similarly, that positivity turns out to consist of a set of negatively defined relational attributes subjected to a misleading ontologisation.

Consideration of a more closely related analogy – the Russian Formalists' attempt to theorise the specificity of poetic language in terms of its differentiation from practical language – may help make the point. The result of this endeavour, Medvedev and Bakhtin argue, was an entirely negative definition of poetic language (its capacity to defamiliarise the automatism of practical language) whose cogency depended on an unwarranted ontologisation of an arbitrarily selected set of differences between poetic and practical language. In being called on to serve the purpose of providing a standardised form of communication in relation to which the *differentia specifica* of poetic language might then be theorised, practical language was able to fulfil this function only because it was itself subject to an arbitrary definition. In focusing purely on narrowly technical forms of utterance in which the communicative function is dominant, Medvedev and Bakhtin argue, the Formalists suppressed those aspects of practical language which included a de-automatising propensity. Once such attributes are included as a part of practical language use and, accordingly, of its definition, then they are clearly unable to serve as criteria whereby practical and poetic language might be differentiated as ontologically distinct realms.

Similarly, then, if literature is to be defined negatively in relation to both science and ideology, these latter must be capable of being defined on their own terms and in a definite relation to one another. There are now more than sufficient grounds for doubting this to be the case. Quite apart from the difficulties associated with the concept of ideology in its own right – its assumption of the attributes of the subject it is supposed to account for, for example, as well as its conventional association with a dualistic ontology of the social, divided between 'the real' and its representations[26] – the very organisation of the epistemological space in which ideology is theorised as the opposite of science has been tellingly called into question in recent debates.[27] Frow, reflecting on these criticisms and urging the need for the category of ideology to be redefined to take account of them, suggests this might be achieved if ideology, rather than being ontologised as a particular kind of discourse, is thought of 'as a *state* of discourse or of semiotic systems in relation to the class struggle'.[28] This ideological state of discourse, he further suggests, consists in 'the tactical appropriation of particular [discursive] positions by a dominant social class'.[29]

While this avoids many difficulties, others remain. Two might usefully be singled out here: first, the arbitrary restriction of the category to the sphere of class relations; second, the equally arbitrary reservation of the term for those tactical appropriations of discourse associated with the dominant class. The effect of these two considerations taken in combination is to equate ideology with dominant ideology, thereby attributing to it the function of reproducing relations of class power via the organisation of consent, and to envision, as its opposite, not truth but resistance. Frow is careful not to ontologise the terms of this distinction. Resistance, like ideology, is, for Frow, a specific use of discourse rather than discourse of a particular kind. Thus understood, he argues, resistance is 'the possibility of fracturing the ideological from within or of turning it against itself . . . or of reappropriating it for counterhegemonic purposes'.[30] None the less, the dichotomous organisation (domination/resistance) he proposes for the field of discourse seems unlikely to account for the full complexity of the different states in which discourse is appropriated and mobilised in the context of different fields of political and power relations.

If these difficulties are to be avoided, and the conditions Frow specifies be met, my own view is that the term ideology must be accorded a much looser and more general function. Capable of specifying neither a particular kind of discourse nor a state of discourse produced by specific forms of its political appropriation, it serves a useful purpose in suggesting that discourse can never be neutral with regard to power relations. To refer to discourse as ideological is thus not to attribute specific properties to it but serves rather as a way of indexing that it is to be examined with a view to disclosing its functioning as a component of the rhetorical strategies through which particular forms of power – and not solely those associated with class relations – are organised or opposed. This is by no means saying nothing; the risk of trying to pin the concept down more tightly, however, is that this seems invariably to result in theoretically arbitrary restrictions of the term which obscure its value at this more general level.

What is certain, however, is that if we cannot fix ideology as a particular kind of discourse defined in terms of an identifiable set of properties which exhibit a definite and unchanging relation to science, the very attempt to define literature in terms of its differences from these two categories collapses. It is important to be clear about the nature of this objection. For it applies not merely to this or that Marxist theory of literature's specificity or autonomy. How, in any particular version of the argument, the box of 'literature' happens to be filled is contingent to the objection which concerns, rather, the very procedure of theorising literature's specificity in terms of an epistemologically derived triadic conception of the economy of the superstructures. The objection also applies to those instances where the procedure of defining literature in relation to ideology is uncoupled from the assumptions of epistemology and deployed in historically limited terms. *Formalism and Marxism* offers an instance of this approach in its suggestion that the capacity of literary texts to estrange or defamiliarise ideology should be regarded not as an invariant effect of literature, conceived as a trans-historical category, but rather as true only of historically specific forms of writing associated with the formation of the bourgeois literary system. It is clear, however, that this attempt to operate with a historically limited category of literature whose specific formal attributes might then be grounded within historically specific relations of literary production offers less a way round the classical Marxist procedure for defining literature's literariness than its last ditch. For the structure of the argument remains the same: literature's specificity consists in its relations to ideology which the analysis must take as a given in order to secure a point of reference in relation to which literature's literariness can be defined.[31]

There are, of course, other difficulties with Marxist theories of literature. Not the least of these concerns a strong tendency toward conventionalism when it comes to determining which writings should fall under the category of literature. With isolated exceptions, this question is usually resolved by duplicating the hierarchy of forms posited by bourgeois criticism. So far as its empirical determination is concerned, literature always – or nearly always[32] – turns out to comprise the self-same works which it is conventionally thought to include (the Great Tradition) while also excluding the broader field of fictional writing from which it is conventionally distinguished: popular or mass fiction.

The difficulties with this procedure are now sufficiently well known not to require further rehearsal. The consequences which follow from it, however, have been less remarked upon. At root, these stem from the fact that the procedure sits ill at ease with that through which the category of literature is defined *as a category*. So far as this is concerned, as we have seen, literature's definition is governed by the statements that it is not science and not ideology. However, when it comes to the empirical task of *filling that category*, a different system of not-statements is brought into play: literature is not popular fiction or mass fiction. There is an obvious procedural inconsistency here. In defining the category of literature, it is a matter of fitting it into the space mapped out for it within the already-determined triadic structure of epistemological reasoning. However, the terms in which that category is then empirically fleshed out derive from the quite different system of distinctions posited by a culturally relative hierarchy of forms. The result, not surprisingly, is a series of contradictions and torsions at the points where these different systems of not-statements meet and, since they cannot entirely be reconciled, mutually abrade one another.

The most obvious casualty of this abrasive collision consists in Marxist theorisations of popular fiction. For since, in the second system of not-statements, popular fiction is distinguished from literature, there is then no way in which this system can be reconciled with the first, in which literature is distinguished from science and ideology, except to argue that, as popular fiction isn't literature and as it clearly isn't science either, it must fall under the category of ideology. The endless reiteration of this argument, in other words, is entirely the effect of a definitional necessity. If the literature/popular fiction distinction is to be inserted into the already mapped-out set of epistemological distinctions between science, literature and ideology, then there is literally nowhere else that popular fiction could be placed except under the category of ideology which would not call into question the terms in which the category of literature has already been theorised.

As a consequence of these contradictory definitional procedures, Marxists have been constrained to approach popular fiction as merely a disguise system for the reproduction and relay of ideology. The effects of this can best be seen by contrasting the procedures deployed in Marxist approaches to literature with those characterising Marxist analyses of popular fictions. In the former, to take the Althusserian version of the argument, the study of literature is an occasion for demonstrating its non-coincidence with ideology. Attention thus focuses on the functioning of those formal devices specific to literature which initiate a process of ideological distanciation through which the contradictions of particular ideologies are rendered perceptible. The Marxist analysis of literature thus offers us a knowledge of the way literary texts work to nudge into our field of vision those aspects of their relations to history, as known by Marxism, which ideologies occlude or repress. When it comes to the study of popular fiction, however, this double relation is denied or, if admitted, rendered inconsequential: since, for definitional reasons, popular fiction cannot be differentiated from other ideologies, its relation to these is one of simple duplication.

An early essay by Roger Bromley, written from within an Althusserian framework, offers a convenient illustration of this argument.[33] Popular fiction, Bromley suggests, 'should be regarded as a specific ideological practice within an ideological apparatus (publishing, communications, media, etc.), and as such participates in the permanent insertion of individuals and their actions in practices governed by ideological apparatuses'.[34] The specificity of popular fiction, however, consists entirely in its secondariness: popular fiction 'is not a primary site of ideology (cf. the educational system) but is one of the secondary areas where ideological components are represented and reinforced. . . .'[35] This secondariness, however, is one without specific consequence since its only effect is to do again what ideology, in its own definition, does to and for itself: represent itself as a natural horizon. Popular fiction thus functions complicitly with ideology, assisting it to pass unnoticed, 'uniform, unambiguous and non-contradictory'.[36]

The task of Marxist analysis, accordingly, is to read through popular fictions in order to identify the ideologies they transmit and for whose transmission they serve as otherwise empty vehicles. Extrapolating from a discussion of late nineteenth-century romance fiction, Bromley thus suggests that popular fictions are typically characterised by a system of absences and presences:

ABSENT	*PRESENT*
The current relations of production.	Personal relations.
The bourgeoisie (the real ruling class) as personified in economic categories.	Aristocracy (fraction offered at the level of style and code as *real* ruling class).
The working classes, defined in relation to capitalism as economic personification of *labour*. That is to say: Capital and Labour in its fundamental relations of antagonism under capitalism.	The petit-bourgeoisie personified in the *woman* particularly (and in authorial ideology).
Exchange relations in the economy.	Marriage: non-antagonism. House as property, self-owning and self-growing.
Division of labour.	No divisions other than natural.
Society.	Nature Self-consciousness.[37]

It is clear, here, that the master-text governing the left-hand column is none other than *Capital* and that the effect of the analysis is to demonstrate that popular fiction does not represent social relations in the same way that Marxism does: in other words, that it is *not* Marxism (science) but *is* ideology. What is most important to note, however, is the absence of a third column charting the fictional modes in which the ideological themes comprising the second column are represented. For this absence is a definitional requirement if it is to be demonstrated that popular fiction is, indeed, ideology, and, thereby, the terms of its own differentiation from literature can be reconciled with the contradictory terms in which literature is differentiated from ideology.

LITERATURE WITHOUT AESTHETICS

To summarise: the purpose of the foregoing has been to query not merely this or that Marxist theory of literature but the logic governing the procedures through which, however it may be formulated, a conception of literature's specificity is arrived at. The central problem, I have suggested, thus concerns less how the space of literature is filled within any particular theory than the way in which this space itself is conceived. The inherent instability of the science/ideology couplet undermines the ground necessary to secure a conception of literature either as a form of writing that is invariantly distinct from ideology or as a historically specific form of writing whose differentiation from ideology is the effect of a specific configuration of the field of ideology in general.

Does this mean, then, that there can be no such thing as a theory of literature? Terry Eagleton takes this view. After reviewing the difficulties associated with attempts to differentiate literature from other semiotic systems so that it might serve as a bounded object of knowledge for a specific science, he concludes that the logic of 'recognising that literature is an illusion is to recognise that literary theory is an illusion too'.[38] Given the impossibility of securing the boundaries of the literary, Eagleton argues, the point is not to counter conventional theories of literature with a Marxist theory. Rather, it is to rethink the study of literature as part of a larger intellectual project concerned with the study of discursive or signifying practices, a project which would include analysis of those texts conventionally called 'literature', albeit that the ways in which these would be investigated in being viewed in this wider context would be significantly transformed.

While in general agreement with this conclusion, it is none the less important to insist that, within this broader project, there should be reserved a place for a theory of literature – but for a non-literary theory of literature which will theorise its object as a set of social rather than formal realities and processes. For that there may not be a *literary* theory of literature does not rule out the possibility of there being *other* kinds of theory of literature. The significance of the distinction I have in mind here can perhaps best be clarified by looking more closely at Eagleton's reasons for issuing literary theory/theories of literature with their obituary notices. The root objection to literary theory, he argues, is that 'the one hope it has of distinguishing itself – clinging to an object named literature – is misplaced'.[39] Since there is no such thing as literature, there can be no literary theory nor any theory of literature except as discourses which deal entirely with their own self-generated problems.

Stephen Heath, pointing to the respects in which this still leaves Eagleton with the practical difficulty as to how, then, to negotiate his own relation to the literature which he has declared non-existent, but which still so obviously supplies the condition for his activity, argues he pays a high price for this iconoclastic gesture. Unable to offer a *political* retheorisation of literature – that is, one in which literature is not argued away as non-existent but is rethought as a non-essentialist ensemble of textual articulations of language and experience – Heath suggests that Eagleton's options are reduced to those of reviving old forms of criticism (rhetoric) or contriving new and ever more radical readings, thereby, in either case, leaving literature in much the same place that it was before issued with its obituary: 'an academic object for the oldest criticism or the newest readings'.[40] A further difficulty with Eagleton's argument consists in its empiricism. Christopher Norris, commenting on the application of a related argument to the more general concerns of aesthetics, usefully identifies its shortcomings. To dismiss the concerns of aesthetics as being 'wholly self-induced by the discipline which sets out to explain or resolve them', he argues, runs the risk of missing the point that 'the same is true to some extent of any branch of knowledge that defines its subject area by singling out questions of especial theoretical interest'.[41]

It should be noted, in the light of these considerations, that my critique of the logic of aesthetic overdetermination has not rested on the empiricist argument that there is no such thing as literature or art. Rather, it has rested on a demonstration of the theoretical inconsistencies which result from the attempt to translate the transcendental distinctions of philosophical aesthetics into the typically triadic structure of Marxist conceptions of the economy of the superstructure. The objection is thus less that literature, as a special kind of writing, does not exist – although this is surely true – than that the system of concepts upon which this construction of literature depends is itself flawed. The problem, in other words, lies in how the space of the literary is theorised. Yet if this is so, it then remains at least a possibility that this space may be rethought and a cogent conception of literature elaborated which is disabled neither by the theoretical objections I have rehearsed nor by the argument that literature, as a special kind of writing, does not exist. The critical question here concerns the nature of the distinctions the category is used to effect. That the category cannot designate an ontologically distinct realm of writing is clear.

However, this need not hinder its capacity to designate distinctions of another kind. Let me indicate some possibilities:

1. That the term literature be used to refer to a particular socially organised space of representation whose specificity consists in the institutionally and discursively regulated forms of use and deployment to which selected texts are put, the empirical question as to the actual identity of those texts being regarded as a contingency which does not affect the definition. Clearly, a theory of literature proceeding from this definition would have no need to secure, either theoretically or empirically, literature's existence as a special kind of writing. Its concerns would rather centre on the constitution of a region of social practice whose specificity consists in the modes of use and deployment of the texts it constitutes as its occasions rather than in a set of formal properties. The effect of this move is to rethink the ontological status of literature such that it is taken to refer to an observable set of social processes rather than to an (as it has proved so far) unfathomable essence.

2. That literature, so defined, be regarded as a historically specific set of institutional and discursive arrangements regulating the use and deployment of the texts it constitutes as its occasions. In effect, this is to limit the concept of literature to the modern period, distinguishing it from earlier institutional and discursive organisations of the field of writing. This is not, however, the same thing as a distinction between modern and premodern forms of writing. The processes whereby forms of writing deriving from earlier periods are retrospectively literarised by abstracting them from the sharply different institutional and discursive forms regulating their initial use and organising their relations to adjacent fields of social practice would form a part of literature under this definition.

3. That literature, so defined, be regarded as a set of social realities and processes which interact with other spheres of social practices *on the same level*. This is to deny those depth models of the social structure which support the hermeneutic project of deciphering literary texts in terms of the underlying realities they express. The grounds for this denial consist in the contention that all social practices are simultaneously institutional and discursive in their constitution.

141

It can be seen how, if these steps are taken, the way is opened for a theory of literature that will construe its object as a historically specific, socially organised and maintained field of textual uses and effects. And if it is important to insist, in this sense, on the specificity of literature, this is because, thus understood, it is by no means a mere illusion. Although we can already see beyond its rims, this socially organised field of textual uses and effects has had very real consequences, historically, and continues to function as an influential set of social practices which have inescapably to be taken into account in present-day political/critical calculations. To conclude, because literature cannot be secured as a formal reality, that its analysis should be dissipated into an undifferentiated study of signifying practices is to miss what ought properly to have been the focus of analysis in the first place: the functioning of a definitely organised field of uses and effects in which strategies of boundary construction and maintenance are central to the functioning of a *socially differentiated region of textual uses and effects* (rather than kind of writing).

I shall return to consider the kinds of shift of focus these perspectives might induce in chapter 7. First, however, I want to examine another aspect of the influence of philosophical aesthetics on Marxist literary theory. For there are, in addition to the theoretical considerations examined so far, quite pressing political reasons why the connection between the two should be severed.

6

REALLY USELESS 'KNOWLEDGE': A POLITICAL CRITIQUE OF AESTHETICS

AESTHETICS AND TRANSCENDENCE

In an essay he wrote in 1928, P. N. Medvedev argued that the aesthetic theory of Hermann Cohen, a prominent neo-Kantian, resulted in the analysis of 'the whole concrete entirety of the artistic work and its concrete links with other ideological phenomena' being replaced by an exposition of 'the systematic links between the three parts of the system of philosophy – logic, ethics and aesthetics'.[1] The remark could have, and ideally should have, provided a fitting epitaph to the history of philosophical aesthetics – a history which ought long ago to have been regarded as finished and ready for writing up – inasmuch as the kind of analytical diversion to which Medvedev points is a necessary consequence of aesthetic discourse *as such*, whether neo-Kantian, Hegelian or, for that matter, Marxist. Indeed, the problem is especially acute in relation to Marxism. Wherever the commitment to founding a Marxist aesthetic has been made, the task of developing concepts and methods appropriate to the analysis of the functioning and effects of artistic practices in the context of the historically variable social relations regulating their production and consumption has been evacuated in advance of its commencement.[2] In its place, there has been substituted the attempt to deduce such matters from general and abstract principles concerning the relations between Science, Ideology and Art, the holy trinity of the super-structures which, in Marxist discourse, has too often served in the place of philosophy's triad of logic, ethics and aesthetics.

How could the effects of this be other than diversionary? Where the concerns and procedures of aesthetics prevail, artistic practices are differentiated in terms of their formal properties as theorised in relation to some conception of the aesthetic as a distinct mode of the subject's mental relation to reality. The disposition of Marxism, by contrast, is to establish a social, historical and, above all, political basis for theorising the internal economy of the sphere of artistic practices and their ideological articulations. The resulting 'political economy' of artistic practices would analyse the production, functioning and effects of such practices by locating them not merely within the relations of their production but also within the spheres of social and cultural action that are produced for them by the forms of classification, valorisation and institutional use through which they are inscribed within, and articulated across, different regimes of power, its exercise and its contestation.[3] However, this socialising and historicising impetus is held in check wherever aesthetic categories are imported into Marxist thought, since these require that certain distinctions, conceived in essentialist terms – such as that between art and non-art – be regarded as either underlying or overriding the conjunctural organisation of the field of practices at any given historical moment.

These contradictory pulls between the historical and materialist bias of Marxism and the idealist, ahistorical tendencies of philosophical aesthetics are nowhere more clearly foregrounded than in Herbert Marcuse's *The Aesthetic Dimension*. Marcuse readily admits the dependency of artistic practices on historically variable social relations conditioning both the production of works of art and the manner in which they are socially circulated and received, and he evidently regards the study of such matters as worthwhile. However, it is clear that, for Marcuse, the 'real work' lies elsewhere, in the elucidation of those aspects of the work of art which constitute its essence *as art*. These, in Marcuse's estimation, are always determined in advance by the trans-historical substance of art, a substance which particular works of art invariably embody, albeit in different ways. Accordingly, the most that the analysis of the social relations conditioning artistic practices might accomplish is to account for the varying and contingent ways in which the same transcendental essence of art manifests itself. In true Hegelian fashion, material factors are thus granted a subordinate role in modulating the concrete forms in which an ideal essence is realised:

These historical conditions are present in the work in several ways: explicitly, or as background and horizon, and in the language and imagery. But they are the specific historical expressions and manifestations of the same trans-historical substance of art: its own dimension of truth, protest and promise, a dimension constituted by the aesthetic form.[4]

In brief, to the degree that 'art is largely autonomous *vis à vis* the given social relations',[5] a Marxist analysis, while it may offer supplementary illumination, can never touch the truly essential questions.

The only oddity here consists in Marcuse's claim that this position constitutes a critique, rather than an accurate characterisation, of Marxist approaches to the study of artistic phenomena. Except for the respects in which his argument is directed against the official Soviet codification of the doctrine of socialist realism, it is surely misdirected: Marxist approaches to the study of art, when taking the form of an attempt to develop a distinctive Marxist position within the tradition of philosophical aesthetics (Lifshitz, Lukács, Vazquez, della Volpe, Althusser), have entirely conformed to the dualistic logic of analysis which Marcuse proposes. Socio-historical analysis may reveal this, that or the other interesting particular about individual works of art, but never anything about Art itself which, in the last analysis, is the ultimately determining force behind, or within, every individual work of art: the individual formulations may vary, but each of the major traditions of Marxist aesthetics developed to date offers a restatement of this central and shared proposition.

The resulting tension between the historical and materialist impetus of Marxist categories and concerns and the idealist pull of aesthetics is nowhere more clearly manifest than in the peculiar inflection to which the problem of relative autonomy has been subjected in Marxist aesthetic theory where, in contrast to other regions of Marxist theory, it has been regarded less as being concerned with how to conceive the relations between a number of interacting levels or sites of determination (such as the state and the economy) than with how to secure, for Art, some defining, inner essence which is free of any external or prior determination. Indeed, it is scarcely an exaggeration to say that *the* main problem of Marxist aesthetics, and one round which it has spun idly, has been that of seeking to reconcile two contradictory propositions – that artistic practices are socially determined, and that Art is not. This reconciliation, moreover, has always been effected by means of a discourse of transcendence which purports to account for the respects in which Art *qua* Art always exceeds its determinations. Here is Lukács, for example:

> if the genesis of every work of art is defined in society according to class, still the art-work will shatter – the more forcefully, the more important it is – the social limitations of its birth.[6]

There is scarcely a single text within the tradition which does not contain statements like this, their rote-like repetition betraying the nervousness of a practice which has often staked its all on the terrain of apologetics.

All of this is bad enough and scarcely promising for the prospects of a sober materialist analysis of the relations between artistic practices and social processes. The political consequences of such discourses of transcendence, however, are even worse in lending support to the supposition that the political effects of artistic practices might be deduced from an immanent analysis of their formal properties. 'The criteria for the progressive character of art', as Marcuse puts it, 'are given only in the work itself as a whole: in what it says and how it says it.'[7] And, needless to add, art's progressive character is bestowed on it precisely by its autonomy, its transcendence of its determinations. To cite Marcuse again:

> the radical qualities of art, that is to say, its indictment of the established reality and its invocation of the beautiful image (*Schöner Schein*) of liberation are grounded precisely in the dimensions where art *transcends* its social determination and emancipates itself from the given universe of discourse and behaviour while preserving its overwhelming presence.[8]

The particular formulations may vary, but every major variant of Marxist philosophical aesthetics has similarly attributed to art a critical function derived from precisely those autonomous characteristics which constitute it as art. In the *Grundrisse*, Marx argued that thought must strive to comprehend the concrete as 'the concentration of many determinations'.[9] Marxist aesthetics has followed the opposite path in promoting the illusion that concrete questions of cultural and artistic policy can be read off from a general theory of the aesthetic arrived at entirely by means of the abstract procedures of philosophical speculation, quite independently of any concrete analysis of the variable functioning of artistic phenomena within specific socio-historical relations. Indeed, there is a sense in which the programme and procedures of aesthetic discourse, Marxist or otherwise, obviate the need for the concrete analysis of anything. To take the case of Marcuse again, it is clear that the progressive function he claims for art applies only to 'authentic' or 'great' art. Nor is it any embarrassment to Marcuse that the construction of the category of 'great' or 'authentic' art is dependent on, as he himself puts it, 'a self-validating hypothesis':

> I term those works 'authentic' or 'great' which fulfill aesthetic criteria previously defined as constitutive of 'authentic' or 'great' art.[10]

Marcuse is well advised in admitting to the evident circularity of this procedure. As Jurij Lotman notes in *The Structure of the Artistic Text*, the production of a corpus of 'great literature' is always a matter of establishing one text as 'literary' or of artistic value by referring it to other texts which, it has already been decided, exemplify the criteria of 'literariness' or artistic value.[11] In other words, the question as to what constitutes great art can only be resolved provided that it has already been determined. Yet a good deal – indeed, politically, everything – hinges on this tautology. All issues pertaining to the political effects of works of art are resolved at a single, definitional stroke merely as a result of positing a distinction between 'authentic' and 'counterfeit' art. This is true, albeit in varying ways, of Lukács, Althusser and Fischer, with their essentialist oppositions between authentic art on the one hand and degraded art/ideology on the other. However, it is, again, Marcuse who states the logic of this position most succinctly:

> The authentic *oeuvre* is not and cannot be a prop of oppression, and pseudo-art (which can be such a prop) is not art.[12]

Given formulations such as these, the programme of a critical aesthetics happily turns out to be one which is already accomplished the moment it is announced. The first task, since everything depends on it, is to sort out 'authentic' from 'inauthentic' art – but this is hardly necessary since the two can be distinguished merely by invoking criteria previously used to differentiate them, so the job is already done. Once this 'already done' has been done again, the next step is to elaborate those unique, trans-historical essences which incline 'authentic' art to be inherently critical of the existing social order. But there is no real need to do this either, for all the elements of such a critical aesthetic are already there, pre-formed in the aesthetic writings of Kant, Hegel, Schiller or whoever: they merely await their political awakening. All that is necessary to this end is to shape these elements into a new configuration, sprinkle liberally with a few judicious quotations from the young Marx and, in Marcuse's case, with a dash of Freud also, and hey presto! the job is done. A Marxist aesthetic springs ready-made from bourgeois aesthetics, like Athene from the head of Zeus, without its feet ever touching the ground and without ever completing the passage from its bourgeois origins to its would-be Marxist destination. For where is there a Marxist aesthetic which does not derive its distinctive characteristics from a set of operative concepts culled from some pre-Marxist body of aesthetic theory? In aesthetics, as in philosophy, Marxism's rhetorical claims to have transcended its forebears have been denied by its practical subordination to the dominating influence of one or another version of bourgeois aesthetics.

All of this ought, by now, to be perfectly obvious. To announce a requiem for aesthetics *in toto* would, no doubt, be premature inasmuch as, although its theoretical credentials are thoroughly tattered, it still has an undeniable political use-value – but only for the right. It is not too surprising, therefore, that notwithstanding – indeed largely ignoring – the criticisms to which it has been subjected, aesthetic discourse has found a number of champions in recent years. René Wellek concludes *The Attack on Literature* firm in the conviction that 'aesthetic experience differs from other experiences and sets off the realm of art, of fictionality, of *Schein*, from life' and urges critics to attend to their proper business: that of distinguishing 'between art and nonart'.[13] The essays collected in Laurence Lerner's *Reconstructing Literature* are replete with similar sentiments.[14]

The time is long past, however, when the project of a Marxist aesthetic ought finally to have been laid to rest. Not only has this not happened, but there are signs that aesthetic discourse is likely to assume a renewed significance as the, by now, evident crisis of Marxism deepens. The more the totalising ambit of Marxism is called into question in the domains of economic, social and political analysis, the more aesthetics will be called into service to provide a principle of totality capable of shoring up the conceptual edifice of classical Marxism. This is most conspicuously evident in the recent work of Fredric Jameson whose *The Political Unconscious* band-aids Marxism's totalising claims, but only at the price of transforming Marxism into a local instance of a generalised critical-aesthetic discourse.

At a more mundane level, aesthetic discourse has also recently recruited a left-wing publicist in the form of Peter Fuller. Fuller is, he assures us, 'of the Left',[15] and, conjuring the prospect of (Heavens to Betsy!) 'a General Anaesthesia which may engulf us all',[16] has ranged himself against this threat in the name of a biologically based aesthetic. For Fuller, correctness of aesthetic response is a political question. It is too much to hope that my arguments might nip the worm in the bud, but my main purpose here is to argue that, to the contrary, nothing whatsoever of any practical political consequence hinges on the establishment of an aesthetic by whatever means, biological, social or historical. By way of anticipating my later comments on this, Alan Durant, noting that aesthetic discourse is always ultimately based on the 'discernments of a hypothetical posterity', economically summarises its capacity to obscure contemporary political questions:

> When qualities of aesthetic forms are projected primarily forwards in time towards an imaginary audience for assessment and value, contemporary judgements become simply temporary obstacles; and relevant, practical questions are exchanged for long-term professions of faith.[17]

In brief, assessed from the point of view of its yield for a socialist politics, aesthetic discourse, I want to argue, constitutes a really useless form of knowledge, and one which would be quite appropriately satirised, in William Cobbett's terms, as 'heddakashun'.[18] By way of advancing this claim, and also substantiating the polemical burden of my argument so far, I turn now to consider the organisational properties of aesthetic discourse, paying particular attention to the peculiar variant of the subject form which such discourse constructs.

THE PROPERTIES OF AESTHETIC DISCOURSE: VALUE AND THE VALUING SUBJECT

In his *Immanuel Kant*, Lucien Goldmann cites the early Lukács's view that 'the *Critique of Judgement* contains the seeds of a reply to every problem of structure in the sphere of aesthetics; aesthetics need thus only clarify and think through to the end that which is implicitly there to hand'.[19] This was precisely what Lukács did in subsequently historicising Kant's conception of the subject and object of aesthetic judgement. The approach adopted here is rather different. The *Critique*, I shall argue, *does* provide a clear statement of 'every problem of structure in the field of aesthetics', but less by way of resolving those problems, or anticipating their resolution, than by specifying the conditions that would need to be met were they to be resolved. Viewed in this light, Kant's treatise is most fruitfully read as a commentary on the necessary conditions, properties and requirements of aesthetic discourse.

Before doing so, however, it is necessary to distinguish between aesthetic discourse and discourses of value in order to register a distance from, and resist the gravitational pull of, Kant's transcendental method. By aesthetic discourse, I have in mind the many variants of philosophical aesthetics which exhibit related properties in their attempts to distinguish some unique faculty, lodged within and constitutive of human subjectivity, which would serve as a basis for establishing the potential, if not actual, universality of aesthetic judgement. Aesthetic discourse, that is to say, construes the aesthetic as a distinctive mode of the subject's mental relation to reality. The means by which this is accomplished vary from Kant's transcendental critique of the faculty of judgement to the analysis of the progressive historical construction of a unified subject and object of aesthetic judgement favoured by Hegel and Lukács, to attempts to locate the basis of aesthetic judgement in the biological substratum of the human individual as, for example, in Peter Fuller's work. Whatever the methods used, however, aesthetic discourse exhibits a substantially identical structure: an analysis of the constitution of the subject, whether this be conceived as self-wrought or culturally produced, provides the justification for the view that aesthetic judgement is, ought to be or one day will be universal just as this, in turn, supports the contention that there is a distinctive aesthetic mode of the subject's appropriation of reality. This circularity is an inherent property of aesthetic discourse. Susceptible to neither logical nor empirical demonstration, the existence of a distinctive aesthetic faculty is always ultimately sustained, but entirely intra-discursively, by the projection of a set of conditions in which the subject of value can be represented as universal.

By discourses of value, by contrast, I mean the much more numerous and heterogeneous array of discourses which regulate the social practice of valuing within different valuing communities. Such discourses typically constitute systems for the classification and valuation of persons effected by the means of systems for the classification and valuation of objects and practices. They delimit a set of valued objects and practices and produce, for these, an appropriate valuing subject; that is, a subject marked out from other subjects by his/her ability to recognise the value which such objects and practices are said to embody. This subject is also a *valued* subject, valued precisely because of its ability to correctly apply the rules for valuing which are legislative within a particular valuing community. In this way, the valuing subject functions, ultimately, as the primary valued object also. To the degree that discourses of value address the individual as always-already, either wholly or in part, the valuing subject they produce and require, they constitute a means for the individual's valuation of self as both subject of discernment and ultimate valued object. Their structure is thus narcissistic.

Such discourses are by no means limited to the sphere of artistic practices. Nor, from a sociological point of view, is this necessarily the most important sphere of their operation. As Pierre Bourdieu shows in *La Distinction*, discourses of value may be organised in relation to a wide variety of objects and practices, including sporting and culinary pursuits, for example. Moreover, in Bourdieu's analysis, such discourses, in transforming objects and practices into signs of differentiated social identities, play an important role in relation to more general mechanisms of group formation and group differentiation. They are, in effect, practical social ideologies. As such, Bourdieu focuses on their role in relation to class differences in offering both different modalities for the transformation of economic into cultural capital and supplying the means for the self-differentiation of the bourgeoisie and petit-bourgeoisie from the popular classes as well as from each other. However, discourses of value may also function similarly in relation to national, regional, ethnic or gender differences. Whatever the sphere of their operation, though, they work by constructing an ideal of personality, in both its mental and physical aspects, in relation to which the individual is interpellated as valuing, valued and self-valuing subject.

There are no necessary connections between such discourses of value and aesthetic discourse. In most cases, the two operate in different registers. The rules for valuing as well as the subjects and objects of value which discourses of value propose are legislative and have effects solely within the limits of particular valuing communities. Such discourses are prescriptive, but only for those who occupy or take up the position of the valuing subject they construct, a position which may be refused since such valuing subjects are identifiably socially specific. Aesthetic discourse, by contrast, is the form taken by discourses of value which are hegemonic in ambition and, correspondingly, universalist in their prescriptive ambit and which have, as their zone of application, those practices nominated as artistic. The position of universal valuing subject which is necessary to such discourse – and, invariably, such a position is produced by generalising the attributes of the valuing subject associated with a socially specific discourse of value – can be refused *to* but not *by* the individual. Such refusals, however, always leave open a route whereby the valuing practices of each and every individual may be conformed to the principles of judgement embodied in the universal valuing subject. This is achieved by the deployment of cultural, and hence remediable, criteria which permit the disqualification of those individuals whose judgements are assessed as being wayward or incomplete from the point of view of the position of the universal valuing subject which such discourse constructs. Such criteria, while maintaining a liberal façade, provide a means of discounting as impertinent any and all aberrant systems of aesthetic evaluation which would otherwise call into question the universalising constructions of aesthetic discourse.

As such, aesthetic discourse rests on two specific conditions. First, there must already be cleared a space within which the construction of a universal valuing subject can be located. It is epistemology which clears this space in securing a general conception of the subject form which enables rules for valuing derived from particular valuing communities to be theoretically represented as universally legislative, either actually or tendentially. This is not merely to suggest that, historically, epistemology provided the surface of emergence on which the problems of aesthetics could become visible, although this is certainly the case.[20] The more important point is that theories of the aesthetic logically presuppose an already elaborated theory of knowledge. The *differentia specifica* of the aesthetic as a specific mode of the subject's mental relation to reality, that is to say, can only be established in relation to some prior conception of the knowledge relation between subject and reality, for it is this which provides the co-ordinating centre of philosophy's theorisation of the mental economy of the subject in supplying a self-supporting point of anchorage in relation to which the characteristics of the other modes of the subject's relations to reality can be specified. Moreover, this knowledge relation must already be secured to provide the necessary conditions for an inquiry into the constitutive properties of the aesthetic, for such an inquiry presupposes a subject that is capable of investigating its own constitution. As Catherine Greenfield has put it, epistemology establishes a conception of 'the subject as both the known object of its own introspection and simultaneously the principle which makes such knowledges possible', thereby producing the necessary preconditions for 'the proper activity of mind as the study of its *own* contents'[21] – which aesthetics pre-eminently is.

As its second precondition, aesthetic discourse presupposes the existence of the artistic as an identifiably distinct institutional sphere within society for there to be something, on the object side of the equation, for aesthetic discourse to latch on to. To paraphrase Habermas, we might say that aesthetic discourse can acquire momentum and a social purchase only when there exists a 'public artistic sphere' produced by the deployment of specific forms of classification and exhibition in such separated exhibition contexts as art galleries and museums.[22]

The combined effect of these two conditioning factors is that, more frequently than not, aesthetic discourse fetishises the object of value in ways which serve as a complement to, and are produced by means of, its universalisation of the valuing subject. This point requires some elaboration. Since it is clear that value is a relational

153

phenomenon produced in the passage between subject and object, it is readily admitted in most forms of aesthetic discourse that beauty neither is nor can be a natural property of the object. As Kant puts it:

> If we wish to discern whether anything is beautiful or not, we do not refer the representation of it to the Object by means of understanding with a view to cognition, but by means of the imagination (acting perhaps in conjunction with understanding) we refer the representation to the Subject and its feeling of pleasure or displeasure. The judgement of taste, therefore, is not a cognitive judgement, and so not logical, but is aesthetic – which means that it is one whose determining ground *cannot be other than subjective*.[23]

Even so-called objectivist aesthetics, which construe the aesthetic as a distinct set of mental effects produced by those practices nominated as artistic, secure their determining ground in the properties of the subject in assuming a general subject form capable of experiencing or recognising those effects. Once this determining ground has been universalised, however, aesthetic discourse tilts on its axis as the properties of the subject which guarantee the universality of aesthetic judgement are transferred to the object. Value, transfixed in the singular gaze of the universal subject, solidifies and takes form as a property of the object just as, once the universal valuing subject has been constructed, its active, value-constitutive role becomes passive: all it can do is to recognise the value that was already there, secreted somewhere in the dense folds of the object.

David Hume's essay *Of the Standard of Taste* (1757) provides an economical example of many of these regulative procedures of aesthetic discourse, and one in which their association with the exercise of cultural power stands forth particularly clearly. Hume's starting point is to dispute the view that varying judgements of taste should be ranked equally since their claims cannot be adjudicated by appealing to the properties of objects:

> Whoever would assert an equality of genius and elegance between Ogilby and Milton, or Bunyan and Addison, would be thought to defend no less an extravagance, than if he had maintained a mole-hill to be as high as Teneriffe, or a pond

as extensive as the ocean. Though there may be found persons, who give the preference to the former authors; no-one pays attention to such a taste; and we pronounce, without scruple, the sentiment of these pretended critics to be absurd and ridiculous. The principle of the natural equality of taste is then totally forgot, and while we admit it on some occasions, where the objects seem near an equality, it appears an extravagant paradox, or rather a palpable absurdity, where objects so disproportioned are compared together.[24]

The ground for demonstrating that the principles of aesthetic judgement are universal is prepared, here, via the initial disqualification of those whose judgements depart significantly from the standards of agreed taste. Moreover, this is justified by an appeal to the properties of the objects compared. This is confirmed by the next step Hume takes in arguing that true and universal principles of taste can only be derived by removing all the exterior, disturbing circumstances which are likely to disrupt the true operation of the finer aspects of judgement or, as Hume calls it, sentiment. The principles of taste, Hume thus contends, are most clearly manifested in 'the durable admiration which attends those works that have survived all the caprices of mode and fashion, all the mistakes of ignorance and envy'.[25] In short, the classics. The value of these objects is guaranteed by the universality of their acclaim, and vice versa, within what Bourdieu has characterised as 'the circular circulation of inter-legitimation' in which judgements of value both consecrate and are consecrated by the 'inherently valuable' properties of the objects which they approve.[26] The failure to recognise value where it is thus objectively lodged can therefore, Hume argues, only derive 'from some apparent defect or imperfection in the organ'.[27] Even where there is no congenital defect, however, the capacity for valid judgement may be unequally developed since different individuals have different opportunities and inclinations to exercise and develop this capacity. It is worth quoting Hume's conclusions on these matters in full since they aptly demonstrate the respects in which the qualification of some subjects of judgement is effected by the simultaneous disqualification of others:

Thus, though the principles of taste be universal, and nearly, if not entirely, the same in all men; yet few are qualified to give judgement on any work of art, or establish their own sentiment as the standard of beauty. The organs of internal sensation are seldom so perfect as to allow the general principles their full play, and produce a feeling correspondent to those principles. They either labour under some defect, or are vitiated by some disorder; and by that means excite a sentiment, which may be pronounced erroneous. When the critic has no delicacy, he judges without any distinction, and is only affected by the grosser and more palpable qualities of the object: the finer touches pass unnoticed and disregarded. Where he is not aided by practice, his verdict is attended with confusion and hesitation. Where no comparison has been employed, the most frivolous beauties, such as rather merit the name of defects, are the objects of his admiration. Where he lies under the influence of prejudice, all his natural sentiments are perverted. Where good sense is wanting, he is not qualified to discern the beauties of design and reasoning, which are the highest and most excellent. Under some or other of these imperfections, the generality of men labour; and hence a true judge in the finer arts is observed, even during the most polished ages, to be so rare a character: a strong sense, united to delicate sentiment, improved by practice, perfected by comparison, and cleared of all prejudice, can alone entitle critics to this valuable character; and the joint verdict of such, wherever they are to be found, is the true standard of taste and beauty.[28]

The 'universal' principles of taste, then, may be held in check by a variety of interior and exterior impediments. They develop to perfection only when the internal organs of sensation are correctly balanced and when exterior circumstances permit their full and unimpeded exercise and progressive refinement. The proof – the only proof – that such principles of taste exist is provided by the few 'valuable characters' who manifest them in their fully developed form. Happily, however, everyone (everyone whose judgement is allowed to count, that is) knows who these are: '. . . some men in general, however difficult to be particularly pitched upon, will be acknowledged by universal sentiment to have a preference over others'.[29]

The problem Hume is addressing here is clear. Writing against the arbitrary authoritarianism of earlier aristocratic aesthetic prescriptions, his essay articulates the Enlightenment demand that the principles of taste should be arrived at by means of rational and open debate between members of a public who meet as equals. However, the definition of the relevant public, produced by disqualifying the judgements of the congenitally and culturally defective multitude, results in a cultural partiality that is equally arbitrary and authoritarian. The universality of taste turns out, in effect, to be based on the most insubstantial and flimsy of foundations: the consensus of the drawing room. At this point, Hume's analysis is driven into a further contradiction in the respect that the requirements of rationalism require Hume to allow that, within the defined limits of polite society, genuine and irreconcilable aesthetic disagreements may occur:

> But where there is such a diversity in the internal frame or external situation as is entirely blameless on both sides, and leaves no room to give one the preference above the other; in that case a certain degree of diversity of judgement is unavoidable, and we seek in vain for a standard, by which we can reconcile the contrary sentiments.[30]

In brief, once the judgements produced within the bourgeois public sphere have been generalised to equate with the level of the universal, Hume's discourse turns tail on itself, securing a commitment to the principles of rationality necessary to the constitution of the bourgeois public sphere only by sacrificing the possibility that judgement might be represented as universal even in this limited social domain. Put crudely, the bourgeois public maintains a united front, the illusion of a universality, in face of the masses, conducting its disagreements behind closed – and barred – doors.

Kant's *Critique* is a work of immeasurably greater power and rigour. None the less, in universalising the rules for valuing that are legislative within civilised society, it accomplishes the same ideological work, albeit that it does so in the laundered sphere of the transcendental method. This 'dirty work', moreover is accomplished only hypothetically, for Kant does not so much found an aesthetic as establish the conditions that would be necessary for doing so. The *Critique* is, in consequence, as Lukács would have put it, 'the critical self-consciousness of aesthetic discourse'.

Kant's opening question in the *Critique* is whether the faculty of judgement 'which in the order of our cognitive faculties forms a middle term between understanding and reason' is governed by independent and *a priori* principles which would constitute it as a 'special realm'.[31] The existence of this faculty, it is important to note, is presupposed as is its function: that of mediating between and connecting understanding and reason, the subject of cognition and the subject of moral action. Indeed, its existence is required to support the conception of the subject form as a unified trinity of thought, feeling and action. However, the existence of such a faculty cannot, in Kant's view, be proved logically or empirically. 'It is only throwing away labour', Kant argues, 'to look for a principle of taste that affords a universal criterion of the beautiful by definite concepts. . . .'[32] Moreover, this would defeat the purpose of the exercise since the faculty of judgement itself must furnish the means of specifying its own distinctive properties. Otherwise, if these could be known by concepts, then judgement would be subservient to understanding and would not, Kant contends, constitute a 'special realm' within the mental economy of the subject. As for the empirical evidence favouring the view that the sensation of delight or aversion is universally communicable, Kant concedes that this is 'weak indeed and scarce sufficient to raise a presumption, of the derivation of a taste, thus confirmed by examples, from grounds deep-seated and shared alike by all men, underlying their agreement in estimating the forms under which objects are given to them'.[33]

Kant therefore ostensibly places in brackets the specific application of the faculty of judgement and the particular objects to which it is applied within specific valuing communities, in favour of a transcendental analysis of the principles regulating its exercise no matter what the circumstances of its employment. However, the brackets are soon removed. Kant distinguishes the beautiful from the agreeable and the good, both of which imply a concept of an end and the interest of the subject in that end, as that which pleases without regard to any interest of the subject. 'The delight which determines the judgement of taste', he writes, 'is independent of all interest.'[34] Bourdieu has argued that Kant, in making disinterestedness a defining attribute of the aesthetic, merely rationalises a bourgeois class ethos as manifested in the sphere of taste. This view is based on his empirical studies of different class-based valuing practices. These show, at least in the case of contemporary France, that the premium placed on disinterestedness as an appropriate aesthetic attitude correlates directly with the degree to which a class or class fraction is distanced from the practical need to secure the necessities of life. Indeed, it is a way of *displaying* that distance.

For Bourdieu, then, disinterestedness constitutes a particular form of posturing on the part of the subject which, while serving specific social interests, simultaneously masks those interests as well as its own use in their service. For Kant, by contrast, the quality of disinterestedness provides the means whereby his discussion shifts from the level of a phenomenology of bourgeois taste to that of a transcendental analysis of the faculty of judgement, but only by equating the two. The crucial step in Kant's argument in this respect consists in his contention that: 'The beautiful is that which, apart from concepts, is represented as the Object of a UNIVERSAL delight.'[35] It is, however, only within discourses of value governed by the attribute of disinterestedness that beauty is and can be so represented:

> For where any one is conscious that his delight in an object is with him independent of all interest, it is inevitable that he should look on the object as one containing a ground of delight for all men. For, since the delight is not based on any inclination of the Subject (or any other deliberate interest) but the Subject feels himself completely *free* in respect of the liking which he accords to the object, he can find as reason for his delight no personal conditions to which his own subjective self might alone be party. Hence he must regard it as resting on what he may also presuppose in every other person; and therefore he must believe that he has reason for demanding a similar delight from every one.[36]

It is not my purpose to develop a social critique of Kant's aesthetics. None the less, it is worth noting that he hitches his own discourse up into the sphere of universality, which the transcendental method requires, by means of the very slippery toe-hold provided by the illusions of the subject of a specific discourse of value. It is only the demand for agreement arising from the subject's feeling of disinterestedness in performing judgements of taste which provides the ground for Kant's supposition that there might be a universal, or universalisable, faculty of judgement constituting a special realm. However, my interest lies mainly in

Kant's clear perception of the properties of such discourse and of the conditions necessary to sustain it at the level of universality to which it aspires. With regard to the former, Kant is quite unequivocal: universalising discourses of value both fetishise the object of value and deploy a discourse of disqualification in relation to those subjects who do not, or refuse to, conform to their edicts. Of the man who speaks of beauty, Kant says:

> He judges not merely for himself, but for all men, and then speaks of beauty as if it were a property of things. Thus he says the *thing* is beautiful; and it is not as if he counted on others agreeing in his judgement of liking owing to his having found them in such agreement on a number of occasions, but he *demands* this agreement of them. He blames them if they judge differently, and denies them taste, which he still requires of them as something they ought to have; and to this extent it is not open to men to say: Every one has his own taste. This would be equivalent to saying that there is no such thing at all as taste, i.e. no aesthetic judgement capable of making a rightful claim upon the assent of all men.[37]

Kant, it is important to add, does not provide a warrant for such claims at the level of their empirical application within specific valuing communities. Indeed, he argues that nothing is postulated in such claims but 'the *possibility* of an aesthetic judgement capable of being at the same time deemed valid for every one'.[38] In his hypothetical deduction of the conditions which must obtain in order to give such claims both a historical and a logical validity, however, Kant is clear that they require a simultaneous universalisation of the object and subject of value, and the identity of the two. They require the former, Kant argues, in the sense that the ideal of the beautiful which regulates the exercise of the faculty of judgement can only be man:

> Only what has in itself the end of its real existence – only *man* that is able himself to determine his ends by reason, or where he has to derive them from external perception, can still compare them with essential and universal ends, and then further pronounce aesthetically upon their accord with such ends, only he, among all objects in the world, admits, therefore, of an ideal of *beauty*, just as humanity in his

person, as intelligence, alone admits of the ideal of *perfection*.[39]

It is, then, man, as the ideal of the beautiful, which provides the standard governing our estimation of the aesthetic value of objects. For the moment, in the here and now, this ideal exists as 'a mere idea, which each person must beget in his own consciousness, and according to which he must form his estimate of everything that is an Object of taste, or that is an example of critical taste, and even of universal taste itself'.[40] However, it is clear that only the actualisation of this ideal in the world of objects − only, that is, the production of man as the ultimately valued object of whose beauty and perfection all other objects partake and to which they testify − can provide a justification for such claims in finally enabling beauty to be predicated as a concept of the object, now universalised and perfected.

It is equally clear that this universalisation of the object must be complemented by a universalisation of the subject of judgement. Kant thus argues that aesthetic judgements both presuppose and project a *sensus communis*: a common sense on which a yet-to-be-realised unanimity of aesthetic judgement can be founded. 'The judgement of taste, therefore,' he writes, 'depends on our presupposing the existence of a common sense.'[41] This is not to suggest that such a common sense actually exists − its status is that of 'a mere ideal norm'[42] − but that the demand for agreement which accompanies aesthetic judgement presupposes the possibility of its eventual existence. 'The assertion is not that every one *will* fall in with our judgement,' Kant says, 'but rather that every one *ought* to agree with it.'[43] It is in the gap between what is and what ought to be, of course, that discourses of disqualification insert themselves: a *sensus communis* will be produced once the various impediments which inhibit others from applying the faculty of judgement correctly have been removed and once, accordingly, unified subject of value meets unified object of value in a mutually confirming and, no doubt, valuable encounter.

With regard to the likelihood of the production of such a *sensus communis*, Kant is, once again, engagingly, if also revealingly, open:

Is taste, in other words, a natural and original faculty, or is it only the idea of one that is artificial and to be acquired by us, so that a judgement of taste, with its demand for universal assent, is but a requirement of reason for generating such a *consensus*, and does the 'ought', i.e. the objective necessity of the coincidence of the feeling of all with the particular feeling of each, only betoken the possibility of arriving at some sort of unanimity in these matters, and the judgement of taste only adduce an example of the application of this principle? These are questions which as yet we are neither willing nor in a position to investigate.[44]

AESTHETICS AND THE REFORM OF THE SUBJECT

In summary, then, the inconclusive conclusion of Kant's *Critique* can be reduced to the following questions: Will the universality of taste, once it has been produced, turn out to be a natural and original property of the human subject? Or will the subject to which a universality of taste can appropriately be attributed turn out to be the product of a process of cultural and historical unification? This Kantian cliff-hanger has provided one of the central cleavages within the history of aesthetics, and has been particularly influential in distinguishing between conservative and radical positions. It is, however, of quite incidental significance since, whichever position is adopted, the structure of argumentation employed is essentially the same. Each requires that some means be found of anticipating, to recall Alan Durant's phrase, the 'discernments of a hypothetical posterity' and further, in order to validate this construct, of disqualifying those whose judgements do not agree with the yet-to-be announced, but constantly deferred, edicts of a unified valuing subject. In Lukács's man-centred aesthetics, in which the questions Kant leaves open are closed in the name of a historicised narcissism, the empirical failure of subjects in the present to anticipate the judgements that will be pronounced once the cultural and historical process of man's unification has been completed is attributed to the effect of false consciousness on social agents. But Peter Fuller, who espouses a form of historicised biologism, is obliged to resort to similar arguments. Although positing an aesthetic sense based on certain innate biological properties, Fuller – given that few people seem to be correctly appreciating as their biologies say they ought to – must project this 'natural and original' property as a post-historical construct, destined to realise itself only in culturally propitious circumstances. Meanwhile, by deploying a many-stranded discourse of disqualification, Fuller ensures that there is no need to take account of any contradictory evidence which might call this theory into question:

> But, of course, despite what some of my critics have said, my position is in no sense whatever ahistorical. I argue that – like so many human potentialities – this biologically given aesthetic potentiality requires a facilitating environment to develop, and to flourish. The trouble at the moment is that the decline of religious belief, and the change in the nature of work brought about by the rise of modern industrialism, and its subsequent development, have combined to erode the conditions under which this great human potentiality can flourish. That's why it is no use going to the man in the street.[45]

Moreover, it matters relatively little, practically speaking, whether the criteria of disqualification which accompany aesthetic discourse are malignant or benign. So far as questions of cultural policy are concerned, the orientation of aesthetic discourse predisposes it to generate proposals directed to the subject rather than the object side of the aesthetic relation, and to do so no matter what its political affiliations. Although in one respect tilted forward in anticipating 'the discernments of a hypothetical posterity', aesthetic discourse is also obliged to be backward-looking since, as a condition of its construction, it must, at least to some degree, accept and endorse the dominant systems of evaluation handed down from the past. If the aesthetic is to be founded as a universally present mode of the subject's mental relation to reality, then, first, the objects valued in the past must be regarded as the right ones and, second, they must also be regarded as having been valued for the right reasons even if only, as Lukács argued, in limited ways, whose real meaning is to be progressively revealed. As a consequence – and Brecht's comments on Lukács demonstrate this most forcibly[46] – aesthetic discourse, when directed to the object side of the aesthetic relation, can result only in a politics of preserving what has already been preserved and consecrated in the judgements of the past, or of emulating, extending and adapting earlier aesthetic models to fit new circumstances. Since, for the reasons outlined earlier, value is ultimately fetishised as a property of the object, an inability to judge correctly must be attributed to a failing of the subject, a failing accounted for by a series of cultural impediments whose removal thus becomes the primary goal of cultural policy – through education in liberal bourgeois aesthetics or, more usually in Marxist aesthetics, through the transformation of social relations. It is not surprising, therefore, that the predominant tendency within Marxist aesthetics has been to constitute the members of oppressed social groups as subjects whose aesthetic judgement needs to be transformed by being conformed to some already elaborated aesthetic norm. There is, as Fuller puts it, no need, in such approaches, to go to the man in the street, no need to articulate a socialist cultural policy to the different discourses of value which circulate within and between oppressed strata. It is therefore small wonder that Marxist aesthetic discourse has proved quite irrelevant outside the academy since it impedes, in its very structure, an adequate theorisation of the field of social-cultural relations within which a socialist cultural politics must intervene.

And it does more than that. Earlier in his exchange with Terry Eagleton, Peter Fuller argues that 'my aesthetics (though not my politics) are closer to those of Roger Scruton and the "Higher Toryism" of Peterhouse than to all that discourse – semiotics and post-structuralist deconstruction – which goes on up the road at King's.'[47] And with good reason, although he is mistaken to believe that aesthetic and political positions might be so clearly disentangled. Indeed, I have tried to show that the structure of aesthetic discourse is inherently suspect in its political leanings no matter how radical the political protocols displayed on its surface. Jan Mukarovsky, writing of the mutual intolerance of aesthetic norms in polemical situations, succinctly summarises the consequences which discrepant judgements of taste bring in their tow:

> The aesthetic norm is replaced by another, more authoritative norm – e.g., a moral norm – and one's opponent is called a deceiver, or else by an intellectual norm, in which case the opponent is called ignorant or stupid. Even when the right of the individual to make aesthetic judgements is emphasised, one hears in the same breath the request for responsibility for them: individual taste is a component of the human value of the person who exercises it.[48]

In making this remark, Mukarovsky has in mind the relative

164

intolerance produced by the functioning, within specific discourses of value, of ideals of personality that are identifiably socially specific in their articulations. In the case of aesthetic discourse, obliged to operate at the level of universality in order to establish the aesthetic as a distinctive mode of the subject's mental relation to reality, such relative intolerance becomes absolute. Within such discourse, the subject who fails to appreciate correctly is regarded as being incompletely human rather than merely being excluded from full title to the membership of a specific valued and valuing community. To fail to appreciate correctly as a proletarian revolutionary, Scottish Nationalist, radical feminist, or, indeed, Peterhouse Tory is one thing − a failure to take up a particular articulated aesthetic, social and political positionality. An aesthetic, by contrast, no matter how benign the discourse of disqualification it deploys, must operate more far-reaching and complete exclusions and do so by virtue of its very structure.

Notwithstanding the scientific claims which often accompany it, aesthetic discourse is ideological in the Althusserian sense that it functions as a discourse producing subjects. The universal valuing subject (man) it constructs interpellates the reader into the position of a valuing subject who is defined, in relation to the valued object (man), within a mirror structure of self-recognition. Yes, indeed, man is manifested in this object; yes, indeed, I recognise myself in it; isn't it/aren't I wonderful? − such is the effect of aesthetic discourse for the subject who takes up the position it offers. As ideology, however, aesthetic discourse is characterised by a number of contradictions and torsions, albeit ones which vary in their consequences depending on the political articulations of such discourse. In the case of bourgeois aesthetics, the production of a unified valuing subject, although necessary in providing a theoretical legitimation for the re-presentation of class-specific aesthetic norms as universally valid, is also, at another level, sham, and necessarily so. Such discourse *requires* its ignorants if it is to fulfill its practical function of social differentiation. The problem associated with attempts to appropriate aesthetic discourse for socialism are, in many respects, the reverse for, willy nilly, such discourse produces its ignorants and, however benign, an accompanying condescension which serve as a blockage to both political analysis and cultural policy formation.

'Shouldn't we abolish aesthetics?' Brecht asked in the title of an article he wrote in 1927.[49] His answer, of course, was: yes. As a

165

producer, Brecht clearly found the prescriptions of aesthetic systems restricting. If you want an aesthetic, he asked two decades later (clearly implying that he didn't), it could be summed up in the slogan that socialists need 'many different methods in order to reach their objective'.[50] This did not imply any neutrality with regard to the question of value on Brecht's part, but his concern was always with political use-value – local, temporary and conjunctural – which he felt able to address without the need to develop any general, universally applicable theory of the aesthetic as a distinct mode. I think Brecht was right. The political utility of discourses of value operating via the construction of an ideal of personality to which broadly based social aspirations can be articulated is unquestionable. There is, however, no reason to suppose that such discourses must be hitched up to the sphere of universality in order to secure their effectivity. To the contrary, given the configuration of today's political struggles, it is highly unlikely that an ideal of personality might be forged that would be of equal service in the multiple, intersecting, but equally non-coincident foci of struggle constituted by black, gay, feminist, socialist and, in some contexts, national liberation politics. In particular conjunctures, to be sure, an ideal of personality may be forged which serves to integrate – but always temporarily – such forces into a provisional unity. But this is not the basis for a generalisable and universalisable cultural politics. Nor is this the time for such a politics.

7

AESTHETICS AND LITERARY EDUCATION

I happened, when working on an early draft of this chapter, to pass a beauty salon called, simply, *Aesthetic*. This served as a timely reminder of the fact that, beyond its modern specialist uses as, variously, the theory of the fine arts, the philosophy of taste or the science of the beautiful, 'aesthetics' is now also commonly used, as Raymond Williams puts it, 'to refer to questions of visual appearance and effect'[1] – as, in this instance, to the cultivation and maintenance of such appearances. It is this sense of the term Foucault draws on in including aesthetics among the practices of the self he discusses in *The History of Sexuality*[2] – practices, he later tells us, which need to be understood as parts of 'technologies of the self, which permit individuals to effect by their own means or with the help of others a certain number of operations on their own bodies and souls, thoughts, conduct, and way of being, so as to transform themselves in order to attain a certain state of happiness, purity, wisdom, perfection, or immortality'.[3]

What if we look at philosophical aesthetics in the same way? What if we consider it not as a theory of judgement whose accuracy has to be assessed but as a discourse which, through the distinctions it organises (between the merely pleasing, the beautiful and the sublime) and the manner in which it relates these to adjacent distinctions (between the true and the false, the good and the bad), produces a space in which the exercise of judgement functions as part of a system of self-fashioning? And, if aesthetics can be so regarded, what are the relations between this technology of the self and, as Foucault puts it, the 'technologies of power, which determine the conduct of individuals and submit them to certain ends or domination . . .'?[4]

I shall take, as my route into these questions, two contrasting

167

accounts of the nineteenth-century educational deployment of aesthetics, one Marxist and the other taking the Foucaultian tack I have just summarised. This is not a gratuitous choice. To the contrary: exploring where, how and why these accounts differ will, I shall suggest, allow a revised estimation of the relations between the history of aesthetics and the organisation of modern literary politics.

THE IDEA OF ART'S AUTONOMY

Critical science does not consist in inventing new categories to set against the 'false' ones of traditional science. Rather, it examines the categories of traditional science to discover what other questions are already excluded at the theoretical level (precisely as a consequence of the choice of categories). In the study of literature, the following question is important: are the categories such that they make possible the investigation of the nexus between literary objectifications and social conditions?[5]

In posing this question toward the beginning of *Theory of the Avant-Garde*, Peter Bürger suggests that, when applied to the work of Lukács and Adorno, the answer must be 'yes' so far as their approaches to individual works of art and literature are concerned. Equally, though, he contends that the answer must be decidedly in the negative with regard to the light they throw on the functioning of art and literature as institutions. For they do not, he argues, adopt a position sufficiently external to these for their functioning as *institutions* to be readily perceptible. 'Lukács and Adorno', as he puts it, 'argue within the institution that is art, and are unable to criticise it as an institution for that very reason. For them, the autonomy doctrine is an horizon within which they think.'[6] To the degree that literary functions 'are not inherent in individual works but are socially institutionalised', Bürger goes on to argue, their examination requires a reorientation of analytical focus, one in which the doctrine of art's autonomy, conceived as 'the normative instrumentality of an institution in bourgeois society', becomes the object of investigation.[7] Analysis must focus not on individual works but on the distinctive organisation of the field of literary functions and effects produced by the institutionalisation of art's autonomy which derives from 'the progressive detachment of art from real life contexts, and the correlative crystallisation of a distinctive sphere of experience, i.e. the aesthetic'.[8]

What such an analysis might look like is only hinted at in *Theory of the Avant-Garde*. However, a fuller indication of what Bürger has in mind is available in the thumb-nail sketch he offers, in a later essay, of 'a sociology of art which sees the autonomy status of art as the necessary institutional frame for the production and reception of art in bourgeois society'.[9] In his approach to the latter of these questions – the reception of art – Bürger's central concern is to reconcile the apparent contradiction between the institutionalisation of art's autonomy and the simultaneous tendency for art to be used as an instrument of pedagogy:

> Nothing seems to contradict the view that art is institution-alised as autonomous in bourgeois society more strongly than the fact that it is precisely in such a society that works of art have been made educational instruments in the socialisation process both inside and outside of schools.[10]

In Bürger's analysis, however, this pedagogic instrumentalisation of art turns out to be a *necessary* requirement of the concept of its autonomy – 'That an art so conceived should find employment in the bourgeois educational system does not contradict its concept; the concept actually calls for it'[11] – just as, in turn, it *depends* on that concept for 'it is precisely because of their autonomous status that works of art can be made the instruments of education'.[12] That art's autonomy and its pedagogic utilisation are thus able to be presented as two sides of the same coin is a function of Bürger's interpretation of Schiller's *Letters on the Aesthetic Education of Man*, a text he construes as the paradigmatic instance of the doctrine of art's autonomy.

For Schiller, of course, aesthetic education is assigned the role of overcoming an ethical division within the subject and, thereby, prefiguring a situation in which man's lost wholeness, alienated through the division of labour, will be restored to him. Its capacity to perform this task derives from the position accorded aesthetic experience as the locus of a mediation between two contradictory tendencies in the constitution of the subject: the transcendental and the empirical. It overcomes the division between, on the one hand, *Die Person*, or Subject, referring to the concept of the human individual in his freedom from determination (*Selbstandigkeit*), and, on the other hand, *Persönlichkeit*; that is, the particular determinate forms of personhood which result from the fact that, as Schiller put it, 'man is not just Person pure and simple, but Person situated in a particular Condition'.[13] What aesthetic experience thus provides, David Lloyd suggests in summarising Schiller's argument, 'is the necessary *via media* between a passive disposition in which man is given over entirely to Condition and is utterly determined by *sensation*, and an active disposition in which Person governs and autonomous *thought* predominates'.[14]

That aesthetic experience is able to operate on the site of this division within the subject derives from its Kantian conception. It results, that is, from the fact that, when experienced aesthetically, the aesthetic object is related to not as an object of desire – for this would root such experience in the empirically conditioned interests of the subject – but as an object of disinterested contemplation, thereby allowing it to be attributed to that component in the make-up of the subject which transcends particular determinations. Yet, since this experience is experienced by particular, empirically determined individuals, it is thereby also able to be represented as the site and medium of a putative harmonisation of the subject's contradictory constitution, overcoming, however temporarily and provisionally, the division between particular forms of *Persönlichkeit* and *Die Person*, between particular socially determined forms of personhood and the transcendental Subject, Man. Moreover, as, at least in principle, this experience is accessible to everyone, it can simultaneously be regarded as a mode of communication capable of uniting society.

Yet all of this is so only potentially in that, in actuality, aesthetic experience is assessed as beyond the reach of a whole range of specific, empirically determined forms of human individuality. 'For aesthetic experience', as Lloyd puts it, 'is a common property of the human species only as a pure potential, and it is an essential part of Schiller's argument that aesthetic feeling may not be developed at all in the savage, and is scarcely more than embryonic in the barbarian or in the bourgeois.'[15] Hence, of course, the need for aesthetic education as a means of bridging the gap between actuality and potentiality.

And hence also, to return to Bürger, the requirement that art be conceptualised and institutionalised as autonomous in order that it might function as 'the advocate of humanity in a society in whose actual life-processes humanity is not realised'.[16] For if art 'is burdened with the demand that it be an alternative to the real world', it can be so only on the condition that it is opposed to 'that real world as the wholly other'.[17] It is this, its antinomial relation to society, that allows the conception of art's autonomy to be regarded as essential to the programme of aesthetic education which, in turn, if art's capacity for individual and social harmonisation is to be realised, it requires. Yet, at the same time, this programme is destined not to be effectively realised to the degree that the real world to which art is opposed is assessed as incapable of producing 'recipients who are capable of the kind of commerce with works of art which Schiller has in mind'.[18] The consequence, Bürger suggests, is that art's autonomy is institutionalised in the form of an *ideology*. In opposing to the means–end rationality of society an institutionalised experience of harmony whose extended social realisation is simultaneously represented as impossible, the autonomy of art embodies an institutionalised form of 'false consciousness' whose effect Bürger likens to that which Marcuse describes in elaborating his concept of 'affirmative culture':

> To accusing questions the bourgeoisie gave a decisive answer:
> affirmative culture. The latter is fundamentally idealist. To
> the need of the isolated individual it responds with general
> humanity, to bodily misery with the beauty of the soul, to
> external bondage with internal freedom, to brutal egoism
> with the duty of the realm of virtue. Whereas during the
> period of the militant rise of the new society all of these ideas
> had a progressive character by pointing beyond the attained
> organisation of existence, they entered increasingly into the
> service of the suppression of the discontented masses and of
> mere self-justifying exaltation, once bourgeois rule began to
> be stabilised.[19]

This conclusion, that the doctrine of art's autonomy functions as a repressive ideology which serves to stem the formation of a revolutionary consciousness by means of the *promesse de bonheur*, is as unconvincing as it is unsurprising. For isn't this, in essence, precisely the view argued by Lukács and Adorno even though, in accepting the doctrine of art's autonomy as a natural horizon, they were supposedly unable to analyse its functioning as an institution? If this is so, it is hard to see why Bürger places so much stress on the novelty of his method. For a new method which proves capable merely of reformulating already familiar arguments hardly seems worth the effort of its fashioning. Moreover, if that is all it can do, there are grounds for suspecting its novelty and, if we look closely, we shall see that, although seeking to represent his approach as institutional and functional rather than aesthetic, Bürger does not succeed in 'severing the aesthetic connection' as clearly as he supposes.

That he does not do so, furthermore, seems foreordained by the way he defines the concerns of institutional analysis:

> In the sociology of art and literature, the concept 'institution' is occasionally used to refer to the establishments such as publishing, the book-trade, the theatre and museums which mediate between the individual work and the public. It is not in this sense that we will speak of art as an institution in what follows. Instead, we will use the concept to refer to the definitions of the function of art in its social contingency and the changes in that function from period to period. This is not to say that there can be no sociology of the mediating agencies. . . . But such an empirical sociology of the mediating agencies would hardly produce insights into the social function of art and its changes through history. For the accumulation of studies of individual agencies cannot replace a theoretical framework which is the very condition for investigating the social function of art.[20]

This is a most unfortunate passage. For in imposing on the field of institutional analysis an *a priori* unity derived from art's own self-definition, it allows an analysis of the *idea of art* to take the place of an analysis of the diverse array of institutional and discursive conditions regulating the uses of literary and artistic texts. This is possible, however, solely because the idea of art is attributed with the capacity to regulate the functions of such texts whatever the spheres of their deployment. It is this that allows an empirical sociology of mediating agencies to be regarded as of secondary importance compared with the theoretical elucidation of the idea of art. For, since it is precisely and only this idea which such agencies mediate and since the most they can do is to moderate its influence in minor ways, the regulative power of this idea guarantees that a set of unified functions and effects will result from the deployment of literary and artistic texts within, between and across these agencies.

172

Yet it is surely clear that the claims of a *theoretical* versus those of an *empirical* sociology of art is not the point at issue here. What rather hangs in the balance is the *kind* of theoretical attention an analysis of art's institutional deployment requires and, accordingly, the nature of the empirical issues to which it points. Bürger's position, another instance of 'idealist reductionism' in the respect that the organisation of the field of textual uses and effects is regarded as deducible from an immanent analysis of the idea of art, entails that, so far as the influence of the conception of art's autonomy on the educational sphere is concerned, analysis stops at precisely the point it should begin: a consideration of the specific mechanisms of connection through which this idea of art enters into and becomes concretely influential within educational practices and institutions. To suppose that the specific patterns and consequences of the educational deployment of art and literature can be read off from an analysis of the idea of art is to suppose that the field of educational institutions and practices operates as an empty vessel, a neutral medium for the transmission of a specific ideology, without imposing conditions and effects of its own.

Consideration of a related argument may help amplify the issues at stake here. In an essay which draws on Foucault, Terry Eagleton has argued that literature needs to be viewed as a moral technology; that is, as a 'particular set of techniques and practices for the instilling of specific kinds of value, discipline, behaviour, and response in human subjects'.[21] What distinguishes the role of literature from that of other moral technologies of self-formation in this regard is that it is concerned less to instil any particular moral values than to inculcate within the subject a particular way of *being moral as such*. Construing literature as heir to the formalism of Kant's moral philosophy, Eagleton summarises the disposition of the subject which it produces as follows:

> The task of the moral technology of Literature is to produce an historically peculiar form of human subject who is sensitive, receptive, imaginative and so on . . . *about nothing in particular*. . . . It is not just that there are, as we all know, types of literary formalism; it is that Literature *is* a formalism. What is important, in this ideology of Literature, is not so much the object being grasped, which can be any kind of object you like, but the lived experience of grasping it, on the part of a particular individual.[22]

What is most alarming here is the rapidity with which the question of the functioning of a moral technology is reduced, as with Bürger, to the operations of an ideology. Rather than consisting in a particular set of institutional and artefactual arrangements whose composition and functioning have to be investigated, literature here again has an idealist unity bestowed on it. It functions, if Eagleton is to be believed, as a set of ideas which organises the experience of the subject. But then one must ask: How, precisely, do ideas do this? Through what mechanisms do they take hold of the subject? What is the machinery through which this moral technology functions? It is not merely that, within the space of a short article, Eagleton fails to provide a detailed analysis of the distinctive institutional arrangements and techniques of the self which characterise the functioning of literature as a moral technology of self-formation. Rather, the difficulty is that the door to such an analysis is prematurely closed by the contention that the *modus operandi* of this technology consists in its transmission of a specific ideology of literature. As with Bürger, this entails that the question of the specific mechanisms of connection through which this ideology becomes concretely influential within specific pedagogic apparatuses and practices is answered before it can even be properly formulated.

A further difficulty consists in the functionalism of the account and the conception of the subject this implies. For literature's role as a technology of self-formation, as Eagleton goes on to develop the argument, is attuned to the requirement of producing a form of subjectivity that will serve the needs of capitalism. The political rationality of this subjectivity, moreover, is assessed in essentially negative terms in that the stress is placed less on the positive effects of those particular forms of conduct it does produce than on their role in impeding the development of alternative trajectories of subject formation. The value of literature to capitalism, Eagleton thus argues, is that of producing a morally and politically empty, but ostensibly free, form of subjectivity which, precisely to the degree that it exults in the illusion of this freedom, is rendered blind to the real determinations which produce it, as well as to the purposes it serves, thus inhibiting the forms of political commitment that would arise were subjects to acquire a self-consciousness of their determinations. In this respect, Eagleton's assessment of literature's functioning as a technology of self-formation implies a concept of another process of self-formation, one which, resting not on an alternative technology of the self but arising 'naturally' through the subject's acquisition of a self-consciousness of its determinations, will lead the subject in another direction: revolution. For it is only in relation to this supposition that it makes sense to argue that the moral technology of literature functions to trap and waylay the subject, diverting it from the path of the beckoning *rendez-vous* with itself promised in the moment of its self-recognition.

LITERATURE, AESTHETICS AND SELF-FORMATION

It is precisely in its tendency toward arguments of this type, Ian Hunter has argued, that Marxist cultural theory has remained most deeply in the thrall of Romantic aesthetics in having adopted, as a part of its conception of history, a collectivised version of the Schillerian dialectic whereby the production of a division within the subject is held to be liable to a process of historical overcoming. The influence of this aspect of nineteenth-century aesthetic theory on the thought of Marx and Engels is, of course, well known. There is, moreover, wide recognition of its bearing on their conception of history as a process which traces the production of a division within the subject (alienation) only to restore to it its lost fullness in communist society when the various splittings which have rent it asunder (between the sensuous and the rational, the subject and the object, freedom and necessity, culture and society) will be harmoniously reconciled at the moment the subject understands itself as the product of the forces which both initially divided it from itself and subsequently restored it to completeness. Indeed, this lineage is often positively celebrated as demonstrating both that Marxism is the genuine heir to the universalist aspirations of bourgeois aesthetics and that it fulfils its filial obligations in this respect in urging that these aspirations can be realised only in the transition from aesthetics to politics. It is, finally, precisely by virtue of the way in which it has thus positioned itself within this lineage that Marxism, in assigning bourgeois aesthetics its class particularity and partiality, has thereby been able to assess its functioning as ideological in the senses proposed by Bürger and Eagleton.

Familiar though it may be, however, Hunter argues that this way of approaching the history of the relations between aesthetics and education, in which the latter is regarded as an imperfect realisation of the dialectic of full human development posited by Romantic aesthetics, induces a double blindness. First, it entails that the effects of educational apparatuses and the pedagogical techniques deployed within them are either overlooked or theorised purely negatively as constituting an interruption within, and impediment to, the unfolding of this dialectic of human development. Second, Hunter suggests that to broach the analysis of the relations between aesthetics and education by means of an examination of the functioning of a specific idea of art, assessed as a class ideology owing to the inadequacy of its conception of the relations between culture and society, is to fundamentally misrecognise the nature of Romantic aesthetics. For what Romantic aesthetics provides, he argues, 'is not a *theory* of culture and society but an *aesthetico-ethical exercise* aimed at producing a particular kind of relation to self and, through this, the ethical demeanour and standing of a particular category of person'.[23] Or, more fully, it provides

> a minority of 'ethical athletes' with a means for dividing the ethical substance (into the disfiguring drives of thought and feeling, freedom and necessity, didacticism and spontaneity); and a practice of mutual modification or dialectics in which each side was successively played off against the other as a means of shaping the many-sided character.[24]

While in agreement with Bürger in according Schiller pride of place within the paradigm of Romantic aesthetics, Hunter, proceeding from this perspective, reads Schiller's writings differently, stressing the respects in which they constitute the relation between the work of literature (or art) and the reader as 'the focus of an ethical practice in which the individual shapes a relation to his self by overcoming its divisions'.[25] If the divisions held to be constitutive of the work of art − between form and meaning, feelings and ideas − echo those within the ethical substance of the subject, reading, in so far as it is directed to seek a means of reconciling these divisions within the literary work, is simultaneously organised as a practice of character formation which seeks constantly to moderate the imbalance which threatens from the unceasing pull of these contradictory tendencies within the constitution of the subject. The function of criticism, when conducted under the aegis of Romantic aesthetics, Hunter thus suggests, is 'to bring the reader into that relation to the work in which he "becomes aware of his own incompleteness", and is thus forced to begin the endless task of self culture'.[26]

Here, then, is an instance of the Foucaultian view of aesthetics as a practice of the self. It is, however, the part this conception plays in the account Hunter offers of the genealogy of modern literary education that is of most relevance to our concerns here. For it is not, he argues, the pedagogical deployment of the ideology of art as autonomous that should be attended to in this respect. Rather, modern literary education is said to be shaped into being through the contingent coming together of two disconnected histories, as those practices of the self developed in association with Romantic aesthetics undergo a transformation in their functioning as they come to be inscribed within the machinery of popular education as part of a new set of pedagogic relations between teachers and pupils. In this way aesthetic forms of self-fashioning come to function as integral components of developed technologies of self-formation accorded a central role in the governmental processes whereby the attributes of modern citizenries are formed.

There is not space, here, to do more than summarise the rudiments of this thesis. Tracing the formation of popular schooling in its nineteenth-century English context, Hunter's primary concern is to reconcile the apparent contradiction between, on the one hand, the encouragement of self-expressive techniques of learning within the post-monitorial system of popular schooling and, on the other hand, the functioning of popular schooling as a governmental apparatus of moral regulation and normalisation. This contradiction is resolved, Hunter suggests, when it is realised how the development of new pedagogic relations between teachers and pupils allowed the school to function as an apparatus for the normalisation of conduct precisely *through and by means of* encouraging children to express their individuality within an environment in which, in taking place under the surveillance of the teacher, such expressions of individuality could also be subjected to a normalising correction. But not an imposed one: the moral landscape of the popular school, Hunter argues, is one in which the pupil, in making manifest forms of behaviour, thought, feeling and sentiment which are then subject to correction via the normalising gaze of an ethical exemplar – the teacher – is induced to embark on a programme of infinite, non-coercive, self-correction, to become the active agent of his/her own moral normalisation. The development of pedagogic techniques based on the principles of learning through play and self-expression and the deployment of these within a new and sympathetic relation between the child and the teacher resulted in the formation of a moral technology of the self which worked via the pupil's internalisation of a programme of self-correction based on the emulation of the teacher, newly invested with the status of an ethical exemplar. The result, as Hunter puts it, was 'an apparatus in which new social norms for the government of the population could surface inside the formation of the individual conscience'.[27]

It was, then, the organisation of the popular school as a space of moral management that provided the context for the emergence of modern literary education as the pedagogic deployment of literary texts assumed an increasingly important role within this 'machinery of moral training'. That this was so, however, was not attributable to any essential property of literature. Rather, it resulted from the degree to which, owing to contingent considerations (the increasingly widespread availability of both popular and 'serious' reading matter, for example), the literary text presented itself as a suitable vehicle for pedagogic fashioning – through exercises of writing and reading – harnessed to the purpose of facilitating expressions of self in forms that would be amenable to correction and revision. Hunter thus argues in relation to the mechanisms of 'supervised freedom' and 'correction through self expression':

> They were the means by which the 'self' that the individual brought in from a problematic social environment could be exposed to a normalising regimen embodied in the teacher's 'moral observation': an observation which the child learned to take over and internalise as conscience. It was by absorbing these disciplines that English was able to emerge as a powerful ethical technology characterised by four attributes: a special ethical privilege which it acquired as the inheritor of the socio-moral disciplines ('closeness to life'); a pedagogical strategy characterised by correction through self expression; a purpose-built teacher–student relationship combining identification and correction ('detached warmth'); and a new relation to the literary text in which the immediacy of its surface lured the reader into the unfathomable depth of the norms he was corrected by.[28]

In the light of these considerations, Hunter suggests that the key questions to be examined in deciphering the relations between aesthetics and literary education concern the mechanisms of connection through which the techniques of self-cultivation developed in association with Romantic aesthetics come to be inscribed within this specific pedagogic utilisation of literary texts. Initially, as we have noted, Romantic aesthetics comprised a voluntary form of elite self-fashioning which, in representing itself as aiming at the attainment of human completeness, served to mark out, as a special category of person, those who sought to cultivate their personalities by means of the dialectic of self-improvement which the aesthetic life prescribed. This aspect of the legacy of Romanticism is clear enough in the stress Arnold places on the practices of the self through which the aliens were to differentiate themselves from the Barbarians, Philistines and Populace. Of those who exhibit 'the love and pursuit of perfection', he thus writes:

> And this bent always tends to take them out of their class, and to make their distinguishing characteristic not their Barbarianism or their Philistinism, but their *humanity*. They have, in general, a rough time of it in their lives; but they are sown more abundantly than one might think, they appear where and when one least expects it, they set up a fire which enfilades, so to speak, the class with which they are ranked; and, in general, by the extrication of their best self as the self to develop, and by the simplicity of the ends fixed by them as paramount, they hinder the unchecked predominance of that class-life which is the affirmation of our ordinary self, and seasonably disconcert mankind in their worship of machinery.[29]

It is not, however, Arnold's conception of the role of the aliens that Hunter looks to in order to account for the influence of Romantic aesthetics within the educational sphere. Rather, he disputes the traditional view in which the history of English is regarded as an outcome of the diagnostics of Romanticism – in which, that is, the social diffusion of culture's improving balm is prescribed as an antidote to the eroding advances of industrial civilisation. Instead, Hunter looks to another history – the administrative history of the formation of the school inspectorate, from Kay-Shuttleworth through to Arnold – for the specific mechanisms of institutional connection through which the practices of Romantic aesthetics migrated into the educational sphere. Recruited from among the literary intelligentsia, and therefore usually the products of a Romantic training, Her Majesty's Inspectors were selected primarily for their ethical bearing in order that they might represent the 'special social personality – the ethical exemplar – required by the tactics of moral administration'.[30] While initially embodied in the inspectorate, the development of literary education witnessed the transference of these attributes to the English teacher, thereby allowing the construction of a set of relations between text, pupil and teacher in which the pupil, in exposing his/her inner life to normalising scrutiny by means of literary exercises, could embark on a course of self-improvement by adjusting his/her inner life in the light of the corrective readings proposed by a teacher invested with the status of an ethical exemplar. In this way, through its inscription in this new set of pedagogic relations, the literary text becomes the site for a technology of sensibility formation which takes the form, essentially, of an endless programme of rereading conducted in the light of normatively sanctioned corrections of earlier readings.

In pursuing his analysis into the twentieth century, Hunter accords particular attention to the parallel development of educational psychology which, in connecting up with the sphere of literary education, particularly through its influence on Richards, allowed Romantic techniques of ethical self-shaping to be finally transformed into a series of systematically administered tests for the detection of misreadings construed as symptoms of a personality imbalance in need of corrective revision. This, in turn, allows Hunter to offer an account of the development of criticism, as an autonomous university discipline, which views its role as essentially a supplement to the machinery of moral training within which literary education had become inscribed in the sphere of popular schooling. For within criticism, the nature of the pedagogic deployment of literary texts is subtly modified. In popular schooling, the 'régime of reading is managed by the teacher, who must allow the student to "find himself" in the poem while remaining the repository of an authoritative interpretation against which the student's response can be corrected'.[31] So far as the teaching of criticism is concerned, by contrast, the teacher's central task is to determine how, when and where to withdraw from this mediating position so as 'to allow the machine of surveillance to work by itself, as the student finds in the reading and teaching of literature the rhythm of empathy and correction in himself.[32] In this way, criticism serves to produce those moral mentors, adept in the use of literary texts as a part of a disciplined culture of the self, which the machinery of popular education requires. In summarising his argument, and stressing its distinctness from both conventional and Marxist accounts of the rise of English, Hunter thus suggests:

> These changes produced neither a body of missionaries capable of bestowing the promise of culture on 'society as a whole', nor an ideological elite bent on sublimating the democratic social realisation of this promise into the moral excellence of the few. Instead, they produced an ethical technology directed to forming the moral attributes of a citizenry, but a technology also capable of forming a stratum of ethical exemplars from this citizenry: the teachers of English.[33]

Bürger, it will be recalled, broaches the relations between aesthetics and education via the doctrine of art's autonomy and, in viewing this doctrine as regulating the circumstances of art and literature's pedagogical deployment, consequently pays scant attention to the institutional mechanisms of connection through which this doctrine enters into and becomes concretely influential within the educational sphere. Hunter, by contrast, in focusing his attention precisely on such mechanisms of connection, is able to suggest that it is not in the form of ideas but as a set of practices of self-formation allied to a machinery of government that aesthetics has concretely influenced the circumstances of art and literature's pedagogic deployment. In this respect, aesthetics, rather than being assessed as an ideology which functions repressively – a view which characterises most Marxist accounts – is viewed as part of a technology of person formation whose effects are assessed as positive and productive in serving as a means of normalising the attributes of extended populations as a part of the more general procedures and apparatuses of government through which, in Foucault's conception, the attributes of modern citizenries have been shaped into being. 'The ethical demeanour of popular education', as Hunter puts it, 'is a function not of the ideas that it purveys, but of the disciplinary techniques around which it is organised.'[34]

OUTSIDE LITERATURE

LITERATURE'S 'POLITICS OF TRUTH'

It is clear, then, that Hunter's thoroughgoing Foucaultianism allows a more concrete and, for that matter, more materialist approach to the relations between aesthetics and literary education than do the accounts of Bürger or Eagleton. It also provides the basis for an eminently materialist recontextualisation of the question of literature's autonomy. This is clear in the evaluation Hunter proposes of those procedures whereby criticism, in constituting itself as an autonomous science, has posited, as its ostensibly autonomous object, the literary text conceived as a semiotic structure of a distinctive type which it is the task of criticism to elucidate. While the forms of this elucidation may vary, they have in common a tendency to represent the literary text as a multi-levelled structure which, while available to be read at the level of ordinary reading, must then be read in a distinctive literary or aesthetic manner if its specific organisational properties are to be properly understood. Thus, in structuralist poetics, critical analysis is concerned with the identification of those unconscious structures which, while making reading possible, simultaneously elude the reader's consciousness, and which, to the degree that the permutations through which such structures are actualised in reading practices are potentially infinite, allow the literary text to be conceived as the generator of a set of endless semantic possibilities. Or, as in deconstruction, the text may be conceived as a set of processes though which, as potentially fixed co-ordinates of meaning endlessly undo themselves, the text is opened up to an unending process of rereading in which new axes and horizons of signification can be found.

The requirement that there be such a distinctively literary semiotic structure for criticism to elucidate is, of course, based on notoriously circular premises. Such a structure is posited as being there, in the text, because of the distinctive aesthetic response it evokes. However, since it is the nature of aesthetic experience that it eludes definition by concepts, this response is, in turn, the only justification that can be offered for the supposition that the literary text is characterised by distinctive organisational properties which only the aesthetic response fully and adequately recognises. In this way, as Hunter puts it, aesthetic response 'must therefore function as a justification for the poetic structure that justifies it'.[35] The

182

fresh perspective Hunter brings to this criticism, however, consists in the contention that this circularity results from criticism's failure to realise that the properties of literariness it seeks to theorise are the product of the procedures it must itself deploy in order to organise the literary text as the vehicle for a normalising pedagogy. Rather than viewing the literary or aesthetic reading as a response to a specific set of textual properties, Hunter views it as the product of the forms of response and correction which characterise the deployment of texts within modern literary education. This being so, criticism's concern with the autonomous properties of literary discourse is assessed as a search for a phantom object that is entirely of its own making.

The key point here concerns the respects in which, while seeming to address literature as the object of a specialised knowledge, criticism in fact targets the literary text as a vehicle for the ethical organisation of the reader by virtue of the relations between misreading and approved reading which it posits. For while criticism permits a means of identifying misreadings, those readings are not assessed as such in relation to any definite correct readings. Rather, they count as misreadings only in relation to a normatively prescribed correct *way* of reading – the literary or aesthetic mode – in which there is produced, for and within the literary text, that inexhaustible depth which can allow it to function as a device for the reader's self-improvement by means of the revision and correction of earlier readings.

> If modern criticism has come to construe the literary reading as a 'raid on the infinite', always incomplete, always marking a new beginning, this is not because (as it thinks) the literary text contains an inexhaustible supply of meaning due to its openness to an ever-changing domain of experience. Neither is it a sign that the text is a local manifestation of an ideal linguistic calculus capable of infinite actualisations. Rather, it is a sign of the fact that the modern literary text, unlike the text of rhetoric or philology, is not an object of imitation or description, but a more recently elaborated device opening its reader to endless moral invigilation.[36]

Modern literary education thus gives rise to '*a new formation of the literary text*' – a text which, while 'immediately open to experience is also the text that no reading can exhaust' – and '*a new kind of literary reading*' in that the text elicits a response 'which (as "a valid personal expression") can never be wrong, is simultaneously the response which can never be right; because it marks the point at which the reader is opened to a set of norms relayed through the English teacher's "sympathetic inspection"'.[37] Reading aesthetically, therefore, is not a matter of recognising the text's objective literary and aesthetic properties but a matter of behaving correctly within a particular normative regime of reading. The central concerns of philosophical aesthetics – whether conventional or alternative – are thus dissolved at a stroke; the literary or aesthetic effect turns out to be neither an unfathomable essence nor a scientifically explicable property of literary discourse but the contingent product of the modes of textual use associated with a particular moral technology.

This suggests a perspective from which the concerns of Marxist aesthetics might be revalued. For the point that is made of conventional theories of literariness applies with equal force to Marxist ones. These, too, in positing a distinction between the level of ordinary reading and a correct way of reading which follows from the theory of literariness proposed, inscribe the reader in a tutelary relation to the critic. In prescribing a procedure which the reader is invited to follow, the critical practices which derive from Marxist conceptions of art's and literature's specificity thus serve to initiate and superintend a process of the subject's self-revision and transformation. Where such practices differ from those of conventional criticisms is in the type of subject transformation they envisage and aim to effect.

Most obviously, Marxist criticism has sought to revolutionise the subject rather than to induce aptitudes of moral self-management conducive to the requirements of modern forms of government. It is, however, the manner in which this revolutionary function has been envisaged and the associated conception of the relations between text, reader and critic which have most distinguished Marxist from other schools of modern criticism. For, and it is in this that its uniqueness consists, Marxist criticism so organises the relations between text, reader and critic as to constitute the text as a vehicle for the reader's *epistemological* transformation and the critic as his/her mentor in this regard. If this mapping of the relations between the three elements of the critical apparatus still envisages the uses of literary texts as parts of technologies of self-formation, the vectors of this technology are epistemological and political rather than moral and ethical. The significance, from this perspective, of literature's being placed *between* science and ideology concerns less the theoretical validity of the argument than its technological effect. For it is precisely this positioning of the literary which allows its reading, appropriately guided by the critic, to function as a staging-post on the royal road which leads the subject from the misrecognition effects of ideology to the true knowledge of science. Thus Macherey:

> Science does away with ideology, obliterates it; literature challenges ideology by using it. If ideology is thought of as a non-systematic ensemble of significations, the work proposes a *reading* of these significations, by combining them as signs. Criticism teaches us to read these signs.[38]

Viewed, then, as *practice* rather than *theory*, the distinctiveness of Marxist aesthetics consists in the regions of the subject it targets for transformation and, through criticism, the techniques of the self which it instantiates for this purpose. Unlike its Romantic forebear, the aesthetic reading is not a vehicle for reconciling the antinomies of personality as part of a technique of character formation. Nor is the critic an ethical exemplar. Rather, reading is organised as a process of learning again the difference between science and ideology, of disentangling one's self from the latter and heading towards the former (but without ever actually arriving there) under the guidance of the critic who is refashioned, here, in the image of an epistemological exemplar – one whose activity, in placing him constantly on the road which leads from illusion to knowledge, allows him to function as both spur and guide to those who would plot a similar course across the epistemologised contours of the literary text. In Romantic aesthetics, as we have seen, the ideal of the many-sided personality in whom contending attributes are harmoniously reconciled serves as a device which embroils the subject in an unending career of ethical self-shaping. Similarly, the ideal of personality in Marxist aesthetics – one, essentially, in which the epistemological antinomies (science/ideology) which have racked the subject's erstwhile constitution are overcome as the subject acquires a self-understanding of its own historical construction, an ideal which the critic anticipates but never achieves – serves to enlist the reader in a never-ending process of epistemological self-fashioning via the detection and eradication (never complete) of ideological error.

Viewed in this light, the question as to whether or not literature can be adequately theorised as a special category in terms of the qualities which distinguish it from both ideology and science is less important than the *technological effect* of its being so placed. For, in this case, it is no longer the adequacy of a theory that has to be assessed but, rather, the efficacy of a specific kind of deployment of a particular technological apparatus. To have so constructed literary texts that they might serve as instruments for the subject's ideological self-shaping – vehicles through which the misrecognition effects of ideology are scaled away while, at the same time, the reader is led to acquire a surer knowledge of history – is to have fashioned a political–pedagogic instrument of no mean potential. And yet it is an instrument which has nowhere – in the west – exerted any extended social influence. Whatever the tradition's intellectual achievements, this specific technological ordering of text, reader, critic relations has nowhere been successfully implanted within any developed social apparatus.

Many reasons might be advanced for this. It is not, for example, the kind of political instrument which a state diagnosed as bourgeois could be expected to promote via the education system. There are, equally, constraints on the degree to which such a fashioning of the literary text can function as a political–pedagogic instrument in the organisation of labour movements. After all, there are more direct ways of criticising ideology and acquiring historical knowledge than via the intermediary of literature. And this, perhaps, is the nub of the point I am after: that the limitation of Marxist criticism's social reach to some of the more rarefied sections of tertiary education is neither accidental nor corrigible but, rather, a congenital trait of a criticism formed into being in a technological space whose essential contours were predetermined by the criticisms to which it presented itself as, precisely, oppositional.

Here, then, are the rudiments of an account of the relations between Marxist criticism and aesthetics and the emergence of modern literary education and criticism. Hunter's genealogy of the latter, I am suggesting, allows one to see the respects in which the formulations of Marxist criticism have been dependent on (rather than revolutionising) the text, reader, critic relations developed by modern criticism. Of course, Marxist criticism does occupy a distinctive position within this modern literary technology of subject formation – largely, as I have argued, because of the epistemological and political vectors it constructs for this technology. None the less, it should also be clear that Marxist criticism derives the conditions of its intelligibility from this technology of subject formation just as it reproduces the properties of that technology within and across its own practices. The artefact of the unfathomable text, for example, is thus encountered in another form in Marxist conceptions of the literature/ideology relation which, in the very course of the attempt to define it, always eludes such definition and is represented as in some way unsayable. Yet the ineffability of this relation is not the result of a theoretical failure. To the contrary, in winnowing out a space of indeterminacy within the text, it supplies a necessary condition for the endlessness of the subject's literary detachment from the ideological which the critical reading exemplifies and for which it serves as the instrument.

Nor, of course, is this true solely of Marxist aesthetics. Indeed, one might say that the artefact of the unfathomable text conditions and governs the politics of truth of modern literary criticism in the sense that it supplies the shared ground (even though its unfathomability is differently conceived) on which different schools of criticism compete. This suggests grounds for a revaluation of modern criticism's capacity to absorb and recuperate all forms of radical or oppositional criticism and the conventional Marxist attribution of this to the class nature of the bourgeois academy. For the process involved here is not that of the class co-option of opposition. Rather, it is a product of the 'black-hole' effect of the modern literary text which, in its unfathomability, can draw on all criticisms and never be exhausted and which equally requires of all criticisms that they produce their own domain of the ineffable – an unsayable relation to ideology, or a *semiotic chora* – as a condition of engaging with the politics of truth of the modern literary apparatus.

What are we to make of such a politics of truth? In one view it might be positively assessed as having established a distinctive region and type of subject formation which, in fashioning the literary text as an instrument for an endless career of the self, has facilitated the emergence of a new kind of subject, one which, reflexively aware of its own conditioning, can endlessly open new social possibilities in preventing any particular social imagery from closing in on itself. It is, indeed, in just such terms that criticism's political vocation is often spoken of, a vocation which is ultimately authorised by the status invested in the critic as a special kind of person, an exemplary figure of either a moral or an epistemological kind. In a second view, however, any conception of criticism's political vocation which simply installs itself within the set of text, reader, critic relations established by modern literary education is destined – no matter how radical or oppositional the path of subject formation it envisages – to reproduce the modern literary apparatus and its effects.

Terry Eagleton is, I think, spot on in identifying what I take to be one of the more questionable of these effects, one arising out of the contrived mystery of the text's unfathomable depth:

> In such a situation, Literature presents itself as threat, mystery, challenge and insult to those who, able to read, can nonetheless not 'read'. To be able to decipher the signs and yet remain ignorant: it is in this contradiction that the tyranny of Literature is revealed. . . . Literature is always somewhere else: that which, being literate, we have not read or cannot read. Literacy admits us to reading so that we can take the full measure of our exclusion: its effect is to display the secretive knowledge which is always possible but never possessed.[39]

Yet, if my analysis is correct, and if, as Eagleton suggests, this effect is attributable to literature as an institution, then it must be reproduced in any practice which, even when aiming for alternative status, seeks to install its politics within that institution by proposing an oppositional deployment of its constitutive technology of subject formation.

This is not, to be clear, to castigate such practices as oppressive; rather, it is merely to identify one of the conditions of intelligibility of criticism's conception as an instrument for the transformation of the subject. I argued in the previous chapter that the structure of aesthetic discourse necessarily implies a programme for the reform of the subject in the ideal of personality which it posits. Aesthetic practices and the criticisms which superintend them are also, of course, governed by this structure of aesthetic discourse. Indeed, it is the gap between the self as it is and the ideal of personality posited by aesthetic discourse that opens up a region within the subject – however it may be conceived – as a potential area for self-management. Yet this is not to say that the functioning of such practices can simply be read off from the properties of aesthetic discourse. To the contrary, the perspectives on the educational deployment of aesthetics considered here suggest that it is less the nature of such discourse *as such* than a specific technological ordering of the relations between text, reader and critic that has most to be attended to in order to assess the long-term significance of the historical articulation of the relations between the spheres of education and aesthetics. This, in turn, suggests that the class or other social articulations of aesthetic discourse may be of less importance, from the point of view of criticism's politics of truth, than the role which such discourse has played in fashioning the text, reader, critic relations of the modern literary apparatus.

It is in the light of these considerations that, in the final part of this study, I review some of the more influential formulations of the tasks of Marxist criticism that have been advanced in recent years. While differing in their particularities, all, I shall argue, share a common failing: committed to the grandiose gestures of a criticism which conceives of itself as engaging in a struggle for subjectivity in the abstract and at a macro-political level, they prove unable to take account of the properties of the pedagogical–moral–epistemological technologies which condition the mechanisms of criticism's working. Benjamin, it may be recalled, stressed that the key political question to pose of any intellectual practice concerned less its content than how it stood in relation to an existing apparatus, drawing the decisive distinction between those practices which supplied existing apparatuses with novel goods and those which sought to transform the apparatus's functioning.[40] I have said enough, I think, to explain why – and not as a matter of contingency, but systematically – Marxist criticism should be regarded as having failed Benjamin's acid test. To think critically about criticism requires that account be taken of the actual mechanisms of the literary–pedagogical apparatus, of the techniques of subjectification through which this apparatus works and of the forms of aesthetic, ethical or epistemological self-shaping they support.

To the degree to which, as presently fashioned, these are dependent on inducting the reader into the socially constructed interior of the text as a space in which to exhibit, not correct readings but a *way* of reading in relation to norms which, since their essence consists in their capacity for endless revision, can never be precisely specified, it is this space – and the organisation of alternatives to it – that must be attended to as a condition for the emergence of a more progressive literary pedagogy and criticism. One possibility, for example, might consist in the development of exercises, tests and forms of assessment through which readings can be assessed as definitely correct or not in relation to stated (and hence debatable) criteria, thus constituting the teacher/critic as a technical rather than, say, an ethical exemplar and involving the student/reader in the acquisition of particular technical competences rather than in an unending process of ethical self-correction. This may not, it is true, have the same ring of *bravura* about it as the development of a political aesthetics or a revolutionary criticism; it would, however, be likely to be a good deal more consequential.

Part IV

8

CRITICAL ILLUSIONS

Criticism, in its classical nineteenth-century formulations, was conceived as the site of a universalising discourse. Owing to the privileged place accorded literary texts as both expressing and influencing the general state of a culture or society, practices of commentary which took such texts as their object were regarded as the means for the circulation of discourses which, at least in principle, were as totalising in terms of the readership they imaginarily addressed as in the range of issues they sought to encompass. Matthew Arnold summarised the relations between these two aspects of criticism's function as follows:

> Literary criticism's most important function is to try books as to the influence which they are calculated to have upon the general culture of single nations or of the world at large. . . . Every one is not a theologian, a historian, or a philosopher, but every one is interested in the advance of the general culture of his nation or of mankind. A criticism therefore which, abandoning a thousand special questions which may be raised about any book, tries it solely in respect of its influence upon this culture, brings it thereby within the sphere of every one's interest. This is why literary criticism has exercised so much power.[1]

The objection is less that criticism has never enjoyed quite the power Arnold suggests, than that such power as it has exercised has derived from its selective deployment within specific institutional and discursive contexts. Although proceeding as if speaking to everyone, its circulation has been remarkably restricted with the result that it has often played an important role in the symbolic processes through which social strata are culturally differentiated.

Yet the universalising ambitions which marked criticism's nineteenth-century formation linger on and, strangely enough, nowhere with more weight and persistence than in Marxist thought. Whereas deconstruction tends to reverse Arnold's emphasis in concerning itself with the 'thousand special questions which may be raised about any book' rather than with the more general social or cultural influence of a literary text, the greater part of contemporary Marxist critical theory has sought to enlist literary criticism in support of a generalised form of social and cultural commentary.

There is nothing new in this. The mainstream of the Marxist critical tradition has always placed itself in a direct line of descent from nineteenth-century Romanticism in claiming a theoretical and political disposition which would enable Romanticism's universalising rhetoric to be genuinely realised via discourses which spoke to and for humanity in the making. Yet the tactic remains as rhetorical as ever it was, and seems forever likely to remain so. Accordingly, whereas recent Marxist or neo-Marxist commentaries on the function of criticism have tended to re-align criticism with a totalising conception of social and cultural critique, my purpose here is to put a contrary case: to argue the need for a break with the critical illusions upon which such approaches depend, and which they foster, in favour of a more localised and differentiated approach to questions of critical politics.

While there has been a rush of such studies in recent years, I shall focus mainly on Edward Said's *The World, the Text and the Critic* and Fredric Jameson's *The Political Unconscious*. There are, of course, important differences between these, both in terms of the arguments advanced and the political–theoretical positions from which those arguments are shaped and directed, and I shall come to these shortly. However, to the degree that each offers a set of prescriptions regarding the tasks which criticism should set itself and the means by which it should pursue them, they also invite comparison at the level of the generalised conceptions of criticism's function they respectively advance. This is especially so in view of the fact that, whatever their differences, they share a common impetus and move in the same general direction: that of a going back beyond structuralism, post-structuralism and Marxist theoreticism to a more familiar concept of criticism as a practice of interpretation. The way forward that each constructs, that is to say, is also conceived as a return: criticism is to acquire a revitalised political relevance by going back to being what it once was – a set of interpretative procedures orientated toward the transformation of the consciousness of individual subjects, and hence, in the case of Jameson, of collective subjects also.

In each case, moreover, this movement of return is both enabled and legitimated by a series of blocking or recuperative moves through which the intervening currents of structuralism, post-structuralism and Marxist theoreticism are either discounted as no more than ripples which scarcely disrupt the continuity of criticism's development or are allocated a limited sectoral validity within a revised conception of criticism's traditional function. The consequence is that criticism emerges as a Phoenix from the ashes and stands where, at least imaginarily, it had always stood: as a form of textual commentary which functions as a privileged site of ethical, cognitive and political totalisation. And as a practice which, if not quite essentially radical, is tendentially so. Criticism, when it is true to itself and respects its origins, is ranged against the existing order of things. 'Were I to use one word consistently with *criticism* (not as a modification but as an emphatic),' Said writes, 'it would be *oppositional*.'[2]

In both cases, finally, added force is lent to such arguments – and, correspondingly, to the claims of criticism – via the establishment of an epistemological privilege for the standpoints from which critical activity is ideally to be conducted. For Said, this standpoint is supplied by the individual consciousness of the critic, a consciousness that is nurtured within and by the practice of criticism itself. Criticism thus seems destined to endlessly reproduce itself across the chain of exceptional individual consciousnesses which are the effect of its own activity. To the degree that such individual consciousnesses are also the arbiters of criticism's pretensions to a position of epistemological supremacy over contending discourses, criticism's future as a self-validating practice seems secure.

Jameson's position is somewhat more complex. If, as Jameson argues, criticism is to be regarded as a means to historical understanding, it is History itself which generates the privileged standpoints from which its truths – distilled by criticism – can be rendered intelligible to itself. The argument is a familiar one in the history of Marxist thought, particularly its Hegelian variants, although with one important difference: in Jameson's formulation, the position from which the sense of History is to be distilled does not rest on any identifiable institutional supports. In this respect, *The Political Unconscious* is somewhat like Hegel's *Phenomenology of Mind* but without the state, or like Lukács's *History and Class Consciousness* without the Communist Party. What takes the place of these is criticism, an institutionally ungrounded form of History's self-comprehension. This has profound consequences for Jameson's understanding of Marxism which he converts into a local and contingent instance of a transcendent set of critical operations and procedures. Ultimately, in Jameson's work, it is criticism that provides a support for Marxism and not vice versa.

The steps taken by both theorists to privilege criticism above contending discourses also serve to naturalise it. This is not to suggest that either states or imagines that criticism has always been with us. But each implies that it always will be. While this is not a particularly difficult argument to make in relation to Said, it might seem an odd one to level against Jameson whose appeal is always, in both the first and final instances, to the court of History. But it is precisely History in the grand sense that Jameson appeals to and, as I shall seek to show, his use of the term is so philosophically over-full that it is ultimately deprived of any positive historical content where history is understood in its more mundane and useful sense as the domain of practices which are temporally contingent and variable.

As a consequence, both Said and Jameson tend to attribute to criticism a function that is always there, always waiting to be performed, so that the role allotted considerations of historical contingency is merely that of determining *how* this function is performed in particular circumstances. Against this, I shall argue that the very intelligibility of the concept of criticism, understood as a set of interpretative practices conducted with a view to transforming the consciousness of subjects, presupposes a specific set of institutional and discursive conditions which organise a field of text–reader relations which such practices can latch on to. Criticism, thus understood, is a specific practice occupying a distinctive institutional and discursive space (and one resting on definite social underpinnings) which effects a specific ordering of the relations between texts, readers and practices of textual commentary. As such, its effects are not limitless, either historically or contemporaneously. Such a space has not always existed, nor is there any reason to suppose that it will unendingly continue to do so. Perhaps more important, though: it does not, either, currently provide the only space within which literary texts are socially deployed. In their failure to consider the conditions which underpin the space of criticism, Said and Jameson limit the terms of their discussion to the moves that can be made within this space. Being political is ultimately a question of the hermeneutic stance the Marxist critic adopts, assessed in terms of its relations to rival systems of interpretation operating on the same territory of subject formation. The result, in both cases, is a failure even to raise the kinds of questions that need to be put if political debates concerning the conduct of practices of textual commentary are to be informed by an awareness of the highly differentiated field of institutional and discursive spaces in which literary texts are deployed.

CRITICISM VERSUS THEORY

Said's *The World, the Text and the Critic* is a somewhat evasive book in that it is hard to pin down its central propositions. However, this seems clearly to be intended. Not only does the book shun anything so specific as a clearly stated method or articulated body of theory; it offers itself *against* these. Criticism, in Said's view, is, by its very nature, anti-systemic which, at least in some of Said's formulations, seems also to mean that it need not be particularly systematic either. This is less true of Said's criticisms of other positions, which are often telling, than of the passages in which he elaborates his own views on criticism's nature and function. In these, he proceeds by means of a strategic vagueness which elides theoretical difficulties by establishing a somewhat loose and merely associative set of connections between the different stages of his argument. The best (or worst) example of this procedure is the essay 'Traveling theory' in which the concepts of class consciousness, critical consciousness and criticism are allowed to slide into one another so as to become virtually indistinguishable, thereby suggesting proximities between positions which are conceptually distinct. In this particular case, the practice of criticism comes, via the mediating term of critical consciousness, to be associated with Lukács's concept of class consciousness understood, in its proletarian form, as being inherently critical of capitalism – a meaning which, through this chain of associations, seems then also to be somehow intrinsically attached to the activity of criticism itself.

197

This is not an accidental trait. To the contrary, it is essential to the method by which Said produces a radical pedigree for the concept of criticism he advances. *The World, the Text and the Critic* is, in fact, best characterised as a *pot-pourri* of political credentials derived, mainly, from Lukács, Gramsci and Foucault, into which, as the occasion requires, Said dips a resolutely traditional concept of criticism's function in order to garnish it with a flavour of radicalism. It is not surprising, therefore, that, at first sight, many of Said's formulations seem impeccable in terms of the political sentiments which motivate them. At the most general level, Said argues that criticism must turn away from what has become 'the somewhat mystical and disinfected subject matter of literary theory' — textuality — to concern itself once more with the 'worldliness' of texts: that is, their affiliations with power, the ways in which 'even when they appear to deny it, they are nevertheless a part of the social world, human life, and of course the historical moments in which they are located and interpreted'.[3] Or, more fully:

> The realities of power and authority — as well as the resistances offered by men, women and social movements to institutions, authorities, and orthodoxies — are the realities that make texts possible, that deliver them to their readers, that solicit the attention of critics. I propose that these realities are what should be taken account of by criticism and the critical consciousness.[4]

These, then, are the realities, the realities *beyond* texts but which are none the less incorporated *within* them, with which criticism should concern itself. It should do so, moreover, in full recognition of its own worldliness and circumstantiality, of its limitations to and interests in a particular time and place. The critic, in restoring to the text its worldly affiliations, restores to his/her practice a worldly pertinence in enabling him/her to speak, beyond texts, to and about the worldly realities — the new cold war, militarism, Reaganism's assault on organised labour — upon which the arid world of literary theory has turned its back.

So far, so good: nothing much to object to here, it might seem. However, difficulties accumulate if one probes these general formulations more closely. For example: what type of connection should criticism posit between the text and its worldliness in order to produce, for those texts and for itself, a relevant stake in the worldliness of the present? And how is criticism to order the relations between the worldliness of a text's past 'affiliations' and its 'affiliations' in the here and now? To whom should criticism address itself, and how might it best do so? It is not that Said is silent on these questions. There's no shortage of words, but precious few proposals which suggest any specific direction for the conduct of criticism and precious few concepts, except for that of affiliation, by means of which the relations between the textual and extra-textual orders of reality might be theorised. However, closely examined, this concept proves to be little more than an inflated metaphor which ends up treating texts like persons in attributing their social connectedness to the relationships of association – in Tönnies's sense – into which they seem voluntarily to enter. At one level, Said uses the term to refer to social and cultural forms of human bonding that have been instituted where social bonds based on biological reproduction have failed or been judged insufficient. At this level, the term provides the basis of Said's account of the differences between nature and culture and of the transition from the former to the latter. Affiliative relationships are social and cultural rather than natural in order, albeit ones in which the kinds of authority associated with natural filiative orders (i.e. the authority of the father) have been transferred to the world of social and cultural institutions:

> Thus if a filial relationship was held together by natural bonds and natural forms of authority – involving obedience, fear, love, respect, and instinctual conflict – the new affiliative relationship changes these bonds into what seem to be transpersonal forms – such as guild consciousness, consensus, collegiality, professional respect, class, and the hegemony of a dominant culture. The filiative scheme belongs to the realm of nature and of 'life,' whereas affiliation belongs exclusively to culture and society.[5]

It is difficult to know what to make of this rereading of the Oedipus myth. One would have thought that, at the very least, a certain caution would be in order these days in equating the order of nature with a concept so manifestly patriarchal as that of 'filiation'. The underlying difficulty, though, consists in the sheer amount of work and range of tasks the concept of affiliation is called on to perform. Apart from providing a means of representing the difference between nature and culture in general,

Said uses the concept of affiliation to refer to a specifically modern kind of cultural relationship, a new cultural system. 'Childless couples, orphaned children, aborted childbirths, and unregenerately celibate men and women populate the world of high modernism with remarkable insistence,' Said argues, 'all of them suggesting the difficulties of filiation.'[6] Affiliation, in this sense, is a response to 'the pressure to produce new and different ways of conceiving human relationships' in circumstances where 'biological reproduction is either too difficult or too unpleasant'.[7] Affiliation here is not a set of objective social processes but something the individual subject does in joining or expressing support for voluntary forms of social association. The subject escapes the atomised and alienated conditions of life in capitalism by affiliating himself (for Said provides no examples of women doing the same) to some higher order or cause: Joyce to art, Lukács to the proletariat.

Then, as if this did not stretch the concept far enough, it also transpires that texts have a similar capacity for affiliation. Of the worldly events and circumstances that surround texts, Said argues, 'much that goes on in texts alludes to them, *affiliates* itself directly to them'.[8] The notions of joining, connecting, enlisting, subscribing, supporting: the concept of affiliation combines all of these and, in doing so, simply collapses from overwork. It tells us nothing concrete, nothing that might be preferred above the more precise language of the social sciences as a means of analysing specific social situations and relationships, and implies a good deal that is actively misleading. It is, in brief, the kind of improvised social theory which Leavis specialised in and which, while it is usually as far as the liberal-humanist critic wants to go into such 'technical' matters, has been savaged – or just plain ignored – in the historical and social sciences.

That said, however, an implied mechanism of effects and an underlying theory of the relations between literature, criticism and society runs throughout Said's discussion. Said is adamant that it is through the uniqueness of an author's individuality that a text's worldliness is to be restored to it via the conduct of criticism. It is style, 'the recognisable, repeatable, preservable sign of an author who reckons with an audience' that 'neutralises the worldlessness, the silent, seemingly uncircumstanced existence of a solitary text'.[9] Moreover, this restoration of the text's worldliness is effected from the perspective of another, equally individualised position: that of the critic, the exemplary individual whose consciousness is placed 'at a sensitive nodal point' in being opposed to the prevailing orthodoxy, whatever it might be. And this criticism, finally, is directed toward an abstract reader: that is, to any reader, and therefore to no reader in particular, to a reader who is conceived as a point of individual consciousness within and, putatively, against the world. In brief, in Said's conspectus, the function, and conceit, of criticism is to transform the reader into the subject of the critical consciousness which the critic claims to exemplify, to net the reader in a series of relations between author, text, critic and the world such that s/he is interpellated into the community of criticism, a lonely yet vigilant consciousness turned against the world.

It will be clear from this that criticism is, for Said, an exceedingly loose and elastic term. Less a specific competence acquired through a process of training than a mental orientation, a habit of thought, criticism is indefinable except in the most general terms. To the degree that it is possible at all, its characteristics can be more precisely specified only negatively. It is a practice without positive terms:

> If criticism is reducible neither to a doctrine nor to a political position on a particular question, and if it is to be in the world and self-aware simultaneously, then its identity is its difference from other cultural activities and from systems of thought or of method. In its suspicion of totalising concepts, in its discontent with reified objects, in its impatience with guilds, special interests, imperialised fiefdoms, and orthodox habits of mind, criticism is most itself and, if the paradox can be tolerated, most unlike itself at the moment it starts turning into organised dogma.[10]

Criticism, in brief, is a practice without allegiances of any sort: to a particular method, theory, political party or programme of action; '"solidarity before criticism",' Said opines, 'means the end of criticism'.[11] Its only commitment, predictably enough, is to the text. Auerbach, Barthes, Genette and Benjamin: each of these critics, however different their procedures, is, Said contends, 'a reader whose reading is *for* the text and whose method is *from* the text'; each 'converts what seems to be alien material, or in some cases quixotic and trivial material, into pertinent dimensions of the text'.[12] Criticism, then, is an attitude, that 'certain something', which conjoins the work of the very best critics in spite of the different theoretical apparatuses they employ. More than that, criticism – although only the very best – is produced in *opposition* to theory. If what most defines criticism is what it is not, then what it is not, for the greater part, is theory. This criticism/theory opposition is the organising centre of the negative essentialism which characterises Said's definition of criticism and which, through the chain of metaphoric substitutions he proposes, articulates a related opposition between totalisation in its good sense (ethical and humanistic) and totalisation in its bad sense (the closure of a theoretical system). Criticism is always 'skeptical, secular, reflectively open to its own failings', a constantly mobile and adaptive practice that 'is constitutively opposed to the production of massive, hermetic systems',[13] and gravitates naturally toward the looser, more open-ended, essentially incomplete and ironic structure – or anti-structure – of the essay form. Theory, by contrast, is closed in on itself. It converts the analysis of the world into an auto-inspection of its own properties, spelling the death of criticism:

> Theoretical closure, like social convention or cultural dogma, is anathema to critical consciousness, which loses its profession when it loses its active sense of an open world in which its faculties must be exercised.[14]

However, criticism is not merely different from or opposed to theory; it is also elevated *above* theory, serving as both theory's judge and its corrective. This emerges most clearly toward the end of the essay 'Traveling Theory' where theory is hauled before the court of the essentially messy and sprawling nature of reality:

> But unless theory is un-answerable, either through its successes or its failures, to the essential untidiness, the essential unmasterable presence that constitutes a large part of historical and social situations . . . then theory becomes an ideological trap. It transfixes both its users and what it is used on. Criticism would no longer be possible.[15]

But theory never stands directly before the court of reality. It is the 'critical consciousness' that stands between theory and the world, serving as prosecuting counsel, judge and probation officer, indicting theory for its closures, measuring its inadequacies and initiating a programme of reform to place it back into contact with the worldliness it has lost sight of:

I am arguing, however, that we distinguish theory from critical consciousness by saying that the latter is a sort of spatial sense, a sort of measuring faculty for locating or situating theory, and this means that theory has to be grasped in the place and the time out of which it emerges as a part of that time, working in and for it, responding to it; then, consequently, that first place can be measured against subsequent places where the theory turns up for use. The critical consciousness is awareness of the differences between situations, awareness too of the fact that no system or theory exhausts the situation out of which it emerges or to which it is transported. And, above all, critical consciousness is awareness of the resistances to theory, reactions to it elicited by those concrete experiences or interpretations with which it is in conflict. Indeed I would go as far as saying that it is the critic's job to provide resistances to theory, to open it up toward historical reality, toward society, toward human needs and interests, to point up those concrete instances drawn from everyday reality that lie outside or just beyond the interpretive area necessarily designated in advance and thereafter circumscribed by every theory.[16]

Here we have it: not only a job for life, but the top job within the hierarchy of knowledges criticism itself posits. Said's procedures here are a replica of those which, according to Gaston Bachelard, philosophy deploys in order to be able to lord it over the sciences. By organising a series of oppositions – between the concrete and the abstract, the natural and the artificial, the intuitive and the deductive – and gridding these on to the opposition philosophy/science, philosophy, Bachelard argues, is elevated above the sciences in being made to appear as the representative of, and as having direct contact with, the given, the concrete and the real versus the impoverished, artificial abstractions of science. But it is only the philosopher who places philosophy in this enviable, epistemologically privileged position of having a direct grip on the real. 'In other words,' as Dominique Lecourt summarises Bachelard's conception of the 'self-sufficiency' and 'conceit' of philosophy, 'philosophy installs a system of concepts in which it is sufficient to itself; it is itself the legislator there, ordering the degrees of knowledge by auto-placing itself at the top of a hierarchy which it has itself established.'[17] It is, similarly, the critic, Said, who places criticism in a situation of direct contact with the real in contrast to the schematic abstractions of theory. Criticism is the locus of 'a sort of measuring faculty', which the critic somehow acquires just by reading a book or two — for the faculty is neither the product of nor sustained by a definite system of concepts, since that would deprive it of its immediacy — and which qualifies him to separate the wheat of concrete knowledge from the chaff of theory's arid abstractions. The critic, 'the man of least effort', to paraphrase Lecourt, 'will be able to judge the "heroic work of theory"'.[18]

This is not merely a cautious retreat from the excesses of theoreticism but a determined attempt to reinstate a resolutely atheoretical conception of criticism's nature and function. In the absence of any account of the processes through which this special faculty is to be acquired, one can only assume that it is the product of a 'Munchausen effect' whereby some individuals, but not others, critics but not theorists, pull themselves out of the quagmire of their own discursive determination by their own bootstraps — or, more likely, by reading Jane Austen. We are back, in effect, with the terms proposed by Arnold whose achievement, as Chris Baldick summarises it, 'was to create a new kind of critical discourse which could, by its display of careful extrication from controversy, speak from a privileged standpoint, all other discourses being in some way compromised by partial or partisan considerations'.[19] The main difference is that, for Said, this privileged standpoint is produced by the critic's embroilment in controversy, by his partisanship for humanity in face of the closures produced by the disinterested schemas of theory. For all that Said thus inverts the terms of the Arnoldian conception, the two positions are strikingly similar in constructing for criticism a position of transparency in relation to the real. In the Olympean perspective of Arnold, Baldick argues, facts, 'those innocent objects upon which we seem merely to stumble, speak their innocent language apparently of their own accord, while their ventriloquist is "out of the way"'.[20] In Said's view, it is the critic who speaks the world, rather than the world which speaks itself: but it is the same world, and the critic its same, finely tuned instrument.

It should be added that, in all of this, just as 'criticism' and 'critical consciousness' function as interchangeable terms for Said, so the theory for which criticism is to serve as the corrective slides across from its starting point — the arid stress on textuality of contemporary American literary theory – to encompass *all* and *any* theory: that is, all conceptually systematised representations of the world of social and human affairs, right across the spectrum from Northrop Frye to Foucault. Said's Arnoldian heritage shows through most, though, in his preference for a humanistic learning organised around literature above technical and scientific education. If the critic must oppose the closed dogmas of ideology, he must also prevent knowledge from degenerating into specialisms. 'Between the power of the dominant culture, on the one hand, and the impersonal system of disciplines and methods (*savoir*), on the other,' as Said puts it, 'stands the critic.'[21] It is, of course, only this conception which, to recall the list cited earlier, produces for criticism a possible role in relation to the new cold war, militarism and Reaganism's assault on organised labour. Why else should it be assumed that the criticism of literary texts might be able to speak to or about these matters, or that anyone should be inclined to listen? What else but the moral authority conferred on literature within the Arnoldian tradition could produce the space of criticism as a form of indirect speech about such worldly matters? In these respects, Said simply assumes the naturalness of a practice which constitutes literary texts as the sites for a totalising commentary which aims at the ethical-cum-political transformation of subjects without inquiring into the historically specific conditions which have put such texts into the places – discursive and institutional – where they can be so constituted and from which, today, they are so evidently slipping. Similar difficulties characterise Jameson's concept of criticism. In his case, though, these are not the effect of a mere oversight. Indeed, Jameson goes to considerable theoretical pains to universalise both the concerns and the procedures of criticism.

CRITICAL ACROBATICS

In the preface to *The Political Unconscious*, Jameson states that his 'object of study is less the text itself than the interpretations through which we attempt to confront and appropriate it'.[22] The opposition is, in truth, a little disingenuous, since it is posed only in order to be resolved and, indeed, is tendentially resolved before it is posed. These two paths, the paths of the text and its interpretations, of the object and the subject, are destined to 'ultimately meet in the same place'[23] – the end of history, the final, and only, anchorage point of the band-aided Marxist hermeneutic Jameson proposes. None the less, Jameson's reasons for foregrounding the interpretative systems through which reading practices are organised are interesting enough. He subsequently made these clearer in an interview he gave shortly after the publication of *The Political Unconscious*:

> in undergraduate work one does not really confront the 'text' at all, one's primary object of work is the *interpretation* of the text, and it is about interpretations that the pedagogical struggle in undergraduate teaching must turn. The presupposition here is that undergraduates – as more naive or unreflexive readers (which the rest of us are also much of the time) – never confront a text in all its material freshness; rather, they bring to it a whole set of previously acquired and culturally sanctioned interpretive schemes, of which they are unaware, and through which they read the texts that are proposed to them. This is not a particularly individual matter, and it does not make much difference whether one locates such interpretive stereotypes in the mind of the student, in the general cultural atmosphere, or on the text itself, as a sedimentation of its previous readings and its accumulated institutional interpretations: the task is to make those interpretations visible, as an object, as an obstacle rather than a transparency, and thereby to encourage the student's self-consciousness as to the operative power of such unwitting schemes, which our tradition calls *ideologies*.[24]

The strategic localism of this rationale, the perspective of a committed teacher's political engagement with the conditions of his own practice, commands respect. There are grounds, though, as Samuel Weber has suggested, for querying the politics of the pedagogy it produces: namely, that Marxism should be presented as an alternative within the dominant forms of literary curricula, in which literature functions as a privileged site of subject formation, rather than as the basis for a curriculum organised on different principles.[25] My reason for raising this point here, however, is that it echoes a similar strategic localism in *The Political Unconscious*. Jameson's purpose in this study is to defend, and to retrieve for Marxism, the process of interpretation 'construed as an essentially allegorical act, which consists of rewriting a given text in terms of a particular interpretive master code'.[26] Indeed, he claims for Marxism the status of an untranscendable hermeneutic horizon, representing it as a system of interpretation, in the form of a narrative of History, which is able to subsume all rival interpretative paradigms within itself, making use of their findings but in ways which simultaneously cancel out and preserve their insights by assigning them a purely sectoral validity within its own totalising procedures.

Jameson is fully aware of the objections which this manifestly Hegelian position courts, particularly in view of its liability to the Althusserian critique of expressivist conceptions of the social totality in their dependency on the notion of underlying causes which are revealed through an analysis of their effects. 'What is denounced', he writes with such objections in mind, 'is therefore a system of allegorical interpretation in which the data of one narrative line are radically impoverished by their rewriting according to the paradigm of another narrative, which is taken as the former's master code or Ur-narrative and proposed as the ultimate hidden or unconscious *meaning* of the first one.'[27] Rather than disputing the force of this objection, Jameson grants it and takes up his ground elsewhere, defending such interpretative procedures as having acquired an ontological force – and therefore a degree of validity – in functioning as 'local laws within our historical reality':

> The idea is, in other words, that if interpretation in terms of expressive causality or of allegorical master narratives remains a constant temptation, this is because such master narratives have inscribed themselves in the texts as well as in our thinking about them; such allegorical narrative signifieds are a persistent dimension of literary and cultural texts precisely because they reflect a fundamental dimension of our collective thinking and our collective fantasies about history and reality.[28]

The reasoning here is a little slippery. As John Frow has noted, the passage marks a crucial shift in Jameson's position: interpretations, which were previously distinguished from texts, are here collapsed back into them with the result that criticism's strategies can be said to be dictated by the properties of texts themselves. 'The historical objectivity of structure', as Frow puts it, 'predetermines the appropriate categories of its representation.'[29] While undoubtedly correct, this criticism does not entirely hit its mark since the justification Jameson aims for here, although it aspires to a theoretical legitimacy, is primarily political in intent and, as such, is by no means without force. Earlier in his discussion, Jameson, speaking of the application of allegorical principles of interpretation to the New Testament, argues that these serve:

> as a mechanism for preparing such a text for further ideological investment, if we take the term *ideology* here in Althusser's sense as a representational structure which allows the individual subject to conceive or imagine his or her lived relationship to transpersonal realities such as the social structure or the collective logic of History.[30]

Transposing the terms of this argument to his defence of criticism as a process which rewrites a given text in terms of an interpretative master code, Jameson's point is that, to the degree that criticism organises the reading of literary texts such that these have come to be invested with an ideological function, then Marxists can hardly afford to stand aloof from this preconstituted terrain of ideological struggle. If criticism, in its conventional guises, implicates the literary text in the ideological processes of subject formation, then Marxists must intervene within these processes in an attempt to modify their political inflections.

I have few problems with this position if presented as justifying a function for criticism on localised political grounds which might then be debated and assessed on their merits. The difficulty is that, while Jameson's argument *does* operate at this level, it does not remain there. Indeed, in a manner reminiscent of Leavis, what starts off as a localised conception of criticism's political vocation ends up as a conception of its necessary function at any particular place or time. Worse, such interpretative procedures, far from being assigned a purely sectoral validity within Marxism, come to be defined as constitutive of Marxism as a discourse of the Truth. In effect, Jameson transcodes Marxism into the language of criticism so that Marxist method becomes a localised – but privileged – instance of a set of interpretative procedures which are represented as having a universal force and validity: the narrativisation of desire, of representation and history, which allegorical systems of interpretation effect, Jameson argues, constitutes 'the central function or *instance* of the human mind'.[31] 'Always historicise!' is the opening injunction of *The Political*

Unconscious, yet almost every step Jameson subsequently takes prevents him from doing so.

I will return shortly to the broader implications of Jameson's conception of Marxism. The point I wish to stress here concerns the respects in which Jameson's universalisation of criticism as a set of interpretative practices bearing upon the processes of subject formation systematically evacuates in advance any grounds on which the political function of such practices might be subjected to a more local and more precise calculation. It takes away the space within which questions relevant to such calculations might be put. And it does so in part because, contrary to Jameson's view, it *does* make a difference where the reader's interpretative paradigms come from: whether from the text itself, or as a sedimentation of its previous readings and accumulated institutional interpretations.

To give an example: while it may be granted that criticism organises the reading of literary texts to produce for these a stake in the ideological processes of subject formation, it is by no means clear that this is universally and necessarily so, even within the limits of our current historical reality. Yet Jameson's suggestion that the procedures of interpretative criticism are appropriate to the properties that have come to be sedimented in texts themselves implies this to be so. To the contrary, a better case could be made for arguing that this ideological investment of the literary is the product of a historically specific and institutionally grounded set of discursive practices which produces the literary as a space open to the kinds of interventions Jameson outlines. It could also be argued that the effects of this critical apparatus (for that is what it is, rather than a universal instance of the human mind) are unevenly distributed through different regions of the social, particularly so in the respect that, as Pierre Bourdieu's work suggests, the bourgeoisie, petit-bourgeoisie and working classes are placed differently in relation to this apparatus.[32]

To put this more pointedly: there is no reason to suppose that a political criticism which addresses an undergraduate readership – a readership which has been formed, and is placed within, the apparatus of criticism – need have any relevance, or any possibility of purchase, outside this restricted (but still important) domain. Jameson alludes to this problem in the *Diacritics* interview when he remarks, apropos of the difficulties of his own style, that a popular pedagogy and journalism require quite specific skills, and ones distinct from those appropriate to his own sphere of work and influence as a university teacher. While, again, this manifests an exemplary localism, questions concerning the relations between criticism and popular reading practices are not reducible to matters of style or spheres of influence, as if criticism – of whatever political hue – could increase the range of its social effectivity merely by simplifying or democratising itself.

Jameson's own presentation of the procedures of interpretative criticism lends support to Pierre Macherey's argument that such a criticism derives its cogency from the relationship between the text's visible surface and its hidden depths which that criticism itself posits.[33] It is only these discursively organised spatial co-ordinates which enable criticism to present itself as a practice which delves beneath the text's exteriority to reveal its secreted meanings. The late nineteenth-century history of English criticism bears eloquent testimony to the effort that went into the production of these spatial co-ordinates. Philological criticism was opposed not merely because of its Germanic associations but because its formalistic dissections denied the text any deep structure, depriving it of the rich interiority which the Arnoldian critical project required. 'Philological criticism is to criticism in the proper sense of the term', John Churton-Collins thus wrote, 'what anatomy is to psychology. . . . The scalpel, which lays bare every nerve and artery in the mechanism of the body, reveals nothing further.'[34] It is the defence of this deep structure of the text, moreover, that has provided much of the common ground between Marxists and Leavisites in their opposition to structuralism and post-structuralism.

What such arguments often ignore, however, is the fact that the spatial topography of surface/depth, exteriority/interiority, bears only tangentially, if at all, on the organisation of popular reading practices. Work on cinema's star system and on the personality system of television, for example, suggests that popular readings are governed by a set of hermeneutic co-ordinates within which texts – the text of a film and of a star's biography, for example – are ranged alongside one another, mixing and co-mingling on the same plane, rather than being juxtaposed as front and back, surface and depth, visible form and hidden meaning. If this is so, the failure of even Marxist criticism to reach out significantly beyond the academy is no accident; nor is it corrigible merely by a more accessible style, although this would probably do no harm. Rather, it reflects a failure to theorise the different social relations of reading within which practices of textual commentary might seek to intervene.

Nor is the point I am making here limited in its applicability to the domain of popular readings. While it may be true, historically, that criticism has organised the reading of literary texts such that these have come to be invested with an ideological function of subject formation, it by no means follows that this exhausts the range of practical affairs in which such texts are implicated. To suppose that it does is to assume that literary texts have practical social consequences only in so far as they affect the consciousness of subjects; that is, only in so far as they furnish the sites for a coming-to-consciousness, on the part of the subject, about the world and his/her place within it. The consequences of this assumption are visible in the mechanism of effects which, although never clearly stated as such, permeates Jameson's account of the relations between criticism and literature. This mechanism of effects consists in the two-staged relationship Jameson posits between texts and history. First, he views the experience and consciousness of authors as conduits through which changes in the structure of historical relations are transmitted to the literary text, which then stores these changes in its structure. Jameson then suggests that criticism, in unlocking the text, serves as a further relay circuit through which the text, and, via the text, the history which it stores become effective in promoting changes in the structure of contemporary social relations via their influence on the experience and consciousness of subjects within the present. In effect, literary texts as mediated by criticism thus serve as the vehicle for History's dialogue with, and influence upon, itself.

To the degree that this mechanism of effects is dependent on the services of criticism, rather than a natural process which criticism merely enhances, it is clearly not operative within all of the institutional and discursive contexts through which literary writings are connected to, and made to function within, ongoing social processes. The uses of literary texts in various forms of technical training and in the development of certificated competences; their use as parts of moral technologies in the processes of character training; their use across diverse institutional sites (school, family, church, media): 'nothing', as Ian Hunter has argued, 'is gained by attempting to reduce the host of social technologies and special procedures of the apparatus of literature to the single point of consciousness. . . .'[35] Indeed, there is much to be lost as the possibility of a plural and nuanced politics, of a set of different discursive and institutional strategies orientated to the wide range of practical affairs in which literary texts are implicated, is thereby sacrificed to the blanket, cover-all politics of criticism which aims, in an undifferentiated way, at effecting a transformation in the consciousness of subjects.

In brief, Jameson's localised defence of literary criticism overreaches itself. Not only is there necessarily a function for such a criticism but, in Jameson's conspectus, there are and can be no functions for forms of textual commentary which do not conform to its procedures. Indeed, there is hardly any space for such practices at all. Literary criticism is so thoroughly naturalised as an instance of the supposedly universal tendency for all experience and textuality to be transcoded into the totalising narratives of religious systems or philosophies of history that, in the final analysis, the sphere of commentary is dominated, entirely and monolithically, by such transcoding practices. The necessity of criticism's function is thus guaranteed by representing all forms of textual commentary as akin to criticism in their organisation. If, as a consequence, a continuing role is claimed for Marxist criticism, this is at the price of transforming Marxism into a localised, albeit privileged, instance of interpretative criticism, privileged because of its supposed ability to narrativise History as a single, continuous human adventure. Of the struggles of the past, Jameson thus remarks:

> These matters can recover their original urgency for us only if they are retold within the unity of a single great collective story; only if, in however disguised and symbolic a form, they are seen as sharing a single fundamental theme – for Marxism, the collective struggle to wrest a realm of Freedom from a realm of Necessity; only if they are grasped as vital episodes in a single vast unfinished plot. . . .[36]

This conception becomes the source, as Jameson's analysis unfolds, of a veritable circus of Hegelian acrobatics. The most conspicuous of these are occasioned by Jameson's attempts to anneal any contradiction between feminist and Marxist narrativisations of History. This leads him to argue that sexism and patriarchy, rather than having any specific conditions of existence of their own, 'are to be grasped as the sedimentation and the virulent survival of forms of alienation specific to the oldest mode of production of human history'.[37] Subsisting within capitalism, which is alleged to store up and restate the unresolved contradictions of earlier modes of production, sexism and patriarchy, Jameson suggests, will thus be annulled through the transformation of capitalism since 'the transformation of our own dominant mode of production must be accompanied and completed by an equally radical restructuration of all the more archaic modes of production with which it structurally coexists'.[38] This subtle deployment of the Hegelian category of *Aufhebung* to represent the struggles of radical feminists and socialists as essentially identical in order that they might be construed as parts of 'a single great collective story' cannot disguise the fact that this unity is achieved by the arbitrary denial of other subject positions and narrative possibilities, especially those produced by discourses which insist on the non-coincidence of class and gender struggles.

However, the most telling contortions, at least from the point of view of my concerns here, are produced by Jameson's attempts to deny that the Marxist narrativisation of history is merely one interpretative code among many, for to concede this would entail that Marxism could not be preferred above its rivals except arbitrarily. As a hermeneutic system, Jameson argues, Marxism provides three levels or semantic horizons in which the literary text might be inserted for analysis. Each of these horizons, in constituting the text differently, distils a different facet of its historical meaning. At the first level, the object of analysis is the individual text construed as 'a symbolic act, whereby real social contradictions, unsurmountable on their own terms, find a purely formal resolution in the aesthetic realm'.[39] Here the focus is on the more or less immediate circumstances of the text conceived as an individual utterance. At the second level, where the organising category of analysis is that of antagonistic class relations, the text is conceptualised as a specific execution or manifestation of a class discourse. At this level, the text is grasped less as a symbolic resolution of real social contradictions than as 'a symbolic move in an essentially polemic and strategic confrontation between the classes'.[40] Finally, the organising units of the third and last semantic horizon, where the object of analysis is the ideology of form as instanced by such textual ensembles as genres, are modes of production and the orders of their succession/co-existence.

The relations between these three semantic horizons are such that the last, in providing the ultimate ground of and support for

213

the first and second, also supplies the means whereby the textual histories produced at each of these different levels might be harmonised and dovetailed into a total History. Equally important, it furnishes that History with an ontological foundation in functioning as the point in Jameson's analysis at which discourse enters into contact with, and is ultimately dissolved into, the real. It does so by also serving as the point of Jameson's own imaginary resolution of the contradiction between constructivist and empiricist conceptions of history. This contradiction, which runs throughout *The Political Unconscious*, is one which, for the most part, Jameson deals with by placing his bets both ways. While conceding that we can have no knowledge of History as a total process independently of the forms in which that process is represented or textualised, Jameson maintains that History none the less has a real existence independently of such representational forms and, indeed, invokes this History as the ultimate explanation for the forms in which it is textually mediated and represented – a sure case, as John Frow puts it, 'of having one's referent and eating it too'.[41] In the final analysis, however, empiricism wins out as the referent, if it cannot be known, makes itself felt and experienced as such. History, Jameson argues, is 'the experience of Necessity'.[42] What Jameson means by Necessity is not always entirely clear. In some contexts, he speaks of it as a property of discourse – the illusion, generated by the narrative forms of history writing, that what happened had to happen the way it did. In others, Necessity functions as a set of extra-discursive realities, setting objective limits to what can be achieved in particular circumstances and therefore also – although this time for real – determining that History could not have turned out otherwise than it has. Jameson elaborates this second, and ultimately decisive view of History as Necessity in the following terms:

> History is what hurts, it is what refuses desire and sets inexorable limits to individual as well as collective praxis, which its 'ruses' turn into grisly and ironic reversals of their overt intention. But this history can be apprehended only through its effects, and never directly as some reified force. This is indeed the ultimate sense in which History as ground and untranscendable horizon needs no particular theoretical justification: we may be sure that its alienating necessities

214

will not forget us, however much we might prefer to ignore them.[43]

This, of course, resolves nothing. The invocation of history as 'a text that is identical-to-itself, but whose identity is never immediately present as such' and which therefore 'always requires an intermediary, a critical spokesman in order to be heard', Samuel Weber has argued, necessarily raises the question: who speaks for History?[44] In Jameson's case, moreover, this begets a further question: whom does History hurt? For if hurting is the only way in which History manifests itself and makes its alienating necessities felt, then, unless we can answer this question – and, clearly, we cannot, except arbitrarily – History must remain unspoken and we're back where we started from: with histories – plural, partial and contradictory – among which Marxism may be counted, at best, as first among equals. Just as seriously, by making Necessity the ontological basis of, and therefore epistemological guarantee for, a Marxist narrativisation of History rooted in the category of mode of production, this foundational category is itself radically transformed: no longer an articulated combination of forces and relations of production, it becomes merely a specific expression and organisation of the relations between two ahistorical essences – Desire and Necessity – locked in an eternal and irresolvable antagonism. And it is this conception of History as a process impelled by the couplet Desire/Necessity that is supposed to provide the master narrative into which all forms of human experience and textuality are to be transcoded! Althusser, it may be recalled, argued that Marx was able to open up the continent of history to scientific investigation only by breaking with earlier closed philosophies of history which represented themselves as 'the *truth of* History', as exhaustive, definitive and absolute knowledge of it and which, consequently, could only ever discover in 'the real' the reflections of their own starting points.[45] Jameson's formulations entail that this opening be closed down again. In place of an analysis of the production and functioning of literary texts within history that would be orientated to the production of new knowledges, the criticism he advocates is one which can merely rehearse, and rehearse again, albeit at different levels of analysis and in relation to different texts, the same narrative spinning around the same terms.

Nor is this merely a problem for the concept of literary criticism

Jameson proposes. It profoundly affects his broader characterisation of Marxism as a whole which, to the degree that it is presented as a sub-species of criticism, exhibits the same type of ideological closure. Yet this closure is accompanied, at another level, by an unlimited openness. Like Said, Jameson opposes criticism, and Marxism as criticism, to the aridities and dogmas of theory and, also like Said, his definition of criticism, and so of Marxism also, lacks positive terms. The validity of Marxism, he argues, 'does not depend on some dogmatic or "positive" conception of Marxism as a system' but derives from the fact that it is a kind of thinking which knows no boundaries and which is 'infinitely totalisable'. Marxism, as he elaborates this conception, 'is simply the place of an imperative to totalise, and the various historical forms of Marxism can themselves equally effectively be submitted to just such a critique of their own local limits or ideological strategies of containment'.[46] According to the logic of this account, which might be summarised by saying that s/he who totalises last totalises longest, we have no idea what the Marxism is that serves, or will serve, as Jameson's hermeneutic master-key to History since, whatever Marxism is now, it may shortly cease to be in consequence of the incessant self-critique which results from its infinite self-enrichment. It is merely the empty box of what it might become, a promissory note to be redeemed once the historical process is completed.

However, it is arguably this very openness which accounts for the influence of Jameson's Marxism which becomes, in the movement of its self-totalisation, not merely a narrativisation of History but History itself. As Samuel Weber puts it, if Marxism, as the site and subject of an endless imperative to totalise, 'can be criticised in *its own name*, it is only because its own "place" is co-extensive with another space which bears another name, that of History'.[47] As the narrative of what has been which, when whatever will be has come to pass, will reorganise itself yet still retain its identity, Marxism as History as Necessity happily turns out, Weber continues, to serve as 'the best means of Saving the Text'.[48] The endless mobility of History provides a means of guaranteeing the stable identity of the text whose particularity, to cite Weber again, 'coincides with its *inertia*, the fact that it is, once and for all, in its proper place *within* History, that is within a story waiting to be told, once and for all, in the one and only way'.[49] In this way, Jameson storms the established critical

216

institutions and practices only to leave them unchanged except by way of enriching them and renewing their potential. Even though texts are only given to us through the sedimented layers of previous interpretations, they still remain the source of ultimate and irreducible meanings which criticism will eventually deliver by means of a never-endingly enriched and self-enriching process through which Marxism integrates all contending interpretative paradigms within itself as it unendingly retotalises its own self-negations. Where Said guarantees the critic a top job for life, Jameson guarantees criticism a vocation forever. Viewed in relation to the American university system, *The Political Unconscious* provides a precise complement to the American appropriation of deconstruction. Just as this vouchsafes a future for interpretative criticism precisely by demonstrating its necessary shortcomings so that, as Terry Eagleton argues in *The Function of Criticism*, the job has to be done again and again, interminably, so Jameson posits the endlessness of criticism with the added bonus that it can be expected to get better – semantically richer and more adequate historically – all the time.

CRITICAL CALCULATIONS

Both Said and Jameson, then, subscribe to the view of criticism as a practice of textual commentary which connects with and impacts upon general societal and political processes in treating literary texts as the pre-texts for the elaboration of interpretative paradigms which seek to influence the ethical, cognitive and political formation of subjects. This tendency to resurrect a traditional conception of criticism's function (albeit one subjected to a political inversion: organising subjects *against* the existing social order rather than, as in Arnold's vision, *for* it) is by no means an isolated one – witness Terry Eagleton's *The Function of Criticism*. Nor are its consequences limited to the literary–critical regions of theoretical debate. Rather, where such arguments are articulated to Marxist concerns, they constitute a response to the accumulation of theoretical and political difficulties besetting the view that Marxism offers a totalising understanding of the structure of social relations and the mechanisms of their historical development. Viewed in this light, the return to criticism can be read, at least in part, as an attempt to *suture* the fragments of such a holistic Marxism back into place.

217

Equally, though, the current organisation of the intellectual field is such that it is only in relation to such a reconstructed Marxism that a place can be found for a revived conception of criticism's traditional function. Given the atomising tendencies of post-structuralist and postmodernist debates, criticism needs the kind of holistic space which a totalising Marxism provides in order to find a home for itself. Criticism refurbishing Marxism, Marxism refurbishing criticism: these two processes – especially as enacted in Jameson's work – are symbiotic. Marxism provides a conceptual space in which the place of literary texts in the social can be fixed as the storehouses of the history which determines them and to which there can be attributed a set of general effects on the processes of subject formation which it then becomes criticism's business to modulate.

Questionable in itself, using the rhetoric of criticism to repair the dents within Marxism's totalising armature, and vice versa, has the further consequence of masking the concrete problems posed by the different spheres of effectivity within which practices of textual commentary operate and in relation to which their political effects must be calculated. Three issues pertinent to such considerations might usefully be identified here. The first concerns the status that should be accorded to the concept of 'the literary' and, accordingly, the forms of displacement to which it might most productively be subjected. Said and Jameson differ, of course, with regard to the critical traditions and the associated concepts of 'the literary' to which they subscribe. An Arnoldian conception of criticism as a practice which construes 'the literary' as a domain having a privileged bearing on the ethical formation of subjects is evident in Said's work. Jameson, by contrast, shares Lukács's view of criticism as having a primarily cognitive function in enhancing the ability of literature to serve as a vehicle for the formation of the historical self-knowledge of the subject. None the less, their positions are similar in conceiving 'the literary' as a property of texts in relation to which criticism functions as a secondary process which merely helps to realise its intrinsic tendencies rather than, as I have suggested is more appropriate, regarding it as a sphere of social and cultural action that is produced for those texts nominated as literary by virtue of the ways in which they are constituted within the institutional and discursive space of criticism. In brief, they mistake the sphere of criticism and its product, literature, for a natural horizon with the consequence that they are unable to address the questions raised by the forms in which literary texts are socially deployed outside that space.

The second problem concerns the role accorded history in relation to criticism. The distinctive hermeneutic gambit of Marxist criticism has usually been to invoke history as the ultimate ground of literary texts in the sense that it both furnishes their material supports and provides the key to their meaning. Governed by the conception of literary texts as the mediated reflections of the history that has produced them, Marxist criticism has thus endeavoured both to distil and to explicate the meaning of such texts by returning them, analytically, to that history which, in its turn, is represented as the hidden (but now uncovered) horizon of their intelligibility. Clearly, this procedure derives its cogency from viewing the relations between texts and history through the grid of a series of related oppositions – surface/depth, open/hidden, etc. Of late, this procedure has increasingly been revealed as just that – a set of discursive operations which can no longer secure its warrant through the ontological foundations on which it had earlier claimed to rest. Jameson's *The Political Unconscious*, clearly intended to meet this challenge, conspicuously demonstrates the impossibility of doing so without resorting to procedures for privileging the claims of Marxism which are clearly arbitrary.

Traditional Marxist conceptions of the relations between criticism and history have had a further aspect: namely, that history is posited as the process that will eventually produce the unified subject which a fully developed Marxist criticism will finally address and which, in the interim, it anticipates. This conception, most evident in the work of Lukács but a widespread tendency, has been responsible for one of the most astonishing areas of neglect within Marxist criticism. In imaginarily addressing a universal subject in the making, and consequently proceeding as if speaking to everyone, Marxist critics have paid scant attention to the institutional and discursive factors regulating their relations to the publics they actually do address or, perhaps more important, might wish to address.

It is, above all, this ideal addressee of criticism – Arnold's imaginary 'everyone' – which, even in its historicised variants, constitutes the most effective impediment to an examination of the more specific, multiple and differentiated political questions posed by the differentially constituted institutional and discursive domains in which literary texts are deployed and practices of textual commentary effectively engaged. At the level of everyday politics – and it is everyday politics that are at issue in the question of criticism's function, not the grand gestures of revolutionary criticism or the building of meta-narratives in the sky – this ideal addressee has no concrete existence. To pose the question of criticism's function in the singular and monolithically is to suppose that such an addressee does or might exist. It is only by breaking with this illusion that the question can be dispersed and broken down into a set of calculations regarding what might be accomplished by different practices of textual commentary conducted in relation to different publics, institutions and circumstances.

9

THE PRISON-HOUSE OF CRITICISM

In *The Prison-House of Language*, Fredric Jameson argues that once a formalist or structuralist move is taken in literary studies, there is no way out of it.[1] It is a step that commits the theorist to a long-term sentence within the maze of language, destined to wander endlessly through its passages without ever breaking out beyond them to establish connection with – well, in Jameson's case, History. Criticism, in the sense bequeathed by the tradition running from Arnold to Leavis, has had a similar capacity for incarceration. Even those critics who do try to escape are eventually hauled back to the penitentiary or, equally likely, succumb to critical recidivism and troop back of their own accord.

Such, at any rate, is the conclusion suggested by Terry Eagleton's *The Function of Criticism*. In this brief but provocative study, Eagleton traces the trajectory of English criticism from its origins in the eighteenth century to Leavis and beyond with a view to identifying the implications of that history for the political tasks to be confronted by contemporary critical practice. As such, it is by far the most politically focused account of the vicissitudes of criticism that we have. There is a tendency in other recent Marxist or neo-Marxist definitions of criticism's tasks – those of Said and Jameson, for example – to proceed as if criticism could be regarded as a purely abstract and disembodied practice conducted from nowhere in particular and as if for everyone. By contrast, *The Function of Criticism* performs a useful service in the importance it accords institutional considerations in both its account of criticism's history and its definition of its contemporary function.

There is, however, a countervailing tendency within the

analysis. One consequence of posing the question of the political function which critical practices might perform via an interrogation of their institutional articulations ought to be to suggest that such practices might be differently constituted and so provide the means for different kinds of political work depending on the institutional contexts in which they are applied. It should suggest that the function of critical practices cannot be prescribed independently of the institutional conditions which regulate who is speaking to whom, within and across such practices, and in what circumstances. Yet, although supported by aspects of Eagleton's discussion, many of his formulations run counter to the particularising political logic of such a conclusion. Indeed, Eagleton's prescriptions are nothing if not generalising, and while his discussion encompasses a number of institutional contexts for critical activity, he eventually claims a singular function for criticism and predicates the realisation of that function on a particular network of institutional sites.

That this is so is attributable, ultimately, to the archive which generates Eagleton's prescriptive statements. For, apart from supplying him with the object of his analysis, it is the archive of criticism, in the Arnold to Leavis tradition, which governs the framework within which criticism's current ills are diagnosed and solutions prescribed. Eagleton's recommendations are a move *within* that tradition and, indeed, a return to it. This is clear enough in the text. Eagleton's critical recidivism is anything but furtive. 'The point of the present essay', he writes, 'is to recall criticism to its traditional role, not to invent some fashionable new function for it.'[2] Nothing trendy, then. Criticism is to become again what it once was, where what it once was is regarded as a totalising form of social commentary and critique – delivering a message about and, ideally, for a whole culture – which furnished a site of opposition to the state. And it must be that or nothing:

> Modern criticism was born of a struggle against the absolutist
> state; unless its future is now defined as a struggle against the
> bourgeois state, it might have no future at all.[3]

The political vocation to which criticism is thus summoned, moreover, is conceived as essential to it. It is criticism's true and original function (but one which it has since lost) which, in being restored to it, thereby returning criticism to itself, realises its alienated essence. While this essentialist aspect of Eagleton's discussion is problematic in itself, an added difficulty is that Eagleton does not envisage it as being particularly likely that the task criticism is thus called on to perform will be accomplished – or at least, to borrow a phrase from Leavis, not in our particular time and place. In this respect, *The Function of Criticism* is characteristic of the antinomial way of thinking that has come to govern Eagleton's approach to the question of criticism's function. This is especially clear in a recent interview. 'As far as criticism goes at the moment, in its narrow definition,' Eagleton argues, 'I wouldn't have said there was much politically at stake either way.'[4] Given the actual constitution of criticism in the here and now and (give or take the odd slippage or two into a wider public domain) its restriction to the universities, nothing of consequence seems to hinge on how criticism is conducted. On the other hand, if criticism is redefined and its social articulations modified, then 'an enormous amount is at stake'.[5] The difficulty with such formulations is that, in constructing criticism's options in the form of a polarity without mediating terms, they suggest that the gap between these options can only be closed by an act of will as criticism is invited to chose between 'political impotence and political effectiveness'.[6] Or the gap cannot be closed at all but results, rather, in a fissure between what can be done in the here and now and what a Marxist criticism ought properly to be doing. And this, in turn, leads to questions of critical politics being posed in the form of a dilemma concerning 'the connection between what one is actually doing now, on the spot, and an image of what in the end would count as definitive of the identity of a Marxist cultural critic'.[7]

But why should it be thought that there need be a contradiction between what can be done on the spot and some terminal conception of the true identity and function of the Marxist critic? What is it that converts practical questions concerning what might most appropriately be done in the here and now into a question of the critic's identity? Need Marxist critics think of themselves as having an ultimate and true identity they must incessantly be in search of? That Eagleton formulates the matter in these terms is partly due to the influence of the messianic strain within the Marxist critical tradition. In *The Function of Criticism*, however, that strain is inflected through the governing terms supplied by the archive of criticism in its peculiarly English variants. Thus, although Eagleton's history of criticism is organised around

Habermas's concept of the public sphere, his use of that concept and the lessons he draws from it are strongly influenced by Arnold's and Leavis's conceptions of criticism's function. It is the overlapping of these two traditions on to one another that accounts for a good deal of the book's persuasive power. It provides a Marxist pedigree for a concept of criticism derived from the history of its English variants, and in so doing provides the project of a Marxist criticism with some anchorage and roots in the English critical tradition.

This is clearly a matter of calculated tactics, a way of insinuating Marxist concerns into the inherited vocabulary of Anglo-American criticism. Equally, though, such an insinuation is possible only because of the common indebtedness of both traditions – through the route of Goethe and Schiller in the case of Marxist criticism – to the ethics and politics of Romanticism whose terms are retained but inverted as earlier definitions of criticism's function are bent back on themselves to radicalise their political connotations. As a consequence, certain assumptions derived from these traditions remain unquestioned. Foremost of these is the conception of criticism as a practice of textual commentary with a totalising ambit which acquires a political effectivity by intervening beneficially within the ideological processes of subject formation as these operate at a general societal level. Criticism, as Eagleton puts it, has compelled widespread attention only when, in speaking about literature, it has emitted 'a message about the shape and destiny of a whole culture'.[8] The logic of this conception of criticism's function was most clearly stated by Leavis. The critic, Leavis argued, 'conceives of himself as helping, in a collaborative process, to define – that is, to form – the contemporary sensibility'.[9] However, as Leavis goes on to argue, the critic can only fulfil this function indirectly via the influence of criticism on the public – the intelligently responsive public – it produces:

> It is through such a public, and through the conditions of general education implied in the existence of such a public, that literature, as the critic is concerned with it, can reasonably be thought of as influencing contemporary affairs and telling in realms in which literary critics are not commonly supposed to count for much.[10]

Eagleton, too, is concerned that criticism should be 'telling in realms in which literary critics are not commonly supposed to count for much', and predicates its ability to do so on its success in moulding a public. A different public, to be sure, and one organised by a different politics. For all that, the symmetry is compelling. As such, the major difficulty with Eagleton's analysis is that, while revealing the historically determined co-ordinates of the social and cultural space in which such a conception of criticism could install itself – albeit as an illusory practice which never achieved the goals it set itself – and while charting the dissolution and fragmentation of that space, he also seeks to re-institute that space and, thereby, find criticism a home again. A revolutionary home, for sure, and a home for a revolutionary criticism but one which, like its forebears, is equally unlikely to achieve what is asked of it. Problematic in itself, this has the further unfortunate consequence of foreclosing on the more practical and more readily achievable tasks practices of textual commentary (not all of which need be conceived as sub-species of a general concept of criticism) might be called on to perform across the varying institutional sites which supply the conditions of their existence and domains of application.

Yet the elements of such a particularising political logic can be derived from Eagleton's text but only, as is my purpose here, when read against the grain of the archive which sustains its more generalising formulations. First, though, it will be necessary to elaborate Eagleton's arguments a little more fully. It will be useful, in doing so, to view them in the light of the trajectory of Eagleton's recent work.

IN SEARCH OF A REVOLUTIONARY CRITICISM

Criticism is not an innocent discipline, and never has been. It is a branch of Marxist criticism to enquire into the history of criticism itself: to pose the question of under what conditions, and for what ends, a literary criticism comes about. For criticism has a history, which is more than a random collocation of critical acts. . . . It emerges into existence, and passes out of it again, on the basis of certain determinate conditions. . . . In constructing the history of criticism we are not tracing the exfoliation through history of a linear, if irregular, process: it is the history of *criticisms* which is at issue. . . . The science of the history of criticisms is the science of the historical forms which produce those

criticisms – criticisms which in turn produce the literary text
as their object, as the 'text-for-criticism'.[11]

This passage appears early in *Criticism and Ideology*, prefacing
Eagleton's discussion of Raymond Williams's work. It is echoed, at
the end of that discussion, by the injunction that criticism should
'break with its ideological prehistory' and situate itself 'outside the
space of the text on the alternative terrain of scientific
knowledge'.[12] Published eight years later, *The Function of Criticism*
both applies the perspectives developed in *Criticism and Ideology*
while also announcing a break with its theoreticist tendencies. It
thus poses, in relation to criticism, 'the question of under what
conditions, and for what ends, a literary criticism comes about' as
well as the question of the circumstances in which it atrophies.
Rather than urging Marxist criticism to establish a clear break
with its ideological prehistory, however, Eagleton, in recalling
criticism to a general function of subject formation, returns it to
that prehistory (or at least to selected aspects of it) and, in doing
so, effects a shift from the plural to the singular mood, from
criticisms to *criticism*.

Habermas's theses concerning the relationship between the rise
of literary criticism and the development and subsequent
deterioration of the bourgeois public sphere are central to both
aspects of Eagleton's argument. He is at times, though, sharply
critical of Habermas and usually productively so. Habermas, for
example, suggests that eighteenth-century criticism and the
institutions which supported its development (literary journals,
debating societies, coffee houses) provided a discursive-institutional
site for the formation of a bourgeois public opinion constructed in
opposition to the aristocratic state. Eagleton, by contrast, assesses
the significance of this formative moment in the history of
criticism as that of facilitating an alliance between the bourgeoisie
and the landed classes. The part played by literary–critical
discourse in circulating the codes of rationality between members
of a public presumed to meet as equals, Eagleton argues, played a
crucial role in 'the cementing of a new power bloc at the level of
the sign'.[13] The classical bourgeois public sphere, dissolving the
distinction between bourgeois, squire, aristocrat and the members
of the professions in involving them in the same institutions as co-
discoursing equals, effected 'a discursive reorganisation of social

power, redrawing the boundaries between social classes as divisions between those who engage in rational argument, and those who do not'.[14]

Eagleton does not, then, idealise the founding moment of criticism as one in which criticism could claim a purely oppositional status and function. It was rather the site and medium of a discursive and institutional class compromise. None the less, this moment supplies the model of criticism's function in relation to which Eagleton organises a lapsarian account of its subsequent history. Centrally implicated in the major political issues of the day, eighteenth-century criticism was 'not yet "literary" but "cultural"' – that is, a form of ethical–humanist commentary which, while it encompassed literary texts, did so alongside other issues of vital public concern rather than as a separated domain subjected to 'an autonomous specialist discourse'.[15] It was, albeit in a polite and recondite way, a site of social and political critique.

Subsequently, owing to a narrowing professionalism and the attenuation of the public sphere which shaped its birth, criticism has turned in on itself and petrified as a consequence of its lack of any vital social relevance. At the same time as criticism's scope narrows in being restricted exclusively to the literary, so its institutional basis becomes increasingly constricted until, with the *Scrutiny* group, it is driven to the ultimate contradiction of seeking 'to recreate the public sphere *from within the very institutions which had severed criticism from it*: the universities'.[16] This leads Eagleton to demand that criticism should break free from the dual restrictions of the literary and the university and, by engaging with the products of the culture industry, assist in the development of a counterpublic sphere within which opposition to the administered culture and politics of late capitalism might be nurtured and developed. 'The role of the contemporary critic', as Eagleton puts it, 'is to resist that dominance' – the dominance of the commodity – 'by re-connecting the symbolic to the political, engaging through both discourse and practice with the process by which repressed needs, interests and desires may assume the cultural forms which could weld them into a collective political force.'[17] Staking its future on the development of institutional sites located outside of and in opposition to the state, criticism, in rendering 'human needs and desires into publicly discussable form, teaching new modes of subjectivity and combating received

227

representations',[18] is to assist in a process of revolutionary will-formation by aiding the coming-to-consciousness of a collective political subject.

Here, then, is the break with the theoreticism of *Criticism and Ideology*. Rather than being severed from its ideological prehistory, criticism is to re-install itself on the terrain of ideology as a practice invested in the processes of subject formation and, thereby, in the constitution of social forces. Indeed, the task set Marxist criticism is to realise the function that had been claimed for criticism at the moment of its inception but which it had been able to achieve only imperfectly. This becomes clearer if account is taken of the second and more immediate point of historical reference informing Eagleton's discussion. This is provided by the working-class cultural associations which flourished in Britain in the 1930s (the Workers' Theatre Movement, the Left Book Club, etc.) and which, in their more developed forms in Germany, 'helped to make possible a Brecht and a Benjamin, and to shift the role of critic from isolated intellectual to political functionary'.[19] It is this moment that serves as the organising political centre of Eagleton's analysis in supplying a crystallised realisation of criticism's function, a second high point in relation to which its subsequent development is, again, conceived and organised in lapsarian terms.

The history of criticism is thus marked by two falls. First, the institutionalisation of bourgeois criticism in the universities from the late nineteenth century onwards is represented as a fall from the extended political function it had acquired in the classical bourgeois public sphere. Its subsequent association with proletarian cultural associations in the 1920s and 1930s is then represented as the potential achievement – at least in class terms – of the ability to articulate a validly general opinion which criticism had earlier claimed but which had been denied it by the restriction of the classical bourgeois public sphere to male property owners. Criticism's second fall, finally, is said to have been occasioned by the post-war erosion of this proletarian public sphere as a result of the increased commodification of cultural production and consumption. Counterbalancing this, though, Eagleton argues that the formation of new types of cultural association in connection with the development of post-war feminism has created an institutional space for criticism which has broken free from the gendered exclusivity of earlier public spheres, bourgeois and proletarian. This space, Eagleton suggests, might be amalgamated with that produced by the revival of proletarian cultural organisations, exemplified by the recent development of working-class writers' and readers' associations. Together, these could provide a counterpublic sphere freed from both the class and gender restrictions which have marked – and marred – criticism's earlier institutional articulations. It is in relation to such a counterpublic sphere, Eagleton suggests, that criticism can attain a genuinely universalising function of subject formation in speaking to, for and on behalf of a general opinion in the process of its formation.

Assessed in terms of its revolutionary credentials, the argument is impeccable and, at the level of generalities, it is difficult to take issue with many of Eagleton's suggestions. The need for criticism to engage with texts beyond the literary canon is unarguable. Nor is there any doubt that Eagleton is right to foreground the question of criticism's institutional connections. Difficulties accumulate, however, if one asks how this is to be accomplished. The specific details of many of Eagleton's formulations often stand in the way of convincing answers. Certainly, the view that film, television, advertising and mass publishing impose the monolithic dominance of the commodity form, *repressing* needs, interests and desires rather than *producing* and *organising* them, is unlikely to supply a means of engaging with the real complexity of those institutions and practices. Nor is it likely to sustain critical practices with any extended social reach or popularity. Unfortunately, such passages work *with* rather than *against* the grain of the analysis, and so cannot be discounted as isolated rhetorical flourishes, suggesting that the terms in which the question of criticism's function is posed may be misleading.

This is also suggested by the improbability of the mission to which Eagleton summons criticism – improbable because the terms of his own analysis suggest that what is called for is unlikely to happen. If the future of criticism is staked on the part it might play in relation to the development of a counterpublic sphere, Eagleton also argues that the very existence of such a sphere is increasingly threatened by the dual pressures of the increasing privatisation of social life and the enlarged sway of the culture industry. In consequence, instead of specifying concretely achievable tasks, Eagleton tends to write criticism into a corner where its destiny seems likely to be that of denouncing the conditions which hem it in and restrict it as it claims a function which it cannot realise – at least not yet. 'Socialist criticism,' as Eagleton puts it, 'cannot conjure a counterpublic sphere into existence; on the contrary, that criticism cannot itself fully exist until such a sphere has been fashioned.'[20]

That criticism thus finds itself placed on the horns of a dilemma is less of a problem than the fact that the terms of that dilemma are conceived and organised by the repertoire of options inherited from the Arnoldian–Leavisite tradition. In recalling criticism to its traditional function, Eagleton thus recalls it to its traditional dilemma also. For, at least since Arnold, criticism has always chafed under the restrictions of the limited institutional domains which have supplied the actual conditions and sites of its operation, seeking to break out beyond these to realise the universalising ambit it has claimed for itself. It would not be difficult, in this respect, to trace marked similarities between Eagleton's account of the degeneration of the classical bourgeois public sphere and Q. D. Leavis's account of the deterioration of the reading public, or between Eagleton's view that criticism should promote opposition to the dominance of the commodity form and F. R. Leavis's view that criticism should seek to constitute and organise sources of cultural resistance to the increasing com-modification of social life. In both cases, criticism assigns itself a totalising social function – that of creating a consensus via the influence of an educated public in the case of the Leavises, and that of welding disparate oppositional groups into a collective political force for Eagleton – in relation to which criticism's existing institutional articulations are perceived as inadequate. The task then comes to be defined as one of forging new institutional mediations through which criticism can once again aspire to the totalising function which, in its self-diagnosis, it once had but has since lost. For the Leavises, this meant rejecting the pretensions of the English Association and the Royal Society of Literature to serve as the centres around which criticism's function might be constituted, and seeking instead to develop a missionary network of institutional mediations, spreading outward from the university through the education system, for the diffusion of criticism's benign and humanising influence. It meant, Baldick has argued, the substitution of teaching for politics.[21] While this opposition is misleading, we may – as does Eagleton – accept its terms for the moment. For what Eagleton proposes is, in effect, the substitution of politics for teaching as criticism is invited to shake free of the limiting confines of the educational system and stake its all on the development of a counterpublic sphere. While obviously differing in terms of their political content, then, the two arguments are symmetrical at the level of the structure governing the terms in which criticism's plight is diagnosed and treatment prescribed. This symmetry is even more apparent if Eagleton's position is compared to Arnold's whose terms it retains but inverts: criticism is to re-acquire its totalising function as a force opposed to the bourgeois state rather than, as in Arnold's vision, operating within that state to establish it as a centre of authority whose influence will radiate outwards and downwards through society.

That Eagleton's discussion describes a close orbit around the tradition of English criticism whose rise and fall it traces is, however, self-evident. The purpose of these archaeological excavations is to bring to light the consequences of that closeness for the position that Eagleton takes up in relation to Marxist criticism. In seeking to appropriate the conception of criticism's function as elaborated in the Arnoldian–Leavisite tradition, Eagleton's concern is clearly to stake out the high ground of criticism for Marxism while the official heirs of that tradition are busily engaged, at Yale and Harvard, in the deconstruction of textual minutiae. But the function that Marxist criticism is thus called on to perform is by no means a new one. To the contrary, the notion that criticism should assist in the formation of a revolutionary subject that will command the stage of history in a moment of terminal crisis has been central to the Marxist critical tradition ever since it attained a fully elaborated form in the writings of Georg Lukács. Indeed, Eagleton's strategy is rather similar to Lukács's appropriation of the Goethe–Schiller critical tradition for Marxist criticism and his provision of a concrete institutional articulation for the latter in the form of the Communist Party.

Viewed in this perspective, the political cutting edge of Eagleton's position consists in the degree to which, in recalling criticism in general to its traditional function, he is thereby also able to affirm that Marxist criticism should carry on as before, but with the advantage of seeming to do so in a concrete, realistic and institutionally grounded way appropriate to a changed set of political circumstances. By connecting criticism's role in the processes of revolutionary will-formation to the part it plays in the development of a counterpublic sphere, Eagleton is able to refurbish the classical Marxist formulations of criticism's function while also avoiding the idealist and, not infrequently, messianic conceptions governing the frameworks in which that function has, post-Lukács, been stated and developed. Criticism is not forced back onto the standpoint of redemption (Benjamin) or negation (Adorno) pending the development of institutional mediations that will enable it to productively connect with the political concerns of the moment. Rather, Marxist criticism is to assist in the process of building the sites which, come the day, will be necessary to the realisation of its true function.

This marks a significant and welcome shift from the redemptive concept of criticism which haunts Eagleton's earlier study of Walter Benjamin.[22] However, traces of the earlier position are manifest in Eagleton's interpretation and use of the concept of the public sphere. While sounding a note of caution against the nostalgic and idealising connotations of Habermas's concept of the classical bourgeois public sphere, an idealising impetus remains strongly present throughout Eagleton's analysis. Also, whatever he says to the contrary, Eagleton is insufficiently alert to the problems inherent in the attempt to theorise criticism's contemporary function by means of an analogy with its function in earlier phases of its development. The consequence is that Eagleton places his bets on the institutional sites where, given the current organisation of the field of criticism, practices of textual commentary might be calculated to have the least likelihood of any extended or cumulative social effects.

It will be useful, in developing these arguments, to distinguish between the three major institutional sites in relation to which, adopting the particularising terms suggested by Eagleton's discussion, the question of criticism's contemporary function may most appropriately be posed: the counterpublic sphere, the university and the mass-mediated public sphere of the culture industry. Here, I shall concentrate on the first two.

CRITICISM AND THE COUNTERPUBLIC SPHERE

In Habermas's early writings the concept of the public sphere fulfils both a historical and a critical function. Historically, it refers to the institutional conditions in which a public opinion came to be formed and articulated in opposition to the state authority. However, this aspect of the concept is simultaneously critical in specifying the circumstances which must obtain in order to produce a reasoning public to whose opinion the state can validly be held accountable:

> By 'the public sphere' we mean first of all a realm of our social life in which something approaching public opinion can be formed. Access is guaranteed to all citizens. A portion of the public sphere comes into being in every conversation in which private individuals assemble to form a public body. They then behave neither like business or professional people transacting private affairs, nor like members of a constitutional order subject to the legal constraints of a state bureaucracy. Citizens behave as a public body when they confer in an unrestricted fashion – that is, with the guaranteee of freedom of assembly and association and the freedom to express and publish their opinions – about matters of general interest.[23]

As such, Habermas argues, the public sphere presupposes a clear separation between a state authority standing over society and 'a sphere of bourgeois society which would stand apart from the state as a genuine area of private autonomy'.[24] It presupposes, that is to say, capitalist social relations of production. The development of commodity production and exchange produced, in the bourgeoisie, a class whose members were not directly dependent on or integrated within a state bureaucracy – as was the case with powerful social classes in feudal and absolutist regimes – and whose interests could therefore be constituted in a relationship of opposition to the state authority. This condition, while making the bourgeoisie relatively independent *vis-à-vis* the state, also separated its members from one another to the degree that, in the market place, the conduct of affairs was regulated by the principle of self-interest. As a second condition, therefore, the emergence of the public sphere required the development of a set of institutions and accompanying rules for the conduct of affairs within such institutions (freedom of assembly, equal rights to participation and membership, the conduct of procedures by agreed means which are open to rational debate and revision) within which differences of individual interests and opinion might be negotiated so as to produce an opinion which might claim the status and backing of a public. In brief, then, the institutions comprising the public sphere mediate between society, conceived as the aggregate of separated individuals transacting their affairs in the market, and the state, conceived as the executive public authority. As such, it constitutes the means whereby the separated interests of the former may be co-ordinated into a public opinion and brought to bear on the state authority in order to curb and modify it.

The main points to stress here concern the relations between state and society which are posited as the conditions for the emergence of the classical bourgeois public sphere. With regard to the state, Habermas has in mind the absolutist state which, owing to its authoritarian structure, generated no internal spaces within which an opinion opposed to its own edicts and tendencies might be produced and organised. It was the monolithic structure of the absolutist state which, in exiling all mechanisms for the formation of a counter-opinion from within its own folds, obliged those mechanisms to find their institutional supports elsewhere. At the same time, the development of civil society promoted by the spread of market relations created a social space clearly differentiated from that of the state on which interests distinguished from and opposed to it might be formed. While such interests required the mediation of a separate set of institutions in order to be shaped into a politically effective opinion, it should not be overlooked that it was the singular class and gender (bourgeois, male) determination of those interests which, in exiling contradictions from what counted as the public, enabled that opinion to be represented and to function as the general opinion of enfranchised political subjects.

It is precisely this dual set of conditions permitting the formation of a generalised public opinion which, according to Habermas's later writings and the related work of Claus Offe, have been undermined by the development of bureaucratic forms of state administration in late capitalist societies. To the degree that state bureaucracies increasingly play a direct role in the regulation of economic affairs, so the existence of a distinct sphere of civil society is undermined. Equally, to the degree that economic associations such as corporations and unions increasingly take on political functions in association with state bureaucracies, so the state becomes increasingly socialised. These joint developments unhinge the clear state/society separation upon which the classical bourgeois public sphere depended and which equally supports the idea of a counterpublic sphere conceived as a series of inter-related sites of opinion formation located outside of and in opposition to the state. Related developments in the constitution and funding of cultural organisations similarly render problematic their conception as a set of extra-state agencies which might form the basis for the mobilisation of a generalised opinion against the state. The simple fact of the matter is that many of the forms of cultural association which Eagleton looks to in this respect are either directly or indirectly dependent on state apparatuses for their funding and administration.

This requires that the terms in which questions of cultural politics are put be reconsidered. In his admirably taut discussion of the work of Habermas and Offe, John Keane clearly demonstrates that neither conceives of state bureaucracies as smoothly functioning totalities which exercise an unshakeable dominion over their members. To the contrary, both stress the degree to which multiple disequilibria are produced by the inability of public and private bureaucracies to co-ordinate effectively their relations with one another. Further contradictions are generated as those bureaucracies, driven to enlist the active support and participation of their members and clients, prove unable to satisfy the demands which such support and participation generate. This leads Keane, rather than speaking monolithically about the public sphere, to speak plurally about public *spheres*. A public sphere, he argues:

is brought into being whenever two or more individuals, who previously acted singularly, assemble to interrogate both their own interactions and the wider relations of social and political power within which they are always and already embedded. Through this autonomous association, members of public spheres consider what they are doing, settle how they will live together, and determine, within the estimated limits of the means available to them, how they might collectively act within the foreseeable future.[25]

Public spheres are therefore 'a continuous, if unintended, effect of the processes of pseudomutual recognition inscribed within bureaucratic forms of power'.[26] They are brought into being not merely outside of and in opposition to the bureaucratic apparatuses of the state but also *within* those apparatuses or in varying degrees of quasi-autonomous relations to state bureaucracies. Feminist public spheres, for example, have arguably been most influentially and enduringly constituted within or in relation to the education system and the spaces produced by the funding operations of state agencies with an investment in the sphere of the cultural, exploiting the contradictory niches such sites afford rather than taking up a position of pure externality and opposition to the state. This obviously calls into question the notion that a series of extra-state forms of public association might be constituted into a counterpublic sphere in relation to which, through the intervention of criticism and other practices, a unified collective subject of political action might be formed. This is especially so in view of the fact that, lacking a singular class and gender determination, the constituencies produced by and involved in different sites of struggle within or in relation to the state are not easily conceived as even potentially a unified subject to which a generalised opinion might be attributed.

In brief, then, I am suggesting that the various issues in relation to which public spheres are constituted and the various institutional sites on which they are formed do not cohere in such a way as to yield the possibility of a bi-polar political opposition (people versus state) being constructed around a central contradiction, such as that of class struggle. Nor, equally, can the state be regarded as a monolith to be opposed in its totality. The state, as Ernesto Laclau and Chantal Mouffe put it, 'is not a homogeneous medium, separated from civil society by a ditch, but an uneven set of branches and functions, only relatively integrated by the hegemonic practices which take place within it'. This means, they continue, 'that the state can be the seat of numerous democratic antagonisms, to the extent that a set of functions within it – professional or technical, for example – can enter into relations of antagonism with centres of power, within the state itself, which seeks to restrict and deform them'.[27] If a brief for criticism is called for – and I do say *if* – it is one that will enable critical practices to operate multiply and variably on the sites of such contradictions rather than – in constructing a totalising contradiction of its own – outside and independently of them.

This is emphatically *not* to argue against the part that critical practices might play in assisting the development of collective writers' and readers' associations, film discussion groups and so on, whatever their formal relationships to the state. Nor is it to argue against attempts to articulate the concerns and interests that might be formed within these different public spheres so as to produce, however provisionally and partially, points of intersection between them. What it *is* to argue against, however, is a conception of criticism's political vocation which stakes its all on the part it might play in relation to the development of such forms of cultural association, if this is at the expense of a more widely ranging set of critical interventions conceived in relation to the contradictions, tensions and different publics formed within the critical apparatuses operating on the terrains of either the state or the market. Eagleton would do well to follow the logic of his own analysis of the classical bourgeois public sphere and to expect that the business accomplished within such cultural associations would be more likely to take the form of a complex series of negotiations and compromises between varied interest groups rather than the formation of a collective oppositional subject.

The point that is ultimately at issue behind Keane's and Eagleton's contrasting formulations of the public sphere concerns the concept of politics which shapes them. In Keane's case, politics is conceived not as a separate sphere or level of action which mediates between civil society and the state but rather, as Ernesto Laclau and Chantal Mouffe put it, as 'a type of action whose objective is the transformation of a social relation which constructs a subject in a relationship of subordination'.[28] While not denying the significance of the varied micro-politics which this conception allows for, the ultimate task, for Eagleton, consists in the degree to which they participate in politics conceived as a set of macro-processes which aim at the revolutionary transformation of social relations all at one go. The limitations of this political imaginary are, by now, surely evident. None the less, it is only in relation to such a generalised conception of politics that the idea of criticism having an equally generalised political vocation makes sense. If Eagleton's approach is mortgaged to a nineteenth-century concept of criticism, so it is also to a nineteenth-century concept of politics: the two support and sustain one another.

CRITICISM AND THE UNIVERSITY

That this dual legacy is an encumbrance is most evident in Eagleton's attitude toward the relations between criticism and the university. Commenting on the moment, in the late nineteenth century, when criticism entered into the universities, Eagleton argues that it thus 'achieved security by committing political suicide; its moment of academic institutionalisation is also the moment of its effective demise as a socially active force'.[29] Clearly, this assessment rests on the conception, noted earlier, of politics as a separate sphere or level of activity rather than a specific type of activity which may inform different institutionally organised spheres of human activity. It also rests on a concept of criticism appropriate to such a concept of politics: that is, as a form of textual commentary which acquires its social effectivity by organising the reader as a subject who takes a meaning from a text with corresponding consequences for his/her consciousness of and mode of relating to and acting within a generalised public arena.

If the concept of politics which motivates the analysis is questioned, however, a contrary case could be argued and with equal conviction: namely, that the moment of criticism's academic institutionalisation, particularly when viewed in the light of its subsequent extension throughout the education system, enormously augmented its power as an effective social force. Indeed, to reverse the terms of Eagleton's analysis, the political weight criticism derived from its earlier institutional articulations in the classical bourgeois public sphere seems insubstantial by comparison. If Arnold spoke sometimes as a 'citizen of the republic of letters' and sometimes as a state functionary, we should not follow his own cultural reflexes in mistaking the former for a more powerful and influential voice than the latter which opened up to criticism a new, vastly expanded and more concretely embedded sphere of activity than it had hitherto enjoyed. Nor need we echo Leavis's regret at the disappearance of an educated public by viewing his activities as an educational propagandist as merely compensating for the decline in criticism's function in the public sphere. To so argue would be to concur with the 'false-consciousness' of these theorists as, in adjusting criticism to the new and positive possibilities offered by the development of an extended and public education system, they represented their activities to themselves as a fall from an earlier golden age.

It is true, of course, that, once its position in the universities and the schooling system was consolidated, criticism no longer functioned as an oppositional force, not even in the equivocal sense Eagleton outlines. But neither was the sphere of action thus constituted entirely without its tensions and ambiguities. If, as has been remarked, Leavis substituted teaching for politics, the result was a politicisation of teaching – the production of an oppositional space within the education system – which has subsequently provided by far and away the most important institutional supports for the kinds of critical practices Eagleton advocates. There should be no mistake about this. Work in educational institutions, which involve extended populations for increasingly lengthy periods of their life cycles, is in no way to be downgraded or regarded as less vital politically than the attempt to produce new collective forms of cultural association with which criticism might engage. Politically committed teachers face enough discouragement without the added suggestion that the 'real work' lies elsewhere. Before we all abandon the education system and set up camp in the counterpublic sphere, a little head counting would do no harm. There is little doubt that, if the numbers reached by radical critical practices in the two spheres were weighed in the balance, the scales would tip decisively in favour of the former. Nor is there any doubt that, without the sustenance provided by the contradictory spaces within the education system, the institutions comprising the counterpublic sphere would have a hard time of it: put simply, socialist and feminist publishing houses, radical theatre groups, and so on are massively dependent on the sales and audiences generated, in part, by the contradictory critical spaces that have been won within the education system.

This reinforces my earlier argument that the notion of a counterpublic sphere constructed in a space outside of and in opposition to the state is incoherent. The fate of such initiatives is intimately tied up with the possibility of sustaining, developing and exploiting the multiple contradictions generated within state bureaucracies. This in turn, however, requires that attention be paid to the differing and specific ways in which such contradictions are constituted. In the case of the functioning of practices of textual commentary in the education system, this calls for a history of criticism that is less concerned with the move from one significant critic or school of criticism to another than with the development of institutionally embedded forms of instruction, training and examination. Not all practices of textual commentary acquire their social effectivity by organising the reader as a subject who takes a meaning from the text, with subsequent consequences for his/her consciousness and mode of relating to and acting within a generalised public arena. Others do so by producing the reader as an agent who performs a practice within specific institutional domains to become the bearer of specific certificated competences. Some fulfil these two functions simultaneously.

To broach the matter in these terms produces a significantly different inflection of the political issues at stake in the question of criticism's contemporary function. Paradoxically, Eagleton himself has provided one of the more suggestive pointers to alternative ways in which this question might be most productively posed, at least in so far as it bears on the relations between criticism and class politics. In his *Literary Theory: An Introduction*, Eagleton argues that, assessed in class terms, the most significant long-term impact of the rise of English as a discipline was registered in relation to the formation of the petit-bourgeoisie. Eagleton's contention here is less that English served to cultivate a distinctively petit-bourgeois world-view than that it equipped the petit-bourgeoisie with a set of practical competencies which, in producing a cultural orientation distinct from the frivolous amateurism of ruling-class culture, enabled it to emerge and consolidate its position as a powerful intellectual stratum, albeit one pressed into the service – although equivocally – of the bourgeoisie. Francis Mulhern notes that the period over which English consolidated its institutional power in the universities – roughly, from the 1890s to the 1930s – also saw a vast expansion in the size of the intelligentsia and a significant alteration in its social composition. Lower-middle-class children were recruited, through an expanded education system, into an enlarged range of functions within state bureaucracies, new media and, of course, private corporations.[30] Viewed in this light, the crucial bag of tricks that English delivered was that of enabling a whole social stratum to negotiate its mobility while retaining, but also reorganising, the typical dual class orientation of the petit-bourgeoisie. If, as Eagleton puts it, 'the lower middle class has a deep animus against the effete aristocracy perched above it, it also works hard to discriminate itself from the working class set below it'.[31] English, in its *Scrutiny* moment, Eagleton suggests, fitted the bill in being both 'radical in respect of the literary-academic Establishment' and 'coterie-minded with regard to the mass of the people'; its concern with 'standards' challenged ruling-class dilettantism at the same time as it 'posed searching tests for anyone trying to muscle in on the game'.[32]

None of this, of course, happened because Leavis wrote a few books or because of the functioning of criticism at a general societal level. It happened because of the educational deployment of criticism – a development whose significance cannot be properly appreciated if it is construed as a fall from criticism's earlier function in the classical bourgeois public sphere. Indeed, what is most striking is the symmetry between these two moments for in both criticism is assessed as playing a vital role in relation to the processes of class formation. The fact that, in one case, it did so on the site of institutions formed up outside the state whereas, in the other, it operated within state institutions is no occasion to view the latter as a 'withered' version of the former. To the contrary, such changes need to be assessed in their positivity as having produced a new and historically more pertinent sphere for the social deployment of criticism in response to shifting processes of class formation and their institutional domains and, in consequence, producing new modalities of critical activity also. Of these, the most important was the examination, I. A. Richards's contribution to the development of Cambridge English and, in many respects, the lynchpin of the discipline's practical social function. As Chris Baldick shows, the examination, viewed in relation to Richards's theory of value, was to function as a practical means of assessing the relative value of persons – hence the stress on an atheoretical, direct and experiential response to the text.[33] All the same, the response sought was to be a close and attentive one, alert to the slightest nuances of meaning, thus testifying to a specific cultural competence acquired through a process of training rather than to a generalised familiarity with culture. In thus prizing a petit-bourgeois seriousness and the stress which, according to Bourdieu and Passeron, is placed on the role of effort in petit-bourgeois attitudes to culture, in contrast to a bourgeois dilettantism which prizes an effortlessly acquired general cultural knowledgeability as the sole valid sign of persons of taste, English helped to colonise the educational apparatus for the petit-bourgeoisie.[34] At the same time, it helped to colonise the petit-bourgeoisie for that apparatus and the other state and private bureaucracies into which they were recruited, usually in subaltern functions, in articulating petit-bourgeois anti-capitalist ideologies to bourgeois romanticism.

It is arguable that one of the central issues facing contemporary critical practices concerns the role they have acquired through their educational deployment in relation to the formation of the petit-bourgeoisie – to the formation of its skills, competencies and practical capacities as well to the forms of ideological and political solidarity into which it is compacted. This, however, is to raise questions of a detailed and specific kind regarding the composition of the student body, career trajectories, the effects of different kinds of pedagogy and assessment, or the kinds of ideological dis-articulations and re-articulations that can most productively be made in the light of these considerations. These questions cannot be explored here except to note that the idea of a strategy for criticism that would, in one of the areas of its practice, be conducted with the aim of influencing the formation of intellectual strata has a perfectly respectable Marxist lineage in the writings of Gramsci. Equally, it has a pertinent point of reference in Foucault's conception of the function of the 'specific intellectual' and the part to be played by such intellectuals in contesting 'the microphysics of power'[35] – a project which can hardly be engaged with if critical activity is pitted entirely against the monolithic dominance of the state and commodity form.

These larger considerations to one side, though, my main point is that generalised conceptions of criticism's function such as Eagleton advocates, especially when they rest on lapsarian accounts of criticism's history, deny any space within which questions of such a detailed and specific kind can even be put. If the relations of practices of textual commentary to the varied and dispersed concerns of contemporary cultural politics are to be meaningfully specified, it is necessary to displace the mood of inquiry from the singular to the plural: to ask not what the function of criticism is, as if it *must* have one and *only* one, but rather what roles might be performed by different types of critical practice given the varied institutional domains, and their varied publics, in which such practices are operative. This variable conception of *criticisms* and their *functions* recognises that literary and other cultural texts are differentially inscribed in the social in such a way as to be involved in a range of practical affairs rather than just one: the formation of subjectivities. It is not, though, a recipe for a live-and-let-live, anything goes anywhere anytime pluralism. To the contrary, to pose the question of criticism's functions plurally and therefore specifically is to sharpen critical disputes by giving them a clearer and more practically defined focus. If, as Leavis argued, the idea of criticism cannot cogently be presented as 'a matter of general-ities',[36] this is ultimately because, at this level, there are no practical means of discriminating between competing prescrip-tions. They thus function purely as exhortations rather than being amenable to any critical calculations.

There is, however, a more general difficulty associated with the very generality of the concept of criticism. For the term has both a specific meaning, one limited to the practices of textual commentary generated in the wake of Romanticism, and a more generalised contemporary usage whereby it encompasses any and all practices of textual commentary, from rhetoric through to structuralism and deconstruction. Such is the sedimented cultural weight of the first usage, however, that it tends to be carried over and applied wherever the term is used and, willy-nilly, to inscribe the ethics and politics of Romanticism in the discourses in which it functions as a central term. Certainly, this is so whenever the question of Marxist criticism is at issue in that such discussions – and Eagleton is by no means alone in this – are usually organised around the assumption that Marxism must supply a criticism which can function as an heir to its Romantic forebears and, thereby, supply an alternative to the latter's misbegotten contemporary progeny. While Eagleton's work has supplied the occasion for this essay, it should be clear that its broader purpose is to suggest that the concept of criticism is so massively encumbered with an ineradicable ideological burden as to render its appropriation by Marxism problematic. Like the commitment to developing a Marxist aesthetics, the project of a Marxist criticism with a singular function – no matter how complexly laminated that function might be – should perhaps be laid finally to rest.

10

CRITICISM AND PEDAGOGY: THE ROLE OF THE LITERARY INTELLECTUAL

In *Criticism and Social Change*, Frank Lentricchia advances a conception of criticism's political vocation which takes its bearings from Foucault's and Gramsci's writings on the nature and function of intellectuals. Adopting, initially, a Foucaultian tack, he argues that questions of critical politics can be intelligibly debated only on the condition that they are related to the specific positions and functions of literary intellectuals in advanced capitalist societies. The key question, he contends, is whether the literary intellectual can 'do radical work *as* a literary intellectual'.[1] In posing the question this way, Lentricchia seeks to distance our ways of thinking about criticism from the influence of earlier conceptions of intellectuals, particularly those summarised in the Gramscian polarity of traditional versus organic intellectuals.[2] The political potential of criticism, he thus argues, will remain concretely unachievable so long as the literary intellectual is conceived as a 'bearer of the universal, the political conscience of us all' or, contrariwise, as one whose practice must be 'overtly, daily aligned with and empirically involved in the working class'.[3]

Instead, in order to identify where and how radical critical work might most appropriately be conducted, Lentricchia looks to Foucault's conception of the specific intellectual — to the theory/practice connection represented, as Foucault puts it, by intellectuals who 'have got used to working, not in the modality of the "universal", the "exemplary", the "just-and-true-for-all", but within specific sectors, at the precise points where their own conditions of life or work situate them. . . .'[4] The literary intellectual, Lentricchia thus argues, must be thought of as 'one whose radical work of transformation, whose fight against

244

oppression is carried on at the specific institutional site where he finds himself and on the terms of his own expertise, on the terms inherent in his own functioning as an intellectual'.[5] A conception of critical politics, then, which, in being related to the concrete institutional sites in which critical activity is actually conducted, resists 'the eviscerating notion that politics is something that somehow goes on somewhere else, in the "outside" world, as the saying goes, and that the work of culture that goes on "inside" the university is somehow apolitical. . .'.[6]

Lentricchia's forthrightness in this matter deserves applause. Yet, if questions of critical politics are to be posed in this way, a whole further set of questions regarding the precise forms of politics at stake in the institutional sites within which criticism is conducted needs detailed and specific answers. However, no sooner has Lentricchia secured the ground on which such questions might be put than he dissolves it again as his discussion takes another tack, a Gramscian one this time. Rewriting Marx's XIth Thesis on Feuerbach to suggest that 'the point is not only to interpret texts, but in so interpreting them, change our society', Lentricchia argues that criticism's function needs to be thought of as integrally enmeshed within struggles for hegemony. Its role here is partly that of undermining existing forms of hegemony via its capacity to produce 'a culturally suspicious, trouble-making readership'.[7] Yet it is also envisaged that criticism may contribute positively to organising an active counter-hegemony by participating in 'the establishment of consent, of a "we"'.[8] To do so, Lentricchia further ventures, entails that criticism incorporate the texts of which it speaks into a discourse of history even though, as he frankly concedes, such a discourse cannot be validated, cannot be guaranteed as history's truth. Suggesting, rather, that historical discourse be understood as 'rhetorical and without foundation',[9] Lentricchia underscores its lack of epistemological supports:

> It is not a question of whether there is a teleology in history . . . but a question of forging the rhetorical conditions for change, a question of forging a teleological rhetoric, of creating, through the mediations of such discourse, a collective will for change, for moving history in the direction of our desire.[10]

One problem with this argument consists in its theoretical eclecticism. For it is by no means easy to see how a conception of criticism's function derived from Foucault's perspectives on the specific intellectual might be harmonised with Gramsci's theory of hegemony. While by no means the first to propose a subsumption of Foucaultian categories within the political logic of Gramsci's work, there are good reasons for doubting whether such a theoretical merger can ever be effected. As Barry Smart argues, Foucault's conspectus on the functioning of power/knowledge relations within governmental apparatuses undoes the very terms of the theoretical machinery which the political logic of Gramsci's theory of hegemony requires:

> In short the 'State'/'civil society' dichotomy is displaced by an analytic focus upon the 'governmentalisation' of power relations, that is the development of individualising techniques and practices which are reducible neither to force nor to consent, techniques and practices which have transformed political conflict and struggle through the constitution of new forms of social cohesion.[11]

Of course, there are some similarities between Foucault and Gramsci. The most important, to my mind, consists in their common focus on the minutiae of everyday life. If Gramsci is concerned with the ways in which consent to ruling-class values is secured via the ways in which those values permeate the tissue of everyday life, Foucault is equally attentive to the capillary mechanisms through which power is dispersed throughout the social so that it gets everywhere, organising the seemingly most incidental aspects of everyday behaviour. Yet even these similarities are more apparent than real. For the theoretical assumptions from which Foucault and Gramsci proceed are so sharply contrastive as to belie any significant points of contact between the perspectives from which this seemingly shared ground is approached.

Thus, whereas Foucault is concerned with the social role of *knowledges*, conceived as discourses which function as 'the truth' in a particular set of social relations, Gramsci remains committed to the general Marxist conception of *ideology* as the opposite of true knowledge. Similarly, Foucault examines the deployment of knowledges as components of the power relations of specific and localised *social technologies* – the prison, the asylum and so on – and stresses the respects in which these do not function in a unified manner as the expressions of a general form of power. By contrast, Gramsci is concerned with the functioning of ideologies within different branches of *the state* which, although not expressing an achieved unity, he none the less sees as characterised by a strong tendency toward the unification of a power emanating from a relatively unified source: the power bloc. So far as the terrain of the everyday is concerned, Foucault emphasises the role of social technologies in regulating the conduct of *the populace* conceived as *objects of social administration*. This, in turn, leads to a concern with the *body/soul* nexus: with how power relations invest the body, train it, force it to perform tasks with a view to effecting a modification of the soul in the production of self-monitoring and self-regulating agents of conduct. For Gramsci, by contrast, the emphasis falls on the role which ideologies play in organising cultural, moral and intellectual leadership over *the people* conceived as *subjects of political action* – on the struggle, that is, for *hearts and minds* where ideologies are assessed for their 'psychological' influence in organising the consciousness of political subjects.

Most telling of all, however, is Foucault's well-known hostility to attempts to organise a unified source of opposition to a generalised conception of power. In stressing the dispersed and relatively uncoordinated structure of power relations, so Foucault also stresses the multiple and dispersed forms of resistance to power; a micro-physics of power begets a micro-politics of resistance. Yet the possibility of unifying oppositions to a generalised form of power, centred on the state, under the leadership of the working class is central to the Gramscian project of a counter-hegemony. Given this, together with Foucault's equally strong objections to continuist narratives of history, the prospects for marrying his conception of the specific intellectual to a political brief for criticism which assigns it the role of contriving historical teleologies to organise 'a collective will for change', are not auspicious. To take Lentricchia's references to the specific intellectual seriously would entail – as Lentricchia himself proposed in *After the New Criticism* – that criticism's function be thought of in terms of detailed and specific strategies for contesting the 'politics of truth' within the apparatuses in which literary intellectuals are most concretely engaged.

Of course, differing from Foucault is not the same thing as being in error.[12] My point is rather that Lentricchia cannot have it both ways. If he seems able, in *Criticism and Social Change*, to claim both Foucaultian and Gramscian credentials for his conception of criticism's political function, this is because he invites these traditions into a shotgun marriage which neglects their theoretical incompatibilities. Moreover, it is by virtue of what this mis-match suppresses that Lentricchia, while seemingly moving in the direction of the specific and the concrete, remains strongly under the influence of traditional concepts of criticism as a generalisable practice of subject formation. For, contrary to the expectations engendered by his opening formulations, Lentricchia has relatively little to say regarding how critical practices should most appropriately be conducted in the light of the specific political and power/knowledge relations of the various institutional sites – universities, journals – within which it is primarily conducted. Rather, these are conceived more in the form of the particular places from which the literary intellectual is to engage in the general task of 'changing society' by influencing the consciousness of individuals.

Yet, I think Lentricchia is right to suggest that the Foucaultian and Gramscian traditions provide useful resources for theorising the different types of political relations in which – to use a less-loaded term – practices of textual commentary are actively implicated. I say this for two reasons. First, of the many challenges to Marxist thought in recent years, Foucault's work has proved the most productive in terms of the new forms of historical inquiry it has enabled. Far from subjecting Marxism to a purely abstract critique, Foucault's work has called Marxist thought into question concretely and specifically in providing a developed alternative to traditional Marxist accounts of the mutations in the structure of power relations associated with the development of capitalism. It has thus disputed 'historical materialism' on grounds which are consistently – indeed, painstakingly – historical and materialist. Second, however, it is equally true that Gramsci's work has served as the point of departure for what has proved to be one of the most open and adaptable traditions of contemporary Marxist thought. This is especially true of Marxist cultural studies in which the now extended phase of 're-thinking Gramsci' in the light of contemporary developments in deconstruction and discourse theory has resulted in many of the founding assumptions of classical Marxism being pushed to, and beyond, their breaking points. To use these resources productively, however, it is necessary to respect their differences. Rather than forcing them into a marriage of convenience, therefore, I shall seek to weave a way between them, to rub them against one another with a view to considering the role of the literary intellectual, as both critic and pedagogue, in the light of the theoretical friction which results from their mutual abrasion.

CRITICISM AND THE 'CRISIS' OF POSTMODERNITY

Few would quarrel with Lentricchia when he argues that criticism should aim to produce 'a culturally suspicious, trouble-making readership'; to so comment on literary texts as to produce an active interrogation of the ways in which they are written into, are written by, and support strategies of power: on this, at least, there is fairly widespread agreement between the main schools of contemporary 'left' criticism – Marxist, feminist, Foucaultian, deconstruction. The difficulty, however, is that Lentricchia seems to have in view a culturally suspicious reader who will, so to speak, only ever have one eye open. For what else are we to make of his further suggestion that criticism should contribute to creating a collective will for change by forging (making/inventing) a teleological rhetoric without foundations? For is not this to envisage a reader who, while vigilantly alert to bourgeois myths of history, will willingly consent to being hoodwinked by progressive myths of history? As if the reader who is culturally suspicious *vis-à-vis* one region of discourse should behave as a cultural dope when confronted by another which, although differing in content, exhibits the same structure.

The position embodies a misjudged response to the postmodernist contention, most forcefully argued by Lyotard, that the procedure of justifying claims to knowledge through 'an explicit appeal to some grand narrative, such as the dialectics of Spirit, the hermeneutics of meaning, the emancipation of the rational or working subject, or the creation of wealth' is now discredited.[13] As we have seen, one response to this argument consists in the attempt to keep such narratives in place by insisting on their historical groundedness. Jameson's endeavour to incorporate postmodernism itself within an epochal conception of history by construing it as the cultural dominant of late capitalism is a case in point.[14] More characteristically, however, Marxist responses to postmodernist critiques have showed the orientation of 'yes, but . . .' which Lentricchia articulates. While conceding the theoretical force of such critiques in accepting that grand narratives of

249

history and the subjects they produce cannot be sustained in the form necessary to legitimise claims to knowledge – cannot, that is, be secured as anything other than discursive effects – this response still insists that the production of a subject, of a 'we', a community, is necessary in the organisation of political action and views the insertion of such a subject within a totalising narrative of history as necessary to this end.

Yet, it is simply no use conceding, in one breath, that progressivist narratives of history are merely discursive effects rather than the reflections and outcomes of 'real processes', while going on, in the next, to say: well, let's re-invent them anyway and hope that no one will notice this change in their status. Or, that if they do, they will voluntarily submit to such narratives in order, through this subjective compliance, to put the motor-mechanisms of History back into place and start them going again. This is merely to cast Marxist thought in the role of a discursive trickster destined to pull the same old rabbit out of the hat every time. On second thoughts, though: a different rabbit. In classical Marxism, it is the movement of History that produces the collective subject which enables History to be moved – to move itself – on to its next stage. Here, by contrast, the process of subject formation is envisaged as entirely spectral. The subject's solidity, so to speak, has melted into air. Entirely dependent on a will to discourse, its substantiality has evaporated. A subject with no name, for its identity cannot be specified in advance of its discursive constitution, its phrase constantly exceeds its content. The classical Marxist discourse of subject formation is retained, but only at the price of a radical hollowing-out of its substantive kernel.

The political and cultural resonances of the argument are also disquieting. For to argue that a collective subject is to be produced through a will to discourse, through forging teleological rhetorics without foundation, comes perilously close to competing with right-wing appropriations of postmodernism on their own terms. 'To speak of things that one wants to connote as real,' Umberto Eco writes with such practices in mind, 'these things must seem real. The "completely real" becomes identified with the "completely fake". Absolute unreality is offered as real presence.'[15] When, as Deborah Silberman has shown, 'faking it' becomes a central component in the cultural strategy of the right, the only appropriate response is one of painstaking and meticulous historical scholarship.[16] To suggest, in these circumstances, that socialists should 'fake it' too reduces politics to a contest between big black myths and little white ones.

Responses to postmodernist arguments from within Marxist cultural studies have displayed a greater degree of openness in conceding that postmodernism has established a genuinely new ground for theoretical debate as well as requiring that the ends toward which socialist cultural politics are directed, and the means through which such politics should be pursued, be rethought. In contrast to Lentricchia's 'yes, but . . .' – which allows the theoretical force of the postmodernist critique of narrative, but then denies it any political pertinence – Marxist cultural studies has related itself to postmodernism more in the mood of 'yes, and . . .' Consequently, where the force of postmodernist criticisms of Marxist thought is granted, these have served as the basis for elaborating new ways of theorising the field of political practices – following their implications through to produce a new political logic rather than stemming their import so as to *suture* an old one back into place.

At the same time, however, such responses have also been characterised by their refusal to take postmodernism entirely on its own terms.[17] Stuart Hall, in particular, has emphatically rejected postmodernism's epochal sense of itself in claiming to embody a 'final rupture or break with the modern era'.[18] More generally, the postmodernist tendency to weave together often quite disconnected problems to produce a generalised discourse of crisis has been treated with caution and, often, outright scepticism. Perhaps most important, however, has been a tendency to turn postmodernist discourses of crisis back on themselves in arguing that what such discourses register as crises are more appropriately viewed as positively enabling of new forms of thought and political action. This is the tenor of Dick Hebdige's useful survey of the currency of postmodernism which, in spite of variations between its different septs and branches, he argues can be broadly characterised in terms of three oppositions: an opposition to totalising forms of social and historical theory, an opposition to teleological modes of reasoning, and an opposition to utopian representations of the future.[19] Although, in my view, not going far enough in refusing to construe these as symptoms of a general crisis, Hebdige's major concern is to work *with* rather than *against* these arguments in advancing a conception of Marxism whose claims to contemporary pertinence depend precisely on its abandonment of any transcendental theoretical guarantees or fixed finality of political purpose.

The position subtending these arguments derives from the extended process of reworking Gramsci which has defined the central theoretical trajectory of Marxist cultural studies since the late 1970s. While divergent positions have been elaborated in the course of this process, all have shared the view that Gramsci's writings embody a theoretical and political logic that is, in some degree, in tension with that of classical Marxism. They have therefore been regarded as lending themselves more usefully than any other theoretical corpus in the Marxist tradition to reviewing the assumptions of classical Marxism in the light of perspectives selectively culled from discourse theory, deconstruction and postmodernism. Using these latter to highlight the respects in which the Gramscian perspective of hegemony requires a definitive break with classical Marxist conceptions of ideology in order to be consistently theorised, the resulting formulations are often a long way indeed from anything Marx or Engels would have recognised. Hebdige, summarising generally shared ground within the cultural studies position, thus argues:

> From the perspectives heavily influenced by the Gramscian approach, nothing is anchored to the 'grands récits,' to master narratives, to stable (positive) identities, to fixed and certain meanings: all social and semantic relations are contestable hence mutable: everything appears to be in flux: there are no predictable outcomes. Though classes still exist, there is no guaranteed dynamic to class struggle and no 'class belonging': there are no solid homes to return to, no places reserved in advance for the righteous. No one 'owns' an 'ideology' because ideologies are themselves in process: in a state of constant formation and reformation.[20]

Within this model, Hebdige continues:

> there is no 'science' to be opposed to the monolith of ideology, only prescience: an alertness to possibility and emergence – that and the always imperfect, risky, undecidable 'science' of strategy. There are only competing ideologies themselves unstable constellations liable to collapse at any moment into their component parts. These parts in turn can be recombined with other elements from other

ideological formations to form fragile unities which in turn act to interpellate and bond together new imaginary communities, to forge fresh alliances between disparate social groups. . . .[21]

It is to this task of 'forging' fresh alliances that politics is committed, where politics is conceived as a process of ideological articulation – that is, connecting the values and beliefs which circulate among subordinate social strata to socialist values and aspirations which, in turn, must be adjusted to take account of the values and beliefs they must negotiate in order to become hegemonic – through which new communities of political action, incorporating new political constituencies, will be brought into being. Moreover, such articulatory practices must be conducted without any conception of a definite positivity of the social to guide them. Rather than consisting in a definite set of relations between classes whose identities can be specified and which exist in precisely determinable relations to one another, the social:

> is instead a continually shifting, mediated relation between groups and classes, a structured field and a set of lived relations in which complex ideological formations composed of elements derived from diverse sources have to be actively combined, dismantled, bricolaged so that new politically effective alliances can be secured between different factional groupings which can themselves no longer be returned to static, homogeneous classes.[22]

There is no sense, here, of contriving a teleological rhetoric or grand narrative of history as an indispensable means of interpellating subjects for a collective political programme. To the contrary, there is a degree of *jouissance*-like exultation in the fact that subjects need no longer be thought of as being enchained within and by a uni-directional historical process which engenders them. For, if neither history nor the fixed positionality of social classes can guarantee a subject for socialism, then so, by the same token, there are no given or absolutely fixed limits to the constituencies which may be recruited in support of socialist objectives. Freed from the constraint which required that the working class be regarded as ontologically privileged, by virtue of its class position, as the co-ordinating subject in the transition from capitalism to socialism, socialist discourse is now able to multiply its outlets and channels of circulation, proliferating in grasping on to new objects and reaching out to new constituencies in a movement to which, in principle, no definite limits can be assigned.

These are welcome developments in terms of the more open, adaptive and flexible forms of debate that they have produced. None the less, the difficulty cannot be masked that this openness is sometimes produced at the price of a corresponding emptiness. As with Lentricchia, criticism is to take part in a process of subject production. The subject to which this process is committed, however, is not a singular one imaginarily inserted within a narrative of history. Rather, its concern is with the organisation of groups of subjects, imaginary communities, whose interests and identities are to be grafted on to, articulated with, one another to bond them into fragile unities, momentarily fused in the pursuit of common objectives, only then to fly apart awaiting their inscription into new, and possibly quite unrelated discursively constructed political positionalities. It is in this sense that the position involves a positive response to postmodernism, and especially to its opening up of the putative closures of modernist narratives of history, the economy, technology, etc. If nothing is guaranteed, then anything is possible: this, at least in some measure, is the thinking behind a theory of articulation which, in another version of 'the will to discourse' position, set itself the task of discursively organising relations both of equivalence (producing a 'we') and of contradiction (organising that 'we' in opposition to a 'them') but without being able to specify any fixed or positive co-ordinates within which such a politics must be conducted.

RHETORICAL POLITICS

The consequence, however, is often a politics which is all phrase and no content, except for a rhetorically contrived one; a politics in which everything is invested in the production of a 'people versus the power-bloc' antagonism, but one in which it becomes impossible to say who 'the people' are or who they might be, whom this category should include and whom it should exclude. In short, a populism without foundation, a conception to which I must admit my own work has contributed:

> The question as to who 'the people' are, where they/we will be made to stand, line up and be counted, the political

direction in which they/we will be made to point: these are questions which cannot be resolved abstractly; they can only be answered politically. The point is not to define 'the people' but to *make* them, to make that construction of 'the people' which unites a broad alliance of social forces in opposition to the power bloc count politically by winning for it a cultural weight and influence which prevails above others.[23]

The incoherence of this position stems from its attempt to run with two contradictory arguments at the same time. To predicate a politics of articulation on the production of a people/power bloc antagonism requires, as Gramsci argued, that the aspirations of divergent subordinate social strata should be connected to the organic ideologies of 'a fundamental class' which, by virtue of its major structural role within the economy, is able to supply a relatively fixed point of reference around which other popular forces might be nucleated to form a unified force. Yet to conceive of social relations as being pierced by discourse through and through entails a denial of the assumption that the social can be thought of as characterised by a definable structure which generates stable points of anchorage for articulatory practices to latch on to. Instead, the social is thought of as comprising a network of discursively constructed positionalities; that is, points of subject formation linked to discursively constituted social projects rather than fixed positions within a given structure of social relations. Moreover, since such positionalities can be stitched into varying relations to other positionalities, then so their relations to different political projects are constantly mutable depending on the conduct of articulatory practices. Just as the meaning of the signifier cannot be specified except in terms of its differing from and endless deferral to other signifiers, so discursively constructed positionalities are caught up in an endless play of differences and deference in relation to other positionalities.

The points at issue between these contrasting formulations are evident in the different positions of Stuart Hall on the one hand and Ernesto Laclau and Chantal Mouffe on the other. While sharing a commitment to rethink Gramsci in the light of contemporary discourse theory, Hall and Laclau//Mouffe part company with regard to the theoretical positions from which this activity is conducted and the political ends to which it is directed.

For Hall, the leading representative of the Marxist cultural studies position, the purpose is to open up Gramscian categories so as to make them more mobile and flexible, but within a theoretical and political logic which remains substantially the same. Thus Hall remains committed to a conception of the positivity of the social deriving from 'the determining lines of force of material relations' which result from differing modes of the expropriation of nature.[24] In setting a limit to the effects of discourse, this conception allows – when all the necessary qualifications have been made regarding the non-necessary class-belongingness of ideologies – that the more open and multifarious field of political relations which results from according discursive considerations a limited sway may still be thought in terms of their function in relation to a relatively fixed class antagonism which supplies the unifying principle of an extra-discursive real. Yet, as we have seen on a previous occasion,[25] Hall is able to secure this position only at the price of a manifest contradiction. Having identified 'the determining lines of force of material relations' as a point of fixity in relation to which the positivity of the social can be constituted, he immediately undercuts this argument in contending that 'we need to think material conditions in their determinate discursive form, not as a fixed absolute'.[26] Putting discourse on both sides of the equation in this way means that 'material conditions', since they are discursive in form, cannot fulfil the role assigned them of setting limits to discourse.

For Laclau and Mouffe, by contrast, the purpose is to open up Gramscian categories so as to go beyond them to stake out a new theoretical and political logic – one not committed to a conception of the positivity of the social, and one which subsumes socialist projects within what is advanced as the broader political logic of a radical and plural democracy. The connection between these theoretical and political logics is provided by Laclau's and Mouffe's account of the role of discourse in the production of political antagonisms and, thereby, in the production of a political space comprised of multiple, dispersed and essentially non-unified – and non-unifiable – fields of political struggle. So far as the first of these questions is concerned, Laclau's and Mouffe's central problem is, as they define it, 'to identify the conditions in which a relation of subordination becomes a relation of oppression, and thereby constitutes itself into the site of an antagonism'.[27] Defining relations of subordination as ones in which 'an agent is subjected to the decisions of another',[28] they argue that the development of 'struggle against subordination cannot be the result of the situation of subordination itself'.[29] The power embodied in such relations may be resisted in a variety of ways in the daily practices of subordinated agents, but such resistance is unable to take the form of a political struggle directed toward ending the relations of subordination concerned unless those relations come to be perceived as relations of oppression. Yet there is no dynamic internal to relations of subordination – whether between classes or between genders, for example – which guarantees that they will be so perceived. This is dependent on the importation into those relations of a discursive exterior which names and judges them as, precisely, illegitimately oppressive ones. As Laclau and Mouffe exemplify their argument:

> 'Serf', 'slave', and so on, do not designate in themselves antagonistic positions; it is only in the terms of a different discursive formation, such as 'the rights inherent to every human being', that the differential positivity of these categories can be subverted and the subordination constructed as oppression.[30]

In this respect, Laclau and Mouffe interpret the French Revolution as the founding political event of modernity, introducing a new political imaginary which has resulted in the proliferation of new fields of discursively produced political antagonisms. The key significance of the democratic discourse bequeathed by the French Revolution, they thus argue, was that of providing 'the discursive conditions which made it possible to propose the different forms of inequality as illegitimate and anti-natural, and thus make them equivalent as forms of oppression'.[31] From this point of view, the nineteenth-century development of socialist politics rests on the same principle as the parallel development of feminist politics. Both were produced by the discursive transformation of what were previously merely relations of subordination (capital/labour; patriarchy/women) into relations of oppression, thereby enabling their constitution as sites for the development of antagonistic politics committed to the abolition of the relations of subordination which characterise these respective spheres. Nor, since their constitution is equally discursive, can the field of socialist or class politics be privileged above, or act as a rallying centre for, that of feminist or, indeed, any other field of political struggle. It is not the capital/labour relation as such that gives rise to socialist politics but the intervention within that relation of democratic discourse. Far from constituting an organising centre for other spheres of political struggle, therefore, socialist politics is merely a sub-species of the more general form of politicality produced by the fermenting effect of the spread of democratic discourse as it introduces the grit of antagonism into relations of subordination and establishes equivalences between the different forms of struggle against subordination which it begets.

These perspectives, then, provide the theoretical and historical co-ordinates for the political logic of a radical, plural and libertarian democracy. In place of the conception of a singular political space organised around a pre-representational contradiction between capital and labour, Laclau and Mouffe argue that the course of modern politics consists in the multiplication of a series of differentiated political spaces organised in relation to a complex network of cross-cutting, discursively organised spheres of political antagonism. This entails that the autonomy and respective specificities of these different political spheres must be respected, thereby disavowing the claim that the struggles of any particular subordinate group might be constituted as generally representative and so capable of serving as a political centre to which the struggles of other subordinate strata might be articulated. As Mouffe puts the point:

> It is, in fact, evident that we must give up the whole problematic of the privileged revolutionary subject, which, thanks to this or that characteristic, granted a priori by virtue of its position in social relations, was presumed to have some universal status and the historical mission of liberating society. On the contrary, if every antagonism is necessarily specific and limited, and there is no single source for all social antagonisms, then the transition to socialism will come about only through political construction articulating all the struggles against different forms of inequality. If, in certain cases, a particular group plays a central role in this transition, it is for reasons that have to do with its political capacity to effect this articulation in specific historical conditions, not for a priori ontological reasons.[32]

Yet, as is evident from this passage, Laclau and Mouffe are still committed to a politics of articulation as part of a hegemonic project – the construction of a new social order – which, in its turn, requires the organisation of a new historical subject. The task, as Laclau put it in an earlier essay, is:

> the construction of a new hegemony, one which is conceived as a differential articulation, not founded on the necessary centrality of any one sector, but which constructs a new popular historical subject, starting from the points of convergence of the numerous fragments generated by democratic struggles during the past decade.[33]

Viewed from this perspective, a politics of democracy pure and simple is judged insufficient:

> This is because the logic of democracy is simply the equivalential displacement of the egalitarian imaginary to ever more extensive social relations, and, as such, it is only a logic of the elimination of relations of subordination and of inequalities. The logic of democracy is not a logic of the positivity of the social, and it is therefore incapable of founding a nodal point of any kind around which the social fabric can be reconstituted.[34]

A politics of democracy, in other words, can only be a negative, oppositional politics; it lacks a conception of the positivity of the social capable of supporting forms of politics directed toward the construction of a new social order. Laclau's and Mouffe's response to this difficulty is twofold: first, to subsume the concept of socialism within that of democracy and, second, to expand the concept of democracy – insisting that it must be radical, plural and libertarian – so that it can serve as a means of envisioning a new kind of society. Democracy, so defined, thus becomes a way of imagining a new set of social arrangements to be aimed for, while also supplying a set of regulative principles governing the political means by which such political ends are to be pursued. So far as the former is concerned, a society which is radically and plurally democratic will be characterised by relations of equality and democratic self-management in all spheres of social life whose irreducible diversity will be recognised rather than being subjected to any co-ordinating, and therefore coercive, centre of social authority. Such an end is achievable, Laclau and Mouffe argue, only if the principles it embodies inform the political means by which it is pursued. Thus, rather than according any particular

259

subordinate social group a leading role in organising a counter-hegemony, their argument, reduced to its essentials, is that subordinate groups should become democratically self-hegemonising. As the spread of democratic discourse introduces contradiction into relations of subordination, transforming them into relations of oppression, the task for 'the left' becomes that of establishing relations of discursive equivalence or, as Mouffe puts it, solidarity between those forces engaged in struggles within and against such differentially constituted relations of oppression.[35] A new form of hegemonic project, then, whose movement, since it does not envisage that all social antagonisms can be definitively resolved to produce a unifying centre for society's self-management, does not prefigure the establishment of a state.

In this sense, the end is the way. The objective is not to produce a discursive opposition between the people and the power bloc that will be activated in a moment of revolutionary rupture to give rise to the direction of society by a new commanding centre of social authority. Rather, it is to set in motion an ongoing process in which the discursive antagonisation of new spheres of social relations is accompanied by the discursive construction of points of connection between them, but ones which do not militate against the essentially polyphonic structure of these voices in struggle. For this reason, the possibility of a unified discourse of the left is erased:

> Discursive *discontinuity* becomes primary and constitutive. The discourse of radical democracy is no longer the discourse of the universal; the epistemological niche from which 'universal' classes and subjects spoke has been eradicated, and it has been replaced by a polyphony of voices, each of which constructs its own irreducible discursive identity. This point is decisive: there is no radical and plural democracy without renouncing the discourse of the universal and its implicit assumption of a privileged point of access to 'the truth', which can be reached only by a limited number of subjects.[36]

Neither Laclau nor Mouffe has explicitly addressed the implications of their political conceptions for the concerns of cultural criticism.[37] None the less, it is possible to see how their arguments might secure a place for a radical conception of criticism's function that is not dependent on, nor serves as a means for, band-aiding a holistic Marxism back into place: namely, that

260

of so reading cultural texts as to introduce discursive relations of antagonism into a limitless array of social relations while also assisting in organising 'a chain of equivalences between all the democratic demands to produce the collective will of all those people struggling against subordination'.[38] Indeed, in calling for an unending war of position whose instruments are primarily discursive, ideological and cultural, criticism necessarily assumes a central place within Laclau's and Mouffe's conception of politics. Politics and criticism are viewed as intrinsically related activities as the tasks of the former are seen to devolve essentially upon the production of political antagonisms and alliances by primarily discursive means. Moreover, criticism-as-politics is still conceived as directed toward its traditional end – effecting a transformation in the consciousness of subjects – albeit that this activity is now no longer regarded as tending toward the production of a unified subject constituted in relation to a central, pre-discursive antagonism.

In these respects, then, the programme of a radical and plural democracy might seem to offer a means whereby traditional Marxist conceptions of criticism might be negotiated into an acceptable relation with postmodernist and post-structuralist conceptions of the highly differentiated and dispersed structure of the field of social relations. The hegemonic task to which Lentricchia summons criticism might be re-installed within this political space without the need for rhetorically contrived teleologies of historical development. Laclau and Mouffe may insist that utopian thought is necessary for the constitution of a radical political imaginary. 'The presence of this imaginary as a set of symbolic meanings which totalise as negativity a certain social order', they write, 'is absolutely essential for the constitution of all left-wing thought.'[39] None the less, they are equally insistent that the organisation of such an imaginary is not dependent upon, nor even aided by, a discourse of historical necessity. Indeed, such discourses are regarded as fundamentally at odds with their revised conception of hegemony whose very logic, as Laclau summarises it, requires that there can be no guarantees as to the outcome of attempts to articulate particular struggles to a hegemonic project:

if the relationship between various social contents is constituted by an immanent and necessary logic of history, then any struggle to hegemonise these contents would be superfluous; but if, on the contrary, a hegemonic struggle *is* possible, then it can only mean that the *very sense* of such contents is not predetermined.[40]

These perspectives do not, of course, equate directly with those of Marxist cultural studies, not even in its most revisionist forms. As has already been noted, Laclau and Mouffe describe their own work as post-Marxist while their central preoccupations derive from an engagement with the concerns of political theory rather than with those of cultural analysis. If, none the less, I have summarised their arguments at some length this is because there is sufficient common ground between the two positions, and the theoretical trajectories they respectively embody, to allow their juxtaposition to usefully highlight problems shared by both. When asked to outline his reasons for resisting Laclau's and Mouffe's conception of the intrinsically discursive structure of social relations, Hall initially suggests this is because 'the notion of society as a totally open discursive field' is unable to suggest positive directions for political practice since it can offer 'no reason why anything is or isn't potentially articulatable with anything'.[41] As he goes on to elaborate the argument, however, the ground shifts slightly:

> Their problem isn't politics but history. They have let slip the question of the historical forces which have produced the present, and which continue to function as constraints and determinations on discursive articulation.[42]

While conceding that there is no intrinsic or necessary connection between particular ideologies and specific social strata, Hall's contention is that, none the less, such connections are historically secured. Specific ideologies, through their protracted articulation to particular strata, come to be historically embedded in those strata. Just as, in language, the fact that 'there is no one, final, absolute meaning – no ultimate signified, only the endlessly sliding chain of signification' does not mean 'that meaning does not exist' – that particular meanings are not secured for and by language users in particular contexts – so the theoretical potential for ideologies to be detached from an association with one class, say, and be articulated to another does not mean that, in practice, specific class/ideology articulations are not historically secured and have a privileged weight over other possible class/ideology positionalities.[43] It is, moreover, the accumulated historical weight of such articulations which serves as a check on the potential 'moveability' of ideologies and so, also, on the capacity of discursive articulations to produce new historical subjects.

These are important differences leading to significantly different forms of political address and emphasis. For Hall, for example, the historical associations of socialism entail that this be thought of as the leading discourse to which other discursively constructed antagonisms should be articulated rather than, as Laclau and Mouffe suggest, subsuming socialist politics within the broader programme of a radical and plural democracy.[44] None the less, the *form* of politics envisaged is the same in the two cases: that, essentially, of a rhetorical politics which aims at the discursive construction of new political subjects – and at drawing those subjects into new forms of discursive alignment with one another – by means of a struggle for the systems of interpellation which govern the enlistment of subjectivities. Abandoning earlier conceptions of politics in which political actors as well as the lines of alliance/opposition between them are held to follow from structurally determined positions and interests, the logic subtending both positions views political relations as essentially rhetorical constructs. Where and how lines of political alliance/opposition are drawn and who ends up struggling with whom, and against whom, are questions which are not resolvable independently of the ways in which discourse organises political antagonisms and establishes relations of equivalence between them. Indeed, if politics has a by-word, it is, for both Hall and Laclau and Mouffe, articulation: severing the discursive connections which characterise right-wing hegemonic projects and forging new ones which will effectively articulate (that is, bring together and connect) a 'rainbow alliance' of popular struggles – this, in effect, exhausts the tasks of political reasoning as they can be posed within this tradition.[45]

Jeffrey Minson has put his finger on the central weakness of this conception of politics. Given that it can no longer be assumed that socialist politics derive their coherence from an objective (economic) foundation, he argues, much recent Marxist thought has sought to establish a basis for socialist objectives and practices in 'a kind of negotiated ideological common denominator, which would express the current aspirations of a multiplicity of political forces, such as party and trade union organisations, social movements, issue campaigns and significant sections of the electorate'. Even supposing such an ideological formula could be found, however, Minson contends that since 'such political ideological constructions at most are a means of *aligning* political forces under a common banner, they do not address the problems of effectively *allying* socialist forces and the fields of practical activity in which they are engaged'.[46] Effective alliances within differentiated political spheres, that is to say, will not necessarily be assisted by the constructions of banner politics to the degree that common ideological denominators are necessarily unable to take sufficient account of the specific array of agents, practices and issues which define the ground of politics in different areas of social life.

Clearly, this is not to deny that the rhetorical construction of political relations may have an important bearing on the way in which political issues are conceived and on the manner in which political divisions are posed and fought through. It is, however, to insist that the rhetorical components of politics have to be assessed in terms of the spheres of effectivity that are proper to them rather than, in being accorded an unmeasured stress, being equated with the sphere of politics *tout court*. This is, in my view, the root difficulty with the formulations of Laclau and Mouffe. In reducing politics to a struggle for the rhetorical construction of the social, they are unable to offer any convincing account of the mechanisms through which rhetorical constructions of political interests and subjects are able to connect with and concretely influence differently constituted spheres of political relations. Politics becomes a matter of slogans and, in the case of Laclau's and Mouffe's conception of a radical and plural democracy, of slogans which are unlikely to accomplish what is asked of them.

This is partly due to the radical relationalism of their position which, as Hall rightly points out, does logically result in a politics which can provide no positive pointers as to which ideological interpellations should be articulated to one another to produce the new historical subjects which the programme of a radical and plural democracy calls for. Hall, as we have seen, looks to the sedimented historical weight of previous articulations to provide a check and limit on the kinds of articulation of ideological interpellations that can be contemplated in any particular set of circumstances. Owing to their more radical conception of the indeterminacy of the social, however, Laclau and Mouffe can specify no positive limits for the conduct of articulatory practices.

All that can be offered is the general formulation that such practices must seek, first, to transform discursively relations of subordination into relations of oppression, and, second, to establish relations of equivalence and solidarity between the struggles of the different social forces which thus define themselves, or are defined, as oppressed. Since relations of oppression are discursively rather than positively defined, however, there is no limit to the number of fields of oppression that may be produced. All that is required is that relations of subordination, in which one agent or set of agents is subject to the decisions of another, should come to be seen as relations of oppression via the intervention of democratic discourse.

Of the many pressing difficulties this occasions, two are of paramount significance. First, the possible infinite extension of fields of political struggle which this conception engenders militates against the possibility of establishing relations of equivalence between different oppressed strata because those who find themselves constituted as oppressed in one field of struggle will be addressed as oppressors in another. The formulation is so elastic that it is difficult to envisage any individuals who would not find themselves contradictorily addressed as between different relations of subordination. Moreover, and this is the second difficulty, it is impossible, except arbitrarily, to provide grounds on which one particular set of interpellations might be preferred above another. The anti-statist arguments of the small business sector, for example, rest just as much on the logic of the discursive transformation of relations of subordination into relations of oppression as do traditional Marxist representations of the capital/labour relation.

While Laclau and Mouffe recognise these difficulties, their proposed solution merely underscores the problem. Acknowledging that discursive constructions of relations of oppression may be multiple and contradictory, they contend that the key issue then concerns the relative weight of, and struggle between, left- and right-wing articulations of the democratic struggles of different political subjects: women, workers, gays, the social movements, etc. The difficulty is evident. For this is merely to fall back on a pre-given sense of the structure of the field of political relations, as if 'left' and 'right' had some self-evident meaning rather than being relational, and therefore inherently unstable, terms whose meaning depends on the rhetorical context in which they are used. There is, in fact, no logical reason why, from Laclau's and Mouffe's perspective, the struggle of workers versus capitalists should be politically privileged above, or regarded as more left-wing than, the anti-statist arguments of small businessmen – arguments which often claim precisely the radical democratic political lineage upon which Laclau and Mouffe seek to found a new political imaginary. Such a preference could only be based on the view that the relations of subordination involved in the capital/labour relation are fundamentally different in type from those involved in the relations between the state and the private sector. If this is so, however, then it must be for reasons which have nothing to do with the discursive construction of those relations – which, of course, would upset the whole theoretical applecart on which the political logic of a radical and plural democracy is based.

Many of these difficulties have their roots in the libertarian strain of Laclau's and Mouffe's argument. To envisage an end to relations of subordination where such relations are defined as ones in which an agent is subject to the decisions of another is mere day-dreaming. Mouffe gropingly recognises this when she argues that 'the rights of some entail the subordination of the rights of others'. When she concludes that the 'defense of acquired rights is therefore a serious obstacle to the establishment of true equality for all', however, she misses the equally important point that the establishment of new rights requires the coercive subordination of some agents to the decisions of others.[47] Programmes of positive discrimination for disadvantaged groups are unimaginable without the development of new forms of subordination of this type.

The more fundamental problem, however, consists in the pass Laclau and Mouffe have been sold by the postmodernist perspectives with which they seek to engage and to bend to their own purpose. Rejecting the possibility that society can be referred to a transcendental principle (such as the economy) which fixes it as a rationally ordered and knowable totality, Laclau and Mouffe opt for a discursive conception of the nature of the social according to which it is held to consist in the relations of difference/articulation between discursively constructed positionalities. Social relations are thus constitutively relations of meaning and, as such, viewed from the perspectives of deconstruction, are never finally pinned down to a definite fixity and so are constantly in a state of flux. This is only one side of the coin, however. The other, as Laclau elaborates it in proposing a revised understanding of the role of ideology, consists in the interplay between rival hegemonic projects in their attempts discursively to fix the social by imbuing it with a definite content and meaning:

> The social is not only the infinite play of differences. It is also the attempt to limit that play, to domesticate infinitude, to embrace it within the finitude of an order. But this order – or structure – no longer takes the form of an underlying essence of the social; rather, it is an attempt – by definition unstable and precarious – of acting over that 'social', of *hegemonising* it. . . .

> The ideological would consist of those discursive forms through which a society tries to institute itself as such on the basis of closure, of the fixation of meaning, of the non-recognition of the infinite play of differences. The ideological would be the will to 'totality' of any totalising discourse. And insofar as the social is impossible without some fixation of meaning, without the discourse of closure, the ideological must be seen as constitutive of the social.[48]

Yet this is to say that the field of social relations consists in nothing but the interplay and balance between rival totalising discursive constructions of society as they are activated through people's heads. That such totalising constructions exist and are influential in organising constituencies of support for particular courses of action is not in question. But we beg leave to doubt that they can carry the burden which such formulations place on them. There is no need to resurrect the notion that society is founded on a pre-discursive ground to argue that, their discursivity notwithstanding, particular regions of social life are characterised by a definite positivity consisting in the rules, regulations, tactics and strategies whereby conduct is regulated, norms legislated, competing claims adjudicated, decisions made, programmes planned and implemented and so forth – and all without any reference to totalising ideological constructions of the social. Laclau's and Mouffe's error is that of a recidivist individualism. For them, the only possible social agents are individuals or groups of individuals ideologically forged into collective subjects. They are consequently unable to take any account of the activities of institutions and organisations as social agents, or of the activities of individuals – not as ideological subjects, but as functionaries of such institutions and organisations. As a consequence, the possibility of any specific and differentiated politics related to the particular exigencies of specific spheres of social and political management is mortgaged in advance to a totalising politics of opposition which is defined exclusively as a politics of consciousness.

GRAMSCI, FOUCAULT AND LITERARY POLITICS

Political struggle, then, is equated with cultural struggle which, moreover, is conceived as being conducted by exclusively cultural or ideological means – an endless politics of the signifier orientated to the production of new subjects and the articulation of relations of solidarity between them. While many of its advocates would fight shy of the extreme discursivity of Laclau's and Mouffe's position – Hall, for example, characterises it as 'a reductionism upward, rather than a reductionism downward, as economism was'[49] – this is, by and large, the conception of politics which has resulted from the postmodernist rereading of Gramsci undertaken from within Marxist cultural studies. As such, no matter how thoroughly other aspects of Gramsci's work might have been warrened out, it is a position that remains remarkably faithful to the main contours of the Gramscian problematic. For the political conspectus of Gramsci's theory of hegemony is, essentially, that of a politics of consciousness – and one which is, relatively speaking, indifferent to the specific properties of the particular institutional sites in which it is conducted. While Gramsci is conventionally, and rightly, credited with stressing the material and institutionally embedded character of ideologies, the fact remains that specific institutional sites are – again, by and large – conceived merely as empty vehicles for the ideologies they relay. As a consequence, cultural politics are cast in essentially the same light – that of disorganising consent to prevailing forms of hegemony and winning support for a counter-hegemony – no matter what the institutional domain of their occurrence. Institutions, in effect, are conceived as merely places from which to conduct a politics of the signifier as part of a struggle for the terms in which consciousness is organised.

To be clear, the resistance registered here is not to this project as such. Indeed, so far as questions of critical politics are concerned, so reading literary texts as to form subjects in opposition to particular forms of power and to forge lines of mutual support between such subjects is, it seems to me, as much as can and needs to be said about what can be asked of criticism and what it can be expected to deliver. This is not to anticipate that such lines of mutual support will ever eventuate in the production of a new collective actor committed to a common programme which envisages the total transformation of existing social relations. I have already indicated, in the preceding two chapters, why I think such totalising conceptions of criticism's function are mischievous. My point here, however, is that, in so far as literary criticism forms part of a politics of consciousness, its role in this regard is no different in principle from that of other regions of cultural criticism – film or television criticism, for example, or heritage site criticism. As such, therefore, it does not exhaust the sphere of *literary* politics nor even address the questions which might be regarded as being most distinctive of this sphere.

Which brings me back to my reasons for doubting the particular fusion of Gramscian and Foucaultian perspectives Lentricchia proposes in seeking to specify the political functions of the literary intellectual *qua* literary intellectual. When Lentricchia commits the literary intellectual to assisting in the formation of a 'we' so as to move history in the direction of our desire, the model of the literary intellectual he has in mind is patently that of the critic for whom the university is just a place from which to engage in debates in more general and more public arenas. But what are we to make of this as a requirement placed on the literary intellectual as a pedagogue? While it may provide a few suggestions as to the content of the curriculum, what guidance does it offer as to how the literary pedagogue should conduct him/herself within the institutionally structured relations between teachers and taught within which his/her activity is inevitably located? What light does it throw on the relations of correction and supervision – which are also relations of subordination – which characterise the literary pedagogue's orientation to the relations between student and literary text?

Barry Smart, it may be recalled, casts doubt on the kind of subsumption of Foucaultian perspectives within the Gramscian problematic of hegemony which Lentricchia proposes. Hegemony, in so far as Foucault is concerned with it, Smart argues, concerns not the organisation of consent to forms of domination operative at a general societal level. Nor is it secured by means of a psychological struggle for consciousness. Rather, it concerns the achievement of particular forms of social cohesion within the differentiated domains of population management which, in the Foucaultian paradigm, constitute the field of the social. As such, moreover, it is secured not by consent to ruling ideologies but:

> by way of practices, techniques, and methods which infiltrate minds and bodies, cultural practices which cultivate behaviours and beliefs, tastes, desires, and needs as seemingly naturally occurring qualities and properties embodied in the psychic and physical reality (or 'truth') of the human subject.[50]

In short, it concerns the politics of truth peculiar to particular regions of social managment where such politics are understood as concerning the ways in which distinctions between true and false, existing in the form of institutional routines rather than abstract propositions requiring consent, fashion human conduct in ways which operate quite pre-consciously. As Foucault once summarised his concerns:

> To put the matter clearly: my problem is to see how men govern (themselves and others) by the production of truth (I repeat once again that by production of truth I mean not the production of true utterances but the establishment of domains in which the practice of true and false can be made at once ordered and pertinent).[51]

If Foucault has any lessons for cultural theory, it is that the politics of cultural institutions are not reducible to a politics of consciousness; that what goes on within such institutions is not only a struggle for 'hearts and minds' but also concerns, and, more distinctively, the deployment of definite technologies of behaviour and forms of human management. Moreover, given that within the Foucaultian paradigm the functioning of power by and through systems of truth is endemic in society, and that there can therefore be 'no power-free or power-less society, no millenial end of history towards which oppressed, exploited or dominated subjects may be led or guided',[52] the task for the specific intellectual becomes that of examining the truth/power symbiosis which characterises particular regions of social management – with a view not only to undoing that symbiosis but also, and of necessity, installing a new one in its place.

270

This would require that the literary intellectual be concerned with the regimes of truth which regulate the functioning of literary institutions. As has already been argued in an earlier chapter, such questions devolve centrally upon the organisation of a distinctively literary system of truth by means of that artefact of literary criticism – the unfathomable text – which, while allowing that some statements may be disqualified as false, partial, inadequate or incomplete, allows none to be validated as finally true. It is, we have suggested, following Hunter, this regime of truth that governs the organisation of the sphere of literary pedagogy in providing, via the student's guided dialogue with the literary text, a means for a career of corrective self-formation conducted in relation to the values invested in the teacher as an ethical exemplar. It would be premature to conclude that this system of truth is entirely oppressive and should therefore be dismantled. None the less, the question should be raised. The difficulty with Lentricchia's formulations, ultimately, is that they envisage simply using this regime of truth without interrogating its functioning or its consequences. For what else does the programme of conducting criticism so as to form a 'we' amount to except a means of exploiting the cultural authority of the critic and his status as a moral-political exemplar in order to initiate a process of moral and political reform on the part of the reader? This is simply to work complicitly with literature's inside without offering any revaluation of that inside, of the history of its formation or the political logic of its current functioning.

271

11

INSIDE/OUTSIDE LITERATURE

Toward the close of *The End of Art Theory*, Victor Burgin is at pains to stress that theorising art's specificity institutionally and historically, rather than essentially and formalistically, offers no support for a politics of art which would situate itself outside its object. To the contrary, the shift of focus entailed by this perspective deprives 'outsiderism' of any possible coherence. For since, viewed institutionally rather than aesthetically, art comprises a complex heterogeneity of discourses and practices, it 'offers no *singularity* which may be confronted from an unproblematical "outside"'.[1] To recommend art's subversion, therefore, is merely a gestural politics, a form of ultra-leftist posturing which fails to take account of the real conditions − institutional and discursive − with which political strategies must engage if they are to have any effect on the conduct of artistic practices or the reception of works of art. This being so, Burgin concludes:

> Rather than play Samson between the pillars of the museum, − which is, anyhow, futile − we should recognise that the museum is no more 'irretrievably bourgeois' than is, for example, the movie theatre, or the classroom − all such spaces are sites of perpetual contestation over 'what goes on' in them, what gets shown, what gets discussed, what issues get raised and taken out of the museum into the surrounding social institutions: in short, what *truths* are (re)generated as prisms of perception and frameworks of action.[2]

If, similarly, I have sought to get outside 'literature' − outside, that is, its conception as an aesthetic category − it has been with a view to identifying the theoretical and political possibilities which might flow from a revised conception of literature's particularity once this is understood institutionally and historically. Whatever its difficulties, the concept of literature cannot simply be dispensed with. While its conventional understanding as a uniquely privileged kind of writing cannot be sustained, the term does cogently designate a specific, but non-unitary, field of institutionally organised practices – of writing, reading, commentary and pedagogy. 'Outsiderism', when literature is defined in this way, is simply not an option. In its historical and institutional specificity, literature poses particular problems of analysis which, if they are to be effectively engaged with, require particular instruments of theorising. Equally, in constituting a specific set of regimens regulating the forms in which designated texts are socially deployed, literature both invites and requires forms of political intervention which, inescapably, must be located within it. Getting outside 'literature', in the first sense, is the process of coming to *see* it, in the second sense, and so to see also the need for more complex and differentiated forms of theoretical analysis and political engagement than those flowing from positions which, fixed on an essentialist definition of literature, seek either to invert its dominant rhetorics or, *per contra*, to oppose it – monolithically – from a discursively constructed exterior.

In concluding, therefore, I shall briefly review the implications of the shifts of perspective I have advocated by drawing together three lines of argument developed in the foregoing discussion. These concern, first, the purposes of literary history; second, the nature of literature's sociality; and, third, the forms of politics specific to literature.

LITERARY HISTORY: FIXING THE PAST

Had it been 'less terrorised by the spectre of "formalism"', Barthes argues in *Mythologies*, 'historical criticism might have been less sterile. . .'.[3] It might also, he intimates, have been more historical too. 'To parody a well-known saying,' as Barthes puts it, 'I shall say that a little formalism turns one away from History, but that a lot brings one back to it.'[4] The formalism Barthes had in mind here was structuralist semiotics, the progeny of Saussurean linguistics, whose formalist descriptions of semiotic systems served to identify the particularity of those systems more precisely and, thereby, to render them more amenable to historical criticism. Yet

Barthes's argument has not remained tied to this theoretical context. The passage cited above could serve just as well as a motto for post-structuralism in the claim, variously enounced, that it is only when history is conceived as comprising a play of endlessly unresolved and unresolvable differences that its analysis can be genuinely and radically historical.

This appropriation of the mantle of history, however, has so far proved largely rhetorical. Historical in principle and in the abstract, post-structuralism has had relatively little impact on the terms in which particular historical debates are conducted. Nor is it likely to do so: mainly because, at root, its conception of history is a literary one. Transferring the properties of the literary text to the past — understood, in this light, as an unfathomable text, unreadable as such yet also infinitely rewritable — post-structuralism is unable to offer any positive knowledge of the past that is capable of surfacing and having effects within the disciplined procedures of historical scholarship. Instead, history becomes an occasion for extending the sphere of application of literary techniques of reading as the past, redefined as a literary object, is constituted as the site for an unconstrained, diachronised wordplay.

The consequences of this literarisation of the past are readily discernible in the post-structuralist perspective on history proposed by Derek Attridge. Like Barthes before him, Attridge's concern is to dislodge the wedge driven between the concerns of historical criticism and those of formalist analysis by those readings of Saussure — such as Lentricchia's and Jameson's — which view Saussure's separation of the concerns of synchronic and diachronic analysis as having provided the primary theoretical justification for modern forms of ahistorical, formalist criticism. The problem with Saussure's conception of the relations between synchrony and diachrony, Attridge argues, is not that it de-historicises language. To the contrary, the contention that the semantic aspects of language use are regulated by synchronically constituted systems of rules emphasises their historical variability and, hence, mutability. In severing the connection through which earlier etymologists had sought to tie language use down to a presumed set of original — and therefore true — meanings, Saussure allowed the determination of meaning to be thought of as intrinsically social and historical. 'Saussure's insistence on the separation of synchrony and diachrony,' as Attridge puts it, 'replacing "authentic" meaning by the meanings possessed for a specific group at a specific time, opens the door to history, while a naive view of the historicity of language completely closes it.'[5] At the same time, however, since this separation entails that the past is denied any consequential bearing upon the present, there would seem to be no good reasons to pass through the door to history which it opens. The same argument which vouchsafes language its historicality dooms its historical analysis to scholastic irrelevance:

> Although the notion of the arbitrary sign within a synchronic system of differences valuably demonstrates that language is a product of historical forces . . . we seem to be effectively prevented from making anything of that history by the very same notion.[6]

The contradiction, Attridge argues, arises from an inconsistency in Saussure's attitude toward etymology which leads him to deny that the synchronic state of a language may be significantly affected by a community's own interpretation – however erroneous – of its language's history. Thus, rather than including the effects of popular or folk etymology – accounts of word origins and derivations, for example, or the influence of 'incorrect' spelling on pronunciation – as integrally a part of a given synchronic state of a language, Saussure refuses these any systemic significance. They are 'not to be taken seriously into account', have 'only minimal importance or none at all' or are 'monstrosities' which should be placed 'under observation in a special compartment'.[7] Why? Because, Attridge contends, to allow the constitution of the synchronic system of language to be affected by the functioning of diachronic interpretations of its history would undo the rigid separation of synchronic and diachronic which subtends the Saussurean paradigm.

Yet this is so only in a special sense. For, in so far as this distinction refers to different states of a language (past and present), there is no need to disallow the role of such diachronic accounts which, since they concern the influence of presently existing interpretations of past usage rather than past usage as such, can be cogently represented as parts of a language's current synchronic constitution. Their diachronic register is merely an aspect of synchrony. The difficulty lies elsewhere in that to grant such diachronic interpretations a systemic status would deprive language of precisely that systematicity which the synchronic/diachronic distinction was meant to secure. It would entail accepting that language is subject to the influence not merely of abstract and impersonal forces but also to the contingent effects of the practices of language users, including the stories they tell themselves or are told about their language's past:

> What he regards as secondary is history as intellectual construct, the history of the etymologist and the theorist of language (academic or popular), and when history in *this* sense interferes it threatens the whole distinction between synchrony and diachrony, and therefore the stability and self-consistency of the system, and has to be excluded. The stories we tell about the past are all very well in their place, but they have no right to change the way we live.[8]

In this light, then, Attridge proposes a positive revaluation of the role of etymology. Understood not as logic nor as science but as a form of rhetoric, it influences present forms of language use 'not as a series of "real events" (which, having passed, can no longer intrude) but as the only way in which history *can* intervene in the present, as a theory or story of the past'.[9] As such, it is distinguished from other influences on language solely by the fact that the accounts it offers play in the register of history. It is a form of word-play distinguished from others by the fact that the associations it establishes are organised as part of an account of the relations between past and present:

> In both devices, the same process occurs: two similar-sounding but distinct signifiers are brought together, and the surface relationship between them invested with meaning through the inventiveness and rhetorical skill of the writer. If that meaning is in the form of a postulated connection between present and past, what we have is etymology; if it's in the form of a postulated connection within the present, the result is word-play. Word-play, in other words, is to etymology as synchrony is to diachrony.[10]

The same, in essence, is true of history. History influences the present not as a set of real past events but as an account of such events in their bearing on currently existing relationships. 'Similarly,' Attridge thus argues, 'the power possessed by history, whether that of the professional historian, the journalist, or the man-in-the-street, to sustain or alter prevailing value systems depends on the success of the stories it tells.'[11] As such, the principal choice Attridge confronts us with is that between, first, histories which, in offering a particular truth of the past – and claiming an objective status for this truth – close it down and, thereby also, in aligning the present to a particular past, close down the possible futures into which that present might be thought to eventuate; or, second, histories which have an 'unjamming' effect in relation to the closed truths of the past, thereby freeing up the present for new forms of thought and practice. Etymology, if used in a freewheeling way, as a rhetorical technique, can thus fissure 'the synchronic surface of the text, introducing diachronic shadows and echoes, opening the language to shifts of meaning that can never be closed off';[12] it can 'be used to unsettle ideology, to uncover opportunities for change, to undermine absolutes and authority – and to do so without setting up an alternative truth-claim'.[13] And, in this respect, etymology – serving, now, as the paradigm for history in general – is, as Attridge candidly notes, very much like literary criticism. For the literary text, like that of a language's past or any past, can also 'be read for or against absolutes, transcendence, closure, authentic and original meaning'.[14]

The argument is both dexterous and, at many levels, extremely persuasive. It is also close to the view, argued earlier in this study, that the past must be regarded as a particular socially organised zone of representation existing within the present. Yet there are also differences deriving from the post-structuralist gloss Attridge places on this position. These concern, in the main, the exclusively oppositional, critical role Attridge envisages for the histories he favours – undermining existing truths but not establishing new ones in their places; resisting closures in the name of an indefinite openness. The disadvantage of this exclusively contestatory conception of history is that, while opening up new potential areas of practice, it does not offer the prospect of any positive knowledge which may be of service in relation to those practices. If history is to be of any service in the present, then, to recall the respects in which the modes of production of historical truths are similar to those of legal truths, it must be capable of producing an 'actionable' past; statements of past events which function as truths for the purpose of the conduct of present practices.

The establishment of such truths, moreover, is not a matter of mere word-play. This is not to deny the rhetorical aspects of history writing which Hayden-White and others have stressed. It would, however, be foolish to overlook those disciplined procedures, constitutive of scholarly history, which regulate the way in which truth statements are adjudicated in historical inquiry. Diachronised word-play is not a sufficient condition for the production of historical truths: that is, for the emergence of positive knowledges (which need not be thought of as absolute or transcendent) capable of serving as a basis for definite courses of action within the present. Attridge's mistake is to treat the past as a seamless web and, in neglecting its differentiated structure as a zone of representation, to overlook the fact that the past, as historians are concerned with it, is not conceivable simply as a text susceptible – even in principle – to being infinitely rewritten. To the contrary, the past comprises a densely regulated zone of statements and procedures which effectively limit what truths might be established as historical and how these truths might be arrived at.

Lentricchia has put his finger on the point I'm after here in contrasting Foucault's approach to history with Derrida's. For Foucault too, of course, the past exists as a set of presently existing realities while history, rather than being conceived as an act of recovery, of memory, is defined as a particular kind of *work*:

> history is the work expended on material documentation (books, texts, accounts, registers, acts, buildings, institutions, laws, techniques, objects, customs, etc.) that exists, in every time and place, in every society, either in a spontaneous or in a consciously organised form. The document is not the fortunate tool of a history that is primarily and fundamentally *memory*; history is one way in which a society recognises and develops a mass of documentation with which it is inextricably linked.[15]

As Lentricchia notes, Foucault's own work on this documentation is dependent on Derrida's critique of the metaphysics of presence. His freeing of analysis from the unities imposed by such conceptions as tradition, genre, or authorial *oeuvres* in order to open up to investigation that discontinuous field 'made up of the totality of all effective statements (whether spoken or written), in their dispersion as events and in the occurrence that is proper to them':[16] these aspects of Foucault's work, Lentricchia argues, are 'made *possible* by Derrida's revision of traditionalist thought in general and of structuralism in particular'.[17] Yet, as he puts it,

Foucault 'is no champion of the *aporia*, no connoisseur of *abyme*'.[18] The past – the mass of documents on which the historian works – is not approached as an instance of 'textuality as *mise en abyme*' but as a set of discursively regulated statements, 'as that internal and informative setting of statement which is open to definition and determinacy'.[19] The difference is clear enough in Foucault's response to Derrida's criticisms of *Madness and Civilisation*:

> in his reading Derrida is doing no more than revive an old old tradition . . . the reduction of discursive practices to textual traces; the elision of the events produced therein and the retention only of marks for a reading . . . what can be seen here so visibly is a historically well-determined little pedagogy. A pedagogy which teaches the pupil that there is nothing outside the text.[20]

Rather than approaching the past as a set of traces to be read allegorically – reading through the said to uncover an unsaid – or, as in deconstruction, to be read as an endless unsaying of the said, Foucault aims at a definite fixing of the past. Its textuality is pinned down by the application of the principle of the rarity of statements which – although not unproblematically so – provides a means of regularising historical events, of grouping them into clusters and assigning them their spheres of effectivity.[21]

In Foucault's case, of course, this concern is manifested in his analysis of the principles governing the emergence and functioning of the objects of discourse – of madness, criminality, the history of nature – within the historical *a priori* of which they form a part. His concern, as Lentricchia usefully highlights it, is with the conditions for being 'in the truth' – not the truth in general, but particular truths, truths which exist not forever 'but only in time and *for* a time'.[22] 'It is always possible,' Foucault writes, 'one could speak the truth in a void; one would only be in the true, however, if one obeyed the rules of some discursive "policy" which would have to be reactivated every time one spoke.'[23]

Now if this is so in relation to the discursive formations of nineteenth-century psychiatry, criminology and biology, the same is true – to bend these arguments to my own purpose – of the contemporary discursive formation of modern historical scholarship. This, too, has its rules governing the formation of objects, its authorities of delimitation, its grids of specification, its own specific sites and modalities. While these are not permanencies – as in any discursive field, rules of formation are also rules of *transformation* – they do impose their constraints, enjoining particular methods of inquiry and discursive policies if statements about the past are to be within the field of historical truth; that is, to be capable of surfacing and having effects there. Far from being 'dangerously naive',[24] Foucault's historical descriptivism is more appropriately regarded as a calculated strategy; a decision about which discursive policy to follow, about which field of truth to be in.

The same is true of post-structuralist perspectives on history. For, at root, these amount to little more than transferring to the field of the past those rules governing the formation of objects within modern literary scholarship. The conception of the literary text as unfathomable – as the site for an endless practice of rereading which can never be wrong yet never be right – is, we have seen, an artefact of the relations of correction and supervision inscribed at the centre of modern literary education.[25] Viewed in this light, the post-structuralist conspectus on the past as an infinite text which can only be endlessly retextualised rests on a transference to the past of literature's own object and procedures. It is a literarisation of the past which must be judged as an attempt to extend the sway of literature's own regime of truth into that of history.

This suggests a slightly different gloss on my earlier argument that the key point at issue in the question of the relations between literature and history concerns how to order the relations between the evidential procedures of two disciplines.[26] For, at least in the particular sense of literature under discussion here, this formulation might be revised to propose that the key issue concerns whether inquiries into literary history are to be governed by the rules of the contemporary discursive formation of history or those of literature. Or, more fully: whether the procedures of historical scholarship should predominate over those of literature to the point of being carried into and disturbing its own regime of truth or, whether, as I am suggesting is the bottom line of post-structuralism, the reverse should be the case.

My own preference in this matter will not, I think, occasion surprise. Given the difficulties associated with literary conceptions of literature, little is to be gained from granting these an extended sphere of operation such that all documents fall within their compass. Textualising the past in such a way that it can be rendered permanently undecidable serves little purpose. Keeping the past open in the cause of keeping present political possibilities open and fluid serves every politics in principle but none in practice. For the latter requires, however provisionally, that the past be fixed, that what can be said of it – what can surface there and be 'in the truth' – be subject to definite limitations, substantive and procedural, if those truths, and the contest over them, are to count for much. This is not a matter of closing down the past but simply of recognising that its openness cannot be infinite if the truths produced there are to prove actionable.

THE SOCIALITY OF LITERATURE

'When I first began to write on critical theory,' Northrop Frye records in 'The critical path', 'I was startled to realise how general was the agreement that criticism had no presuppositions of its own, but had to be "grounded" on some other subject.'[27] Whether biographical, psychological or social in orientation, criticism's tendency to treat the literary text 'as a document to be related to some context outside literature' reflected 'a determination to find the ultimate meaning of literature in something that is not literature'.[28] Setting his face against this tendency, Frye tells us, he sought to provide a foundation for literary studies within literature itself. Rather than merely relating literature to a social and historical background, criticism 'must develop its own form of historical overview, on the basis of what is inside literature rather than outside it; it must 'see literature as, like a science, a unified, coherent, and autonomous created form, historically conditioned but shaping its own history, not determined by any external historical process'.[29]

As is well known, Frye supplies literary criticism with a foundational context immanent to literature in his discovery of those constantly recurring structural elements in the literary tradition which he calls archetypes. The study of such elements, he argues, 'leads to a conception of poetic meaning which is not allegorical, taking us outside literature, but archetypal, placing the poem in its literary context, and completing our understanding of its structure by relating it to the rest of our literary experience'.[30] The purpose of thus securing for literature an inside, however, is not to neglect its outside. Once literature's inside is identified and accorded its proper foundational place within the critical enterprise, then so the critical relevance of its outside seems to fall naturally into place:

> Criticism will always have two aspects, one turned toward the structure of literature as a whole and one turned toward the other cultural phenomena that form its environment. Together, they balance each other; when one is worked on to the exclusion of the other, the critical perspective goes out of focus. If criticism is in proper balance, the 'centrifugal' tendency of critics to move from critical to larger social issues becomes more intelligible. Such a movement need not, and should not, be due to a dissatisfaction with the narrowness of criticism as a discipline, but should be simply the result of a sense of social context, a sense present in all critics from whom one is in the least likely to learn anything.[31]

While this may seem eminently reasonable, literature's inside and its outside have not remained in the places to which Frye assigned them – mainly because its outside, as Frye defines it, has refused to stay put as an outside. Psychoanalytic criticism, Marxist criticism and some forms of feminist criticism: all, in their different ways, have sought to sully that foundational context immanent to literature which Frye so carefully sought to secure by arguing that literature's very essence – its literariness – is the product of some set of psychical or social relations which exist independently of it. Rescued from the status of a contingent context or backdrop, what was defined as outside literature has been imported to the very centre of its inside; what seemed circumstantial has been redefined as constitutive.

The difficulty with this argument is that, while upending the hierarchical ordering of the relations between literature's inside and its outside which Frye proposes, both inside and outside are defined in essentially the same terms. For while allowing that literature's inside is overdetermined by its outside, that inside is still thought of in the same way and as occupying the same place that Frye envisaged for it – as a set of properties that are there, in the writing, in the form. If Frye sought to clear a space for poetics free from the assumptions of allegorical interpretation as applied at the level of individual works, this response has consisted, essentially, in an attempt to allegorise poetics. To the degree that this enterprise has succeeded in collapsing literature's outside (as conventionally regarded) into its inside, poetic and aesthetic conceptions of that inside have none the less governed how social relations external to literature have been invoked and shaped in order to fulfil the task assigned them of accounting for literature's inner constitution. We can see this logic at work in the terms Eagleton proposes for importing literature's outside into its inside, defined in formal and textual terms:

> We are not merely concerned here with the sociological outworks of the text; we are concerned rather with how the text comes to be what it is because of the specific determinations of its mode of production. If LMPs [literary modes of production] are historically extrinsic to particular texts, they are equally internal to them: the literary text bears the impress of its historical mode of production as surely as any product secretes in its form and materials the fashion of its making.[32]

If I, too, have worried at the inside/outside polarity, this has not been with a view to subordinating the former to the latter while still conceiving them in essentially the same terms – literature as a particular form of writing and its 'outside' as a conditioning set of social relations. Rather, it has been to displace the terms of this polarity by proposing a conception of literature's sociality which by-passes the oppositions it establishes. For to theorise literature as a field of institutionally regulated textual uses, functions and effects is to theorise it not as a formally unified set of practices of writing in need of being explained socially but as, precisely, a specific region of sociality on a par with other regions of sociality. Once literature is so regarded, the sense of its having an outside in the manner envisaged by Frye (or his critics) loses coherence. 'Society' and 'history' can no longer be thought of as the locus of literature's external determinations. What is 'outside literature', in this view, is merely what does not fall within it – not because it belongs to another plane of existence but because it happens to fall elsewhere, within some other institutionally regulated zone of practice. This being so, the question as to how to articulate the relations between literature's 'inside' and its 'outside' is replaced by another: how to analyse the imbricative relations between adjacent zones of institutionally regulated practices.

John Frow has come the closest to the position I have in mind when he argues that the essentialist concept of literature should be replaced by that of the literary formation, which he defines as follows:

> The concept designates a set of practices of signification which have been socially systematised as a unity and which in turn regulate the production, the reception, and the circulation of texts assigned to the category. It thus constitutes a common form of textuality for formally and temporally disparate texts, although this shared space may be riven by antagonistic regimes of signification corresponding to different class (or race or gender or religious) positionings and their different institutional bases.[33]

Literature, so defined, consists not of a formally unified field of writing whose commonality is to be accounted for in socio-genetic terms. For the 'texts assigned to the category' may be 'formally and temporally disparate', displaying no essential commonality which has to be fathomed and explained. Its being consists rather in a particular 'form of textuality' – a socially organised field of textual uses and effects – that is to be accounted for in terms of the 'ensemble of norms, practices, and institutional conditions' which produce and sustain it.[34] Literature – or what Frow would call the modern literary formation – is not something whose social underpinnings must be sought elsewhere; it *is* a set of social conditions and its analysis consists in identifying the effects of these conditions – on the uses and functioning of writings produced in earlier periods just as much as the uses and functioning of the forms of writing they support and call forth.

INSIDE LITERATURE

Toward the end of his discussion of Foucault's conception of being 'within the truth', Lentricchia outlines what this might mean for the modern literary critic:

> An ambitious literary critic who desires to lodge his statements within our current sense of critical truth would seek 'co-existence,' as Foucault puts it, with certain other disciplines – Saussurean linguistics, anthropology in the structuralist mode, deconstructionist philosophies, and so on. And his books and articles will speak from institutionally sanctioned sites: a university press, a scholarly journal, but

284

again this is only minimal, for to be critically *dans le vrai* in 1980 is to speak under the imprimatur of certain preferred presses and journals. Above all, certain doctrines will be paid reverence.[35]

As was stated at the outset, I have neither pretended nor aspired to a position for speaking about literature that is immune to these pressures. I have, however, sought 'co-existence' with a different set of disciplines − broadly speaking, history and sociology − from that suggested by Lentricchia. This has been largely with a view to establishing some distance from aesthetic conceptions of the literary, and thus refusing what remains the primary condition for being 'within the truth' of criticism − that of addressing 'literature' as a given and self-subsistent object. My purpose, in advancing an institutional rather than formalist definition of literature, has been to assist in the formation of positions and strategies that will be within literature, so defined, as an ensemble of practices (of classification, commentary and pedagogy) which serve to organise and regulate a particular field of textual uses and effects.

What difference, practically speaking, do such arguments make? Barthes, it may be recalled, imposed his own conditions for being 'within the truth' of criticism. If literature's function is to institutionalise subjectivity, he argued, then the critic 'must lay the fatal bet and talk about Racine in one way and not in another' and, in so doing, 'reveal himself as an utterly subjective, utterly historical being'.[36] For Marxists, I have suggested, this wager has taken the form of investing criticism with a political significance as a means of assisting in the formation of a revolutionary subject. Questions of critical politics, in this view, devolve centrally around the hermeneutic mobilisation of literary texts in ways that will aid the production of a collective political subject capable of effecting a transition from one type of society to another. However, given that, in the presently prevailing political circumstances, such an eventuality is not assessed as in the least likely, this orientation soon gives way to the imaginative extrapolation of the conditions that would be required to support a genuinely socialist literature and criticism.

Both aspects of this position are, in my view, of little concrete service, and for two sets of reasons. The first concerns an assessment of the forms of politics that are enjoined upon socialists by the conditions currently obtaining within advanced capitalist,

285

democratic and pluralist societies. These offer no alternative to reformist politics that take seriously the need to build constituencies and alliances for socialist arguments within the central institutions – economic, political, educational and cultural – of such societies and by means of an appeal to the political sentiments which have an established currency within them. The substitution of the conception of a broadly based popular force – a 'rainbow alliance' of oppressed groups and strata – for the Marxist–Leninist conception of the insurrectionary proletariat as the instrument that will effect our delivery from capitalism in a moment of heightened social contradictions is, under these circumstances, merely diversionary. The fact that such groups occupy positions which are, structurally, subordinate belies their capacity to produce such momentous change while the fact that, however large they might be both individually and collectively, they do not constitute the basis for a potential political majority means that the interests of other social groups must be taken into account in any practical negotiation of socialist arguments into the agendas of actually existing social, political and cultural institutions.

In this light, the perspectives of revolutionary criticism, of criticism as intrinsically oppositional, or of criticism as the instrument for the narrativisation of our desire through the telling of history as one story which beckons us to a utopian future – all of these options, in merely lending a new twist to the discursive grooves established by mainstream criticism, reflect a fundamental failure to pose questions of literary politics in ways that are sufficiently precise and focused to make a sustained difference to the functioning of literary institutions. While using literary institutions for a revolutionary purpose, such conceptions of criticism are too easily absorbed by those institutions to become harmless fire-crackers, predictable critical explosions set to go off at regular intervals, generating momentary controversies which leave the functioning of literary institutions unmodified.

This – to bring me to my second set of considerations – is fundamentally because literary institutions are not reducible to the structure and content of the critical discourses relayed within them. Rather, they comprise, among other things: particular sets of relations between teachers and students, critics and readers; specific techniques of reading functioning as parts of apparatuses of self-formation; specific forms of examination and assessment with consequences for the modes of production and training of intellectual strata, and so on. There is no singular unity here to be opposed, and dismantled by, a revolutionary criticism but a differentiated field of textual functions and effects requiring forms of analysis and intervention that generalised conceptions of criticism cannot deliver.

It is probably foul play, at this point, to rally support for this position from a classic text within the Marxist tradition. I shall do so, none the less. In elaborating his conception of the role of author as producer, Benjamin praises the dual orientation toward existing apparatuses that Brecht recommended – simultaneously using and transforming them. In doing so, however, he points out that this is not a matter of spiritual renewal; 'what is proposed', he argues, 'is technical innovation'.[37] To raise questions of socialist and democratic politics inside literature today is less a question of a search for a revolutionary criticism (or any other kind of criticism) than a matter of technical innovations capable of registering effects within the differing concrete circumstances within which literary texts are socially deployed.

NOTES AND REFERENCES

1 OUTSIDE 'LITERATURE'

1. Barthes, Roland (1977), *On Racine*, New York: Octagon Books, pp. 171–2.
2. *Ibid.*, p. 161.
3. *Ibid.*
4. *Ibid.*, p.172.
5. *Ibid.*
6. Heath, Stephen (1987), 'Literary theory, etc.', *Comparative Criticism,* vol. 9, p. 287.
7. *Ibid.*, p. 314.
8. Yet, even here, a qualification is necessary for, in their genesis in Marx's work, many of these concepts were undoubtedly influenced by nineteenth-century literary and aesthetic conceptions. I merely mean, here, that these concepts have a subsequent history of use and application which – even though this has often been the case – has not always been marked by or tied down to this aspect of their origins.
9. Bennett, Tony (1979), *Formalism and Marxism*, London: Methuen, p. 104.
10. Heath, Stephen (1987), p. 307.
11. Althusser, Louis (1976), *Essays in Self-Criticism*, London: New Left Books, p. 114.
12. *Ibid.*, p. 112.

2 IN THE CRACKS OF HISTORICAL MATERIALISM

1. Williams, Raymond (1977), *Marxism and Literature,* Oxford: Oxford University Press, p. 1.
2. *Ibid.*, p. 3.
3. *Ibid.*, p. 4.
4. Williams, Raymond (1963), *Culture and Society, 1780–1950,* Harmondsworth: Penguin, p. 269.
5. Williams (1977), pp. 5–6.
6. Williams, Raymond (1979), *Politics and Letters*, London: New Left Books, p. 353.
7. Eagleton, Terry (1983), *Literary Theory: An Introduction*, Oxford: Basil Blackwell, p. 11.
8. Lukács, Georg (1971), *History and Class Consciousness,* London: Merlin Press, p. 1.

9. See, for example, Bottomore, T. B. (1975), *Sociology and Social Criticism*, London: Allen & Unwin, chapter 7.

10. Lukács (1971), p. 1.

11. See Jameson, Fredric (1981), *The Political Unconscious*, London: Methuen.

12. Hall, Stuart (1983), 'The problem of ideology – Marxism without guarantees', in Matthews, Betty (ed.), *Marx 100 Years On*, London: Lawrence & Wishart, p. 57.

13. See Althusser, Louis (1969), 'Contradiction and overdetermination' in *For Marx*, London: Allen Lane; and Poulantzas, Nicos (1975), *Classes in Contemporary Capitalism*, London: New Left Books.

14. This is not to suggest that the sociological concept of 'society' and the Marxist concept of 'social formation' should be regarded as interchangeable. The case for holding them distinct is tellingly argued in Therborn, Goran (1976), *Science, Class and Society: On the Formation of Sociology and Historical Materialism*, London: New Left Books. My point here is merely that, viewed from the perspectives of the criticisms under discussion, they are concepts of a similar type. For a fuller exposition of this point, see Giddens, Anthony (1981), *A Contemporary Critique of Historical Materialism*, London: Macmillan.

15. Laclau, Ernesto and Mouffe, Chantal (1985), *Hegemony and Socialist Strategy: Towards a Radical Democratic Politics,* London: Verso, p. 111.

16. See Rorty, Richard (1983), *Philosophy and the Mirror of Nature*, Oxford: Basil Blackwell.

17. Patton, Paul (1983), 'Marxism in crisis: no difference', in Allen, Judith and Patton, Paul (eds), *Beyond Marxism? Interventions after Marx*, Leichhardt: Intervention Publications, p. 60.

18. Hindess, Barry and Hirst, Paul (1977), *Mode of Production and Social Formation*, London: Macmillan, p. 8.

19. *Ibid.*, p.59.

20. *Ibid.*

21. *Ibid.*, p.61.

22. Laclau and Mouffe (1985), p. 3.

23. Patton (1983), pp. 52–3.

24. Laclau and Mouffe (1985), p. 2.

25. Anderson, Perry (1983), *In the Tracks of Historical Materialism*, London: Verso, p. 32.

26. *Ibid.*, p. 12.

27. *Ibid.*, p. 26.

28. *Ibid.*, p. 105.

29. Aronson, Ronald (1985), 'Historical materialism, answer to Marxism's crisis', *New Left Review*, no. 152, p. 76.

30. Hall (1983), pp. 71–2.

31. *Ibid.*, pp. 76–7.

32. As, for example, in his discussion of Yale deconstruction. See Eagleton (1983), p. 144.

33. Eagleton, Terry (1981), *Walter Benjamin, or Towards a Revolutionary Criticism*, London: Verso, p. 97.

34. Eagleton, Terry (1985), 'Criticism and ideology: an interview', *Thesis Eleven*, no. 12, p. 143.

35. Patton (1983), p. 48.
36. Foucault, Michel (1980), *Power/Knowledge: Selected Interviews and Other Writings, 1972–1977*, New York: Pantheon Books, p. 110.
37. Anderson, Perry (1976), *Considerations on Western Marxism*, London: New Left Books, p. 78.
38. Poster, Mark (1984), *Foucault, Marxism and History: Mode of Production versus Mode of Information*, Cambridge: Polity Press, p. 39.
39. Cited in Ryan, Michael (1982), *Marxism and Deconstruction: A Critical Articulation*, Baltimore and London: Johns Hopkins University Press, p. xv.
40. *Ibid.*, p. 21

3 LITERATURE/HISTORY

1. Selden, Raman (1984), *Criticism and Objectivity*, London: George Allen & Unwin, p. 3.
2. *Ibid.*, p. 5.
3. Eagleton, Terry (1976), *Criticism and Ideology*, London: New Left Books, p. 95.
4. *Ibid.*, p. 80.
5. Bennington, Geoff (1987), 'Demanding history' in Attridge, Derek, Bennington, Geoff and Young, Robert (eds), *Post-Structuralism and the Question of History*, Cambridge: Cambridge University Press, p. 20.
6. Eagleton (1976), p. 75.
7. *Ibid.*, p. 72.
8. Widdowson, Peter (1985), 'The acceptable failure of *Literature and History*', *Literature and History*, vol. 11, no. 1, pp. 15–16.
9. *Ibid.*, p. 13.
10. *Ibid.*, p. 16.
11. *Ibid.*
12. *Ibid.*
13. *Ibid.*, p. 17.
14. See Bommes, Michael and Wright, Patrick (1982), '"Charms of residence": the public and the past' in Centre for Contemporary Cultural Studies, *Making Histories: Studies in History-writing and Politics*, London: Hutchinson, p. 266. See also Wright, Patrick (1985), *On Living in an Old Country: The National Past in Contemporary Britain*, London: Verso Editions.
15. See Holderness, Graham (1984), 'Agincourt 1944: readings in the Shakespeare myth', *Literature and History*, vol. 10, no. 1.
16. See Widdowson, Peter (1983), 'Hardy in history: a case study in the sociology of literature', *Literature and History*, vol. 9, no. 1.
17. The key to the importance of history in this regard consists in the use of historians as 'referees' for representations of the past put into circulation outside the academy – in museums, heritage sites, historic re-enactments, costume dramas, period films and television series. While this use of history as a discipline of accreditation had its roots in the nineteenth century, this form of its employment has increased dramatically in the twentieth century.
18. Widdowson (1985), p. 15.
19. Cited in Selden (1984), p. 11.
20. See Barthes, Roland (1970), 'The discourse of history' in Lane, Michael (ed.),

Structuralism: A Reader, London: Jonathan Cape; and Lévi-Strauss, Claude (1966), *The Savage Mind*, London: Weidenfeld & Nicolson.

21. See especially Norris, Christopher (1982), *Deconstruction: Theory and Practice*, London: Methuen; and Norris (1985), *The Contest of Faculties: Philosophy and Theory after Deconstruction*, London: Methuen.

22. See, for example, Eagleton, Terry (1983), *Literary Theory: An Introduction*, Oxford: Basil Blackwell, chapter 4.

23. Bennett, Tony (1987), 'Texts in history: the determinations of readings and their texts', in Attridge *et al.* (1987), p. 66.

24. Lévi-Strauss (1966), pp. 253–4.

25. See their introduction to Attridge *et al.* (1987), p. 4.

26. Norris (1985), p. 29.

27. *Ibid.*, p. 34.

28. Cousins, Mark (1987) 'The practice of historical investigation', in Attridge *et al.* (1987), p. 129.

29. *Ibid.*, p. 132.

30. *Ibid.*, pp. 132–3.

31. *Ibid.*, p. 133.

32. *Ibid.*, p. 134.

33. As cited in Bennington and Young's introduction to Attridge *et al.* (1987), p. 2.

34. Recent Marxist debates have displayed a marked tendency to be bifurcated along the path of the literature/history couplet in this respect. The concept of history defended by Marxist critics often bears little relation to that which figures in the writings of such Marxist historians as Perry Anderson and E. P. Thompson. Nor are the means through which the concept of history is defended, or the purposes for which such defences are mounted, the same between these two regions of Marxist debate. Although their critical conclusions are somewhat different, the stress in Anderson's and Thompson's defences of history thus falls mainly on the practices of historians. (See Anderson, Perry (1980), *Arguments within English Marxism*, London: Verso; and Thompson, E. P. (1978), *The Poverty of Theory, and Other Essays*, London: Merlin Press.) This lack of commensurability between the functions assigned the concept of history in different regions of Marxist thought is clearly a major impediment to its ability to supply Marxist debates with a common, unifying foundation.

35. Lukács, Georg (1972), *Political Writings, 1919–1929. The Question of Parliamentarianism and Other Essays*, London: New Left Books, p. 14.

36. *Ibid.*

37. *Ibid.*, p. 9.

38. Eagleton, Terry (1981), *Walter Benjamin, or Towards a Revolutionary Criticism*, London: Verso, pp. 72–3.

39. *Ibid.*, p. 73.

40. Gramsci, Antonio (1971), *Selections from the Prison Notebooks*, London: Lawrence & Wishart, p. 377.

41. Lyotard, Jean-François (1986), *The Postmodern Condition: A Report on Knowledge*, Manchester: Manchester University Press, p. 41.

42. See Silverman, David and Torode, Brian (1980), *The Material Word: Some*

Theories of Language and its Limits, London: Routledge & Kegan Paul, chapter 2.

43. Poulantzas, Nicos (1978), *State, Power, Socialism*, London: Verso, pp. 111–12.

44. White, Hayden (1982), 'Getting out of history', *Diacritics*. no. 12, pp. 12–13.

45. While accepting the reality of many of the uncertainties now associated with the currency of postmodernism, Hall argues that the clustering of all these uncertainties under the singular sign of 'the postmodern condition' functions as an ideology with an 'eternalising effect' in its suggestion that history comes to an end in that condition. See Hall, Stuart (1986), 'On postmodernism and articulation', *Journal of Communication Inquiry*, vol. 10, no. 2, p. 47.

46. The postmodernist perspective on the decline of universal narratives is, in my view, of a less compelling political significance than Benedict Anderson's observations regarding the tendency for the universalistic narratives of religious communities to be replaced by the more particularistic and enclosing narratives of national communities. See Anderson (1983), *Imagined Communities. Reflections on the Origin and Spread of Nationalism*, London: Verso.

47. See Althusser, Louis (1973), 'The conditions of Marx's scientific discovery', *Theoretical Practice*, nos 7–8.

48. Hunt, Lynn (1984), *Politics, Culture and Class in the French Revolution*, London: Methuen, pp. 57 and 72.

49. Foucault, Michel (1980), 'Nietzsche, genealogy, history' in *Language, Counter-Memory, Practice*, Ithaca: Cornell University Press, p. 154.

50. Greenblatt, Stephen (1985), 'Shakespeare and the exorcists' in Parker, Patricia and Hartman, Geoffrey (eds), *Shakespeare and the Question of Theory*, London: Methuen, p. 164.

51. *Ibid.*, p. 164.

52. *Ibid.*, p. 164.

53. *Ibid.*, pp. 164–5.

54. Ryan, Michael (1984), *Marxism and Deconstruction: A Critical Articulation*, Baltimore: Johns Hopkins University Press, p. 9.

55. *Ibid.*, p. 9.

56. Derrida, Jacques (1981), *Positions*, Chicago: University of Chicago Press, p. 91.

57. Frow, John (1986), *Marxism and Literary History*, Cambridge, Mass.: Harvard University Press, p. 6.

58. *Ibid.*, p. 60.

59. *Ibid.*, p. 83.

60. Foucault, Michel (1972), *The Archaeology of Knowledge*, London: Tavistock, p. 28.

61. *Ibid.*, p. 109.

62. Greenblatt, Stephen (1980), *Renaissance Self-Fashioning: From More to Shakespeare*, Chicago: University of Chicago Press.

63. Tennenhouse, Leonard (1986), *Power on Display: The Politics of Shakespeare's Genres*, London: Methuen.

64. Indeed, Stephen Bann's work suggests that the very expectation there might

be such a theory is a product of the nineteenth-century emergence of literature and history as differentiated spaces of representation which, in ontologising their own constructs, projected these as realities of different kinds whose general form of interrelation had then to be accounted for. See Bann, Stephen (1984), *The Clothing of Clio: A Study in the Representation of History in Nineteenth-Century Britain and France*, Cambridge: Cambridge University Press.

65. Hindess, Barry and Hirst, Paul (1975), *Pre-Capitalist Modes of Production*, London: Routledge & Kegan Paul, p. 312.
66. *Ibid.*, p. 312.
67. *Ibid.*
68. *Ibid.*, p. 309.

4 THE SOCIOLOGY OF GENRES

1. Lukács, Georg (1969), *Probleme der Ästhetik, Werke*, vol. 10, Neuwied: Luchterhand, p. 118. Cited as translated by John Frow in *Marxism and Literary History* (1986), Cambridge, Mass.: Harvard University Press, p. 10.
2. Kent, Thomas (1983), 'The classification of genres', *Genre*, vol. 16, no. 1, p. 2.
3. Wellek, René and Warren, Austin (1970), *Theory of Literature*, Harmondsworth: Penguin, p. 226.
4. See Lukács, Georg (1971), *The Theory of the Novel: A Historico-philosophical Essay on the Forms of Great Epic Literature*, London: Merlin Books; Goldmann, Lucien (1964), *The Hidden God: A Study of Tragic Vision in the Pensées of Pascal and the Tragedies of Racine*, London: Routledge & Kegan Paul; and Jameson, Fredric (1975), 'Magical narratives: romance as genre', *New Literary History*, vol. 7, no. 1.
5. Bürger, Peter (1984), *Theory of the Avant-Garde*, Minneapolis: University of Minnesota Press, p. 69.
6. Derrida, Jacques (1980), 'The law of genre', *Glyph* no. 7, pp. 59–60.
7. Perry, B. E. (1967), *The Ancient Romances: A Literary-historical Account of their Origins*, Berkeley: California University Press.
8. See Haycraft, Howard (1941), *Murder for Pleasure: The Life and Times of the Detective Story*, New York: D. Appleton Century Co., p. 12.
9. Jakobson, Roman (1971), 'The dominant', in Matejka, L. and Pomorska, K. (eds), *Readings in Russian Poetics*, Cambridge, Mass.: MIT Press, p. 82.
10. Duvignaud, Jean (1965), *Sociologie du Théâtre*, Paris: Presses Universitaires de France, p. 59 (my translation).
11. Watt, Ian (1957), *The Rise of the Novel: Studies in Defoe, Richardson and Fielding*, Berkeley and Los Angeles: University of California Press, p. 9.
12. *Ibid.*, p. 32.
13. *Ibid.*, p. 33.
14. *Ibid.*, p. 60.
15. *Ibid.*
16. *Ibid.*, p. 300.
17. Freadman, Anne (1988), 'Untitled: (on genre)', *Cultural Studies*, vol. 2, no. 1, p. 79.
18. *Ibid.*

19. Goldmann, Lucien (1975), *Towards a Sociology of the Novel*, London: Tavistock, p. 6.
20. *Ibid.*, p. 7.
21. *Ibid.*, p. 11.
22. Vilar, Pierre (1971), 'The age of Don Quixote', *New Left Review*, no. 68.
23. Bakhtin, M. M. (1981), *The Dialogic Imagination*, Austin and London: University of Texas Press, p. 8.
24. *Ibid.*, p. 22.
25. Introduction to Bakhtin (1981), p. xxxi.
26. Wittgenstein, Ludwig (1968), *Philosophical Investigations*, Oxford: Basil Blackwell, sections 66–7.
27. Fowler, Alistair (1982), *Kinds of Literature: An Introduction to the Theory of Genres and Modes*, Oxford: Clarendon Press, p. 41.
28. See Barthes, Roland (1975), *S/Z*, London: Jonathan Cape.
29. Sklovskij, Victor (1971), 'The mystery novel: Dickens's *Little Dorrit*', in Matejka, L. and Pomarska, K. (eds), *Readings in Russian Poetics*, Cambridge, Mass.: MIT Press.
30. Fowler, (1982), p. 133.
31. For a discussion of the consequences of this for the contrasting generic frameworks in which Ian Fleming's James Bond novels were read in Britain and America, see Bennett, Tony and Woollacott, Janet (1987), *Bond and Beyond: The Political Career of a Popular Hero*, London: Macmillan, pp. 76–90.
32. For details, see Murch, A. E. (1963), *The Development of the Detective Novel*, Westpoint, Connecticut: Greenwood Publishers.
33. See Lotman, Jurij (1977), *The Structure of the Artistic Text*, Ann Arbor: University of Michigan Press.
34. Freadman, (1988), p. 90.
35. *Ibid.*, p. 95.
36. *Ibid.*
37. I have distinguished the concept of *inter-textuality* from that of *intertextuality* elsewhere as well as arguing my reasons for holding that the former overdetermines the latter. See Bennett, Tony and Woollacott, Janet (1987), pp. 44–5, 53–9, 248–9 and 260–9. This study also attempts to apply the concept of reading formation understood as a particular kind of inter-textual relation. For a further discussion of this term, however, see Bennett, Tony (1983), 'Texts, readers, reading formations', *The Bulletin of the Midwest Modern Language Association*, vol. 16, no. 1 (reprinted in *Literature and History*, vol. 9, no. 2, Autumn, 1983).
38. Lukács, Georg (1969), *The Historical Novel*, Harmondsworth: Penguin, p. 289.
39. Lukács entered the lists of sociology under the banner of a Simmelian formalism. See Lukács, Georg (1914), 'Zur Soziologie des Modernen Dramas', *Archiv für Sozialwissenschaft und Sozialpolitik*, vol. 38.
40. Lukács (1969), p. 290.
41. Williams, Raymond (1984), *Writing in Society*, London: Verso, p. 2.
42. Heath, Stephen (1982), *The Sexual Fix*, London: Macmillan, p. 85.
43. *Ibid.*, p. 95.
44. See Hunter, Ian (1987), 'At the limits of criticism', *Southern Review*, vol. 20, no. 3.

45. Foucault cites genre distinctions as among the familiar groupings and divisions archaeological analysis would need to suspend. See Foucault, Michel (1972), *The Archaeology of Knowledge*, London: Tavistock, p. 22.

46. Tennenhouse, Leonard (1986), *Power on Display: The Politics of Shakespeare's Genres*, London: Methuen, p. 15.

47. *Ibid.*, p. 5.

48. *Ibid.*.

49. See, for an example of work of this kind, the essays by Alan Sinfield and Graham Holderness in Dollimore, Jonathan and Sinfield, Alan (eds) (1985), *Political Shakespeare: New Essays in Cultural Materialism*, Manchester: Manchester University Press. See also the essays collected in Howard, Jean E. and O'Connor, Marion F. (eds) (1987), *Shakespeare Reproduced: The Text in History and Ideology*, New York and London: Methuen.

50. Frow, John (1986), p. 184.

51. *Ibid.*, pp. 187–8.

5 SEVERING THE AESTHETIC CONNECTION

1. Baxendall, Lee and Morawski, Stefan (1974), *Karl Marx, Frederick Engels: On Literature and Art*, New York: International General, p. 7.

2. Rose, Margaret (1984), *Marx's Lost Aesthetic: Karl Marx and the Visual Arts*, London: Cambridge University Press, p. 1. For other studies of a similar kind, see Prawer, S. S. (1978), *Karl Marx and World Literature*, Oxford: Oxford University Press; and Demetz, P. (1967), *Marx, Engels and the Poets, Origins of Marxist Literary Criticism*, Chicago: University of Chicago Press.

3. See Marx, Karl (1973), *Grundrisse: Foundation of the Critique of Political Economy*, Harmondsworth: Penguin, p. 101.

4. Lifshitz, Mikhail (1974), *The Philosophy of Art of Karl Marx*, London: Pluto Press.

5. Lukács, who had worked with Ryazanov at the Marx–Lenin Institute in 1930–1 in preparing Marx's *1844 Manuscripts* for publication, developed a close friendship with Lifshitz after his emigration to the Soviet Union in 1933 and explicitly acknowledged his indebtedness to Lifshitz for rekindling his interest in aesthetic questions.

6. Vazquez, Adolfo Sanchez (1973), *Art and Society: Essays in Marxist Aesthetics*, London: Merlin Press, 1978, p. 97.

7. Jameson, for example, posits a distinction between the social and historical concerns of musical semantics and those of 'aesthetic value proper' in his introduction to Attali, Jacques (1985), *Noise: The Political Economy of Music*, Manchester: Manchester University Press, p. ix. For Eagleton, see the final chapter of *Criticism and Ideology* (1976), London: New Left Books.

8. Lukács, Georg (1970), *Writer and Critic, and Other Essays*, London: Merlin Press, p. 198.

9. Here, as elsewhere, Marxist thought is content merely to invert dominant aesthetic discourses. The view that genuine literature transcends its social determination, and hence exceeds sociological analysis, whereas popular fiction is riven by its determination, and hence amenable to such analysis, is a commonplace which finds its mirror reflection in this aspect of Marxist aesthetics.

10. I have developed this argument more fully elsewhere. See Bennett, Tony,

'Texts in history: the determinations of readings and their texts', in Attridge, Derek *et al.* (eds) (1987), *Post-structuralism and the Question of History*, Cambridge: Cambridge University Press.

11. Foucault, Michel (1970), *The Order of Things: An Archaeology of the Human Sciences*, London: Tavistock, p. 262.

12. Barthes, Roland (1987), *Criticism and Truth*, Minneapolis: University of Minnesota Press, p. 53.

13. *Ibid.*, p. 57.

14. *Ibid.*, pp. 54–5.

15. More often than not, however, the issue is not posed in these terms. In being conflated with the problem of value, the question of literature's relative autonomy is often translated into a concern with its seeming ability to transcend its determinations. Posed in this way, the analysis of literature's autonomy concerns itself less with the relations between different forms of determination than with stressing the limitations of any account of literature which focuses on its determining conditions, however these might be conceived.

16. Medvedev, Pavlev and Bakhtin, Mikhail (1978), *The Formal Method in Literary Scholarship: A Critical Introduction to Sociological Poetics*, Baltimore: Johns Hopkins University Press, p. 29.

17. *Ibid.*, pp. 16–17.

18. *Ibid.*, p. 17.

19. Frow, John (1986), *Marxism and Literary History*, Cambridge, Mass.: Harvard University Press, pp. 25–6.

20. While Eagleton is sharply critical of Althusser's and Macherey's use of figurative language to express the relations between literature and ideology, his argument is none the less a variant of the Althusserian schema in installing literature, as Frow puts it, in an 'epistemological no man's land' between science and ideology. See Frow (1986), p. 27.

21. Eagleton, Terry (1976), p. 69.

22. There is, however, another aspect to Eagleton's position here: the contention that it is ultimately ideology itself which governs the process of its signification by literature ('The process of the text is the process whereby ideology produces the forms which produce it . . .', p. 84). Still, however, literature enjoys the special status of being the privileged instrument through which ideology thus effects its self-production.

23. While these gendered metaphors are intended only loosely, an investigation of the degree to which the relations between science and aesthetics are typically represented in gendered terms in epistemological and aesthetic discourse would, I suspect, prove amply rewarding. Useful bearings for such an analysis can be found in Lloyd, Genevieve (1984), *The Man of Reason: 'Male' and 'Female' in Western Philosophy*, London: Methuen.

24. An excellent example of the contradictory entanglements produced by this proliferation of not-statements is offered by Frow in his discussion of Macherey. See Frow (1986), p. 26.

25. In the aesthetics of writers such as Lukács, Lifshitz and Vazquez, their (largely speculative) anthropological accounts of the processes of art's differentiation from magic constitute the only point at which historical – or, more

accurately, pre-historical – considerations enter into their specification of the aesthetic mode.

26. For the most sustained development of the first of these criticisms, see Hirst, Paul (1976), 'Althusser and the theory of ideology', *Economy and Society*, vol. 5, no. 2.

27. See, for example, Foucault, Michel (1980), *Power/Knowledge: Selected Interviews and Other Writings, 1972–1977*, New York: Pantheon Books, p. 118.

28. Frow (1986), p. 61.

29. *Ibid.*, p. 62.

30. *Ibid.*, pp. 63–4.

31. In truth, *Formalism and Marxism* places its bets both ways here. While arguing that the Althusserian view of literature's capacity to produce an internal distanciation of ideology is true only of historically specific forms of writing, it then undermines the ground necessary to support this argument in contending that the science/ideology distinction must be understood as political rather than epistemological. This disqualifies ideology from performing the role of a differentiating point of reference for literature's definition even in a historically limited sense.

32. Macherey, for example, is concerned with the more general category of fiction rather than with the conventionally more restricted concept of literature. See Macherey, Pierre (1978), *A Theory of Literary Production*, London: Routledge & Kegan Paul.

33. For a further elaboration of the points which follow, see Bennett, Tony (1981), 'Marxism and Popular Fiction', *Literature and History*, vol. 7, no. 2.

34. Bromley, Roger (1978), 'Natural boundaries: the social function of popular fiction', *Red Letters*, no. 7, p. 42.

35. *Ibid.*, p. 40.

36. *Ibid.*, p. 39.

37. *Ibid.*, pp. 52–3.

38. Eagleton, Terry (1983), *Literary Theory: An Introduction*, Oxford: Blackwell, p. 204.

39. *Ibid.*

40. Heath, Stephen (1987), 'Literary theory, etc.', *Comparative Criticism*, vol. 9, Cambridge: Cambridge University Press, p. 310.

41. Norris, Christopher (1985), *Contest of Faculties: Philosophy and Theory after Deconstruction*, London: Methuen, p. 123.

6 REALLY USELESS 'KNOWLEDGE'

1. Medvedev, P. N. (1983), 'The immediate tasks facing literary-historical science', *Russian Poetics in Translation*, vol. 10, p. 83.

2. To avoid confusion, I should make it clear that the criticisms advanced in this chapter relate solely to attempts to develop Marxist theories of the aesthetic conceived as a specific faculty, mode of cognition or set of effects attributable to artistic practices. While these have often framed and influenced more specific and detailed Marxist analyses of artistic practices, they have rarely done so entirely, with the consequence that a good deal of really useful knowledge has been produced that is by no means invalidated by

the criticisms that can be brought to bear against the more general theories of Marxist aesthetics.

3. To avoid a possible second confusion, it should be stressed that the terrain of a 'political economy' of art and Marxist approaches to the study of art are not coterminous. While the former emphatically requires the contribution of the latter, it is – and equally emphatically – not exhausted by that contribution. Specifically, the political relations within which artistic practices function and have effects are neither limited by nor reducible to the sphere of class relations no matter how such relations might be conceived, whether economistically or as a complex combination of economic, political and ideological determinations.

4. Marcuse, Herbert (1979a), *The Aesthetic Dimension: Toward a Critique of Marxist Aesthetics*, London: Macmillan, p. xii.

5. *Ibid.*, p. ix.

6. Lukács, Georg (1964), 'Reflections on the Sino-Soviet dispute', *Studies on the Left*, vol. IV, no. 1, p. 35.

7. Marcuse (1979a), p. 19.

8. *Ibid.*, p. 6.

9. Marx, Karl (1973), *Grundrisse: Foundations of the Critique of Political Economy*, Harmondsworth: Penguin, p. 101.

10. Marcuse, (1979a), p. x.

11. Lotman, Jurij (1977), *The Structure of the Artistic Text*, Ann Arbor: University of Michigan Press.

12. Marcuse, Herbert (1979b), 'Repressive tolerance', in Wolff, R. R., Barrington-Moore Jnr, G., and Marcuse, Herbert (eds) *A Critique of Pure Tolerance*, London: Jonathan Cape, pp. 102–3.

13. Wellek, René (1982), *The Attack on Literature, and Other Essays*, Brighton: Harvester Press, p. 157.

14. Lerner, Laurence (ed.) (1983), *Reconstructing Literature*, Oxford: Blackwell.

15. Eagleton, Terry and Fuller, Peter (1983), 'The question of value: a discussion', *New Left Review*, no. 142, p. 78.

16. Fuller, Peter (1984), *Aesthetics after Modernism*, London: Writers and Readers Press, sleeve.

17. Durant, Alan (1984), *Conditions of Music*, London: Macmillan, p. 81.

18. Johnson, Richard (1979), '"Really useful knowledge": radical education and working-class culture', in Clarke, John and Johnson, Richard (eds), *Working-Class Culture: Studies in History and Theory*, London: Hutchinson.

19. Goldmann, Lucien (1971), *Immanuel Kant*, London: New Left Books, p. 192.

20. This historical pre-givenness of epistemology to aesthetics is made perfectly clear by Baumgarten, conventionally regarded as the founder of aesthetics, who first introduced the term (in 1735) in the following context:

> If logic by its very definition should be restricted to the rather narrow limits to which it is as a matter of fact confined, would it not count as the science of knowing things philosophically, that is, as the science for the direction of the higher cognitive faculties in apprehending the truth? Well, then, Philosophers might still find occasion, not without ample reward, to inquire also into those devices by which they might improve the lower faculties of knowing, and sharpen them and apply

them more happily for the benefit of the whole world. Since psychology affords sound principles, we have no doubt that there could be available a science which could direct the lower cognitive faculties in knowing things sensately. . . .

Therefore, *things known* are to be known by the superior faculty as the object of logic; things perceived are to be known by the inferior faculty as the object of the science of perception, or aesthetic.

Baumgarten, A. G. (1954), *Reflections on Poetry*, Berkeley and Los Angeles: University of California Press, p. 78.

21. Greenfield, Catherine (1984), 'Theories of the subject: rewritings and contestations', *Australian Journal of Communication*, nos. 5 and 6, p. 40.
22. The reference here is to Jurgen Habermas's concept of 'the public sphere': a critical institutional space within which bourgeois public opinion was nurtured and developed in opposition to the structures of absolutism. For the best account of the relevance of this concept to the concerns of aesthetic theory, see Hohendal, Peter Uwe (1982), *The Institution of Criticism*, Ithaca and London: Cornell University Press. I have drawn heavily on this in my discussion of Hume.
23. Kant, Immanuel (1957), *The Critique of Judgement*, Oxford: Clarendon Press, pp. 41–2.
24. Hume, David (1965), *Of the Standard of Taste, and Other Essays*, Indianapolis: Bobbs-Merrill, p. 7.
25. *Ibid.*, p. 9.
26. Bourdieu, Pierre (1979), *La Distinction: Critique social du jugement*, Paris: Editions de Minuit, pp. 54–5.
27. Hume (1965), p. 9.
28. *Ibid.*, p. 17.
29. *Ibid.*, p. 18.
30. *Ibid.*, pp. 19–20.
31. Kant, (1957), p. 4.
32. *Ibid.*, p. 75.
33. *Ibid.*
34. *Ibid.*, p. 43.
35. *Ibid.*, p. 50.
36. *Ibid.*, pp. 50–1.
37. *Ibid.*, p. 52.
38. *Ibid.*, p. 56.
39. *Ibid.*, pp. 76–7.
40. *Ibid.*, pp. 75–6.
41. *Ibid.*, p. 83.
42. *Ibid.*, p. 84.
43. *Ibid.*
44. *Ibid.*, p. 85.
45. Eagleton and Fuller, (1983), p. 79.
46. Brecht, Bertolt (1974), 'Against Georg Lukács', *New Left Review*, no. 84.
47. Eagleton and Fuller (1983), pp. 78–9.
48. Mukarovsky, Jan (1970), *Aesthetic Function, Norm and Value as Social Facts*, Ann Arbor: University of Michigan Press.

49. Willett, John (ed.) (1978), *Brecht on Theatre*, London: Methuen, p. 20.
50. *Ibid.*, p. 112.

7 AESTHETICS AND LITERARY EDUCATION

1. Williams, Raymond (1976), *Keywords*, London: Fontana, p. 28.
2. See Foucault's comments on the aesthetics of existence in Foucault (1986), *The Use of Pleasure*, New York: Random House.
3. Foucault, Michel, 'Technologies of the self', in Martin, L. H. *et al.* (eds) (1988), *Technologies of the Self: A Seminar with Michel Foucault*, London: Tavistock, p. 18.
4. *Ibid.*
5. Bürger, Peter (1984), *Theory of the Avant-Garde*, Minneapolis: University of Minnesota Press, p. 4.
6. *Ibid.*, pp. lii-liii.
7. *Ibid.*
8. *Ibid.*, p. 23.
9. Bürger, Peter (1985/6), 'The institution of "art" as a category in the sociology of literature', *Cultural Critique*, no. 2, p. 6.
10. *Ibid.*, p. 15.
11. *Ibid.*
12. *Ibid.*, p. 16.
13. As cited in Lloyd, David (1985/6), 'Arnold, Ferguson, Schiller: aesthetic culture and the politics of aesthetics', *Cultural Critique*, no. 2, p. 163.
14. *Ibid.*, p. 164.
15. *Ibid.*
16. Bürger (1985/6), p. 15.
17. *Ibid.*, p. 12.
18. *Ibid.*, pp. 12–13.
19. Marcuse, Herbert (1968), *Negations: Essays in Critical Theory*, London: Allen Lane, p. 98.
20. Bürger (1985/6), p. 7.
21. Eagleton, Terry (1985/6), 'The subject of literature', *Cultural Critique*, no. 2, pp. 96–7.
22. *Ibid.*, pp. 98–9.
23. Hunter, Ian (1988a), 'Setting limits to culture', *New Formations*, no. 4, p. 109.
24. *Ibid.*
25. Hunter, Ian (1988b), *Culture and Government: The Emergence of Modern Literary Education*, London: Macmillan, p. 185.
26. *Ibid.*, p. 187.
27. *Ibid.*, p. 64.
28. *Ibid.*, p. 214.
29. Arnold, Matthew (1971), *Culture and Anarchy: An Essay in Political and Social Criticism*, Indianapolis and New York: Bobbs-Merrill Co., Inc., p. 90.
30. Hunter (1988b), p. 214.
31. *Ibid.*, p. 150.
32. *Ibid.*
33. *Ibid.*, p. 152.

34. *Ibid.*, p. 268.
35. *Ibid.*, p. 223.
36. *Ibid.*, pp. 128–9.
37. *Ibid.*, pp. 127 and 129.
38. Macherey, Pierre (1978), *A Theory of Literary Production*, London: Routledge & Kegan Paul, p. 133.
39. Eagleton (1976), *Criticism and Ideology*, London: New Left Books, p. 165.
40. See Benjamin, Walter, 'The author as producer', in Benjamin (1973), *Understanding Brecht*, London: New Left Books.

8 CRITICAL ILLUSIONS

1. Cited in Baldick, Chris (1983), *The Social Mission of English Criticism 1848–1932*, Oxford: Clarendon Press, pp. 42–3.
2. Said, Edward (1984), *The World, The Text and the Critic*, London: Faber & Faber, p. 29.
3. *Ibid.*, pp. 3–4.
4. *Ibid.*, p. 5.
5. *Ibid.*, p. 20.
6. *Ibid.*, p. 17.
7. *Ibid.*
8. *Ibid.*, p. 4.
9. *Ibid.*, p. 33.
10. *Ibid.*, p. 29.
11. *Ibid.*, p. 28.
12. *Ibid.*, pp. 146–7.
13. *Ibid.*, p. 26.
14. *Ibid.*, p. 242.
15. *Ibid.*, p. 241.
16. *Ibid.*, pp. 241–2.
17. Lecourt, Dominique (1974), *Marxism and Epistemology*, London: New Left Books, pp. 45–6.
18. *Ibid.*, p. 45.
19. Baldick, (1983), p. 25.
20. *Ibid.*, pp. 32–3.
21. Said, (1984), p. 220.
22. Jameson, Fredric (1981), *The Political Unconscious*, London: Methuen, pp. 9–10.
23. *Ibid.*, p. 9.
24. Jameson, Fredric (1982), interview in *Diacritics*, vol. 12, Autumn, p. 73.
25. Weber, Samuel (1983), 'Capitalising history: notes on *The Political Unconscious*', in Barker, F. *et al.* (eds), *The Politics of Theory*, Colchester, University of Essex Press.
26. Jameson (1981), p. 10.
27. *Ibid.*, p. 22.
28. *Ibid.*, p. 34.
29. Frow, John (1984), 'Marxism after structuralism', *Southern Review*, no. 17, p. 35.
30. Jameson (1981), p. 30.

31. *Ibid.*, p. 13.
32. Bourdieu, Pierre (1984), *Distinction: A Social Critique of the Judgement of Taste*, London: Routledge & Kegan Paul.
33. Macherey, Pierre (1978), *A Theory of Literary Production*, London: Routledge & Kegan Paul.
34. Cited in Baldick, (1983), p. 73.
35. Hunter, Ian (1984), 'After representation: recent discussions of the relation between language and literature', *Economy and Society*, vol. 13, no. 4, p. 425.
36. Jameson (1981), pp. 19–20.
37. *Ibid.*, pp. 99–100.
38. *Ibid.*, p. 100.
39. *Ibid.*, p. 79.
40. *Ibid.*, p. 85.
41. Frow (1984), p. 39.
42. Jameson (1981), p. 102.
43. *Ibid.*
44. Weber (1983), p. 255.
45. Althusser, Louis (1973), 'The conditions of Marx's scientific discovery', *Theoretical Practice*, nos 7–8, p. 6.
46. Jameson (1981), p. 53.
47. Weber (1983), p. 255.
48. *Ibid.*, p. 258.
49. *Ibid.*

9 THE PRISON-HOUSE OF CRITICISM

1. Jameson, Fredric (1972), *The Prison-House of Language: A Critical Account of Structuralism and Russian Formalism*, Princeton and London: Princeton University Press.
2. Eagleton, Terry (1984), *The Function of Criticism: From the Spectator to Post-Structuralism*, London: Verso, p. 123.
3. *Ibid.*, p. 124.
4. Eagleton, Terry (1985), 'Criticism and ideology: an interview', *Thesis Eleven*, no. 12, p. 143.
5. *Ibid.*, p. 143.
6. *Ibid.*
7. *Ibid.*, p. 139.
8. Eagleton (1984), p. 107.
9. Leavis, F. R. (1953), 'The responsible critic: or the function of criticism at any time', *Scrutiny*, Winter, p. 178.
10. *Ibid.*, pp. 178–9.
11. Eagleton, Terry (1976), *Criticism and Ideology*, London: New Left Books, p. 17.
12. *Ibid.*, p. 43.
13. Eagleton (1984), p. 14.
14. *Ibid.*, pp. 12–13.
15. *Ibid.*, p. 18.
16. *Ibid.*, pp. 76–7.
17. *Ibid.*, p. 123.

18. *Ibid.*, p. 118.
19. *Ibid.*, p. 112.
20. *Ibid.*, p. 114.
21. Baldick, Chris (1983), *The Social Mission of English Criticism, 1848–1932*, Oxford: Clarendon Press.
22. Eagleton, Terry (1981), *Walter Benjamin, or Towards a Revolutionary Criticism*, London: Verso.
23. Habermas, Jurgen (1979), 'The public sphere', in Mattelart, A. and Siegelaub, S. (eds), *Communication and Class Struggle: Capitalism, Imperialism*, New York: International General, p. 198.
24. *Ibid.*, p. 199.
25. Keane, John (1984), *Public Life and Late Capitalism: Toward a Socialist Theory of Democracy*, Cambridge: Cambridge University Press, pp. 2–3.
26. *Ibid.*, p. 7.
27. Laclau, Ernesto and Mouffe, Chantal (1985), *Hegemony and Socialist Strategy: Toward a Radical Democratic Politics*, London, Verso, p. 180.
28. *Ibid.*, p. 153.
29. Eagleton (1984), p. 65.
30. Mulhern, Francis (1979), *The Moment of 'Scrutiny'*, London: New Left Books, pp. 9–10.
31. Eagleton, Terry (1983), *Literary Theory: An Introduction*, Oxford: Blackwell, p. 36.
32. *Ibid.*, p. 36.
33. Baldick (1983), pp. 148–55.
34. Bourdieu, Pierre and Passeron, C. (1979), *The Inheritors: French Students and their Relations to Culture*, Chicago and London: University of Chicago Press.
35. Poster, Mark (1984), *Foucault, Marxism and History: Mode of Production versus Mode of Information*, Cambridge: Polity Press, p. 53.
36. Leavis (1953), p. 181.

10 CRITICISM AND PEDAGOGY

1. Lentricchia, Frank (1983), *Criticism and Social Change*, Chicago: University of Chicago Press, p. 2.
2. See Gramsci, Antonio (1971), 'The Intellectuals', in *Selections from the Prison Notebooks*, London: Lawrence & Wishart.
3. Lentricchia (1983), p. 6.
4. Foucault, Michel (1980), *Power/Knowledge: Selected Interviews and Other Writings, 1972–1977*, New York: Pantheon Books, p. 126.
5. Lentricchia (1983), pp. 6–7.
6. *Ibid.*, p. 7.
7. *Ibid.*, p. 11.
8. *Ibid.*, p. 13.
9. *Ibid.*
10. *Ibid.*, p. 37.
11. Smart, Barry (1986), 'The politics of truth and the problem of hegemony', in Hay, David Couzens (ed.), *Foucault: A Critical Reader*, Oxford: Blackwell, p. 162.
12. To the contrary. While Foucault's perspective on power/knowledge relations

is undoubtedly of major importance, there are limits to its applicability as also to the degree to which it calls into question Marxist formulations, and particularly those of Gramsci. I have argued this point in detail elsewhere. See Bennett, Tony (1988), 'The exhibitionary complex', *New Formations*, no. 4.

13. Lyotard, Jean-François (1986), *The Postmodern Condition: A Report on Knowledge*, Manchester: Manchester University Press, p. xxiii.

14. See Jameson, Fredric (1984), 'Postmodernism, or the cultural logic of late capitalism', *New Left Review*, no. 146, esp. pp. 56–7 and 88.

15. Eco, Umberto (1987), *Travels in Hyperreality*, London: Picador, p. 7.

16. See Silberman, Deborah (1986), *Selling Culture: Bloomingdale's, Diana Vreeland and the New Aristocracy of Taste in Reagan's America*, New York: Pantheon Books, esp. pp. 108 and 119.

17. Not always, however. There is sometimes a tendency to argue that cultural critique must adjust itself stylistically to the surface textures of postmodernism. For a discussion of the difficulties this occasions, as well as of the issues it evades, see O'Shea, Alan and Schwarz, Bill (1987), 'Reconsidering Popular culture', *Screen*, vol. 28, no. 3.

18. 'On postmodernism and articulation', interview with Stuart Hall (edited by Lawrence Grossberg), *Journal of Communication Inquiry*, vol. 10, no. 2, Summer, 1986, p. 47. Hall argues that the grouping together of a series of problems arising out of the collapse of modernist certainties under the singular sign of postmodernism is, in itself, a form of ideological closure: 'What it says is: this is the end of the world. History stops with us and there is no place to go after this. But whenever it is said that *this* is the last thing that will ever happen in history, that is the sign of the functioning, in the narrow sense, of the ideological – what Marx called the "eternalising" effect.' (p. 47)

19. Hebdige, Dick (1986), 'Postmodernism and "the other side"', *Journal of Communication Inquiry*, vol. 10, no. 2, Summer.

20. *Ibid.*, p. 96.

21. *Ibid.*

22. *Ibid.*, p. 95.

23. Bennett, Tony (1986), 'The politics of "the popular" and popular culture', in Bennett, Tony, Mercer, Colin and Woollacott, Janet (eds), *Popular Culture and Social Relations*, Milton Keynes: Open University Press, p. 20.

24. Hall (1986), p. 57.

25. See chapter 2, pp. 26–8.

26. Hall (1986), p. 57.

27. Laclau, Ernesto and Mouffe, Chantal (1985), *Hegemony and Socialist Strategy: Towards a Radical Democratic Politics*, London: Verso, p. 153.

28. *Ibid.*, p. 153.

29. *Ibid.*, p. 152.

30. *Ibid.*, p. 154.

31. *Ibid.*, p. 155.

32. Mouffe, Chantal (1988), 'Hegemony and new political subjects: toward a new concept of democracy', in Nelson, Cary and Grossberg, Lawrence (eds) (1988), *Marxism and the Interpretation of Culture*, Urbana and Chicago: University of Illinois Press, p. 98.

33. Laclau, Ernesto (1983), 'Transformations of advanced industrial societies and the theory of the subject', in Hänninen, Sakari and Paldán, Leena (eds) (1983), *Rethinking Ideology: A Marxist Debate*, New York and Bagnolet: International General/IMMRC, p. 44.
34. Laclau and Mouffe (1985), p. 188.
35. See Mouffe (1988), p. 100.
36. Laclau and Mouffe (1985), pp. 191–2.
37. Although Mouffe has commented on the tendency of mass culture to generate its own field of democratic antagonisms. See Mouffe (1988), p. 93.
38. *Ibid.*, p. 99.
39. Laclau and Mouffe (1985), p. 190.
40. Laclau (1983), p. 42.
41. Hall (1986), p. 56.
42. *Ibid.*, p. 58.
43. *Ibid.*, p. 49.
44. Although Mouffe's position on this is not constant. The formulations of her most recent essay at the time of writing – see Mouffe (1988) – come close to Hall's in this respect.
45. This stress on the politics of articulation has become especially pronounced as cultural studies has made its transatlantic passage. At times, the urging 'to articulate' becomes obsessive, the recurrence of the verb in American cultural studies sometimes assuming alarming proportions. That it has also found its way quite comfortably into pastiche-type forms of Marxist/postmodernist cultural commentary suggests that its political career is likely to be deeply contradictory. See, for some sign of these dangers, Grossberg, Lawrence (1988), 'Wandering audiences, nomadic critics', *Cultural Studies*, vol. 2, no. 3, October.
46. Minson, Jeffrey (1980), 'Strategies for socialists? Foucault's conception of power', in Gane, Mike (ed.) (1986), *Towards a Critique of Foucault*, London: Routledge & Kegan Paul, p. 142.
47. Mouffe (1988), p. 100.
48. Laclau, Ernesto, 'The Impossibility of Society', *Canadian Journal of Political and Social Theory*, vol. 7, nos. 1–2, Spring, 1983, pp. 22–4.
49. Hall (1986), p. 57.
50. Smart (1986), p. 160.
51. 'Questions of method: an interview with Michel Foucault', *I & C*, no. 8, 1981, p. 9.
52. Smart (1986), p. 169.

11 INSIDE/OUTSIDE LITERATURE

1. Burgin, Victor (1986), *The End of Art Theory: Criticism and Postmodernity*, London: Macmillan, p. 192.
2. *Ibid.*, pp. 192–3.
3. Barthes, Roland (1972), *Mythologies*, London: Jonathan Cape, p. 112.
4. *Ibid.*
5. Attridge, Derek, 'Language as history/history as language: Saussure and the romance of etymology', in Attridge *et al.* (eds) (1987), *Post-structuralism and the Question of History*, Cambridge: Cambridge University Press, p. 188.

6. *Ibid.*, p. 195.
7. Cited *ibid.*, p. 197.
8. *Ibid.*, p. 199.
9. *Ibid.*, p. 198.
10. *Ibid.*, p. 193.
11. *Ibid.*, p. 201.
12. *Ibid.*, p. 203.
13. *Ibid.*, p. 202.
14. *Ibid.*, p. 204.
15. Foucault, Michel (1972), *The Archaeology of Knowledge*, London: Tavistock, p. 7.
16. *Ibid.*, p. 27.
17. Lentricchia, Frank (1980), *After the New Criticism*, London: Methuen, p. 191.
18. *Ibid.*.
19. *Ibid.*, p. 193.
20. Foucault, Michel (1979), 'My body, this paper, this fire', *Oxford Literary Review*, vol. 4, no. 1, pp. 26–7.
21. For a discussion of the difficulties associated with this aspect of Foucault's work, see Brown, Beverley and Cousins, Mark, 'The linguistic fault: the case of Foucault's archaeology', in Gane, Mike (ed.) (1986), *Towards a Critique of Foucault*, London: Routledge & Kegan Paul.
22. Lentricchia (1980), p. 195.
23. Cited *ibid.*, p. 197.
24. See Wordsworth, Anne, 'Derrida and Foucault: writing and the history of historicity', in Attridge *et al.* (1987), p. 118.
25. See chapter 7.
26. See chapter 3.
27. Frye, Northrop, 'The critical path: an essay on the social context of literary criticism', in Bloomfield, Morton W. (ed.) (1972), *In Search of Literary Theory*, Ithaca and London: Cornell University Press, pp. 94–5.
28. *Ibid.*, pp. 95–7.
29. *Ibid.*, p. 103.
30. *Ibid.*, p. 131.
31. *Ibid.*, pp. 103–4.
32. Eagleton, Terry (1976), *Criticism and Ideology: A Study in Marxist Literary Theory*, London: New Left Books, p. 48.
33. Frow, John (1986), *Marxism and Literary History*, Cambridge (Massachusetts): Harvard University Press, p. 84.
34. *Ibid.*
35. Lentricchia (1980), pp. 198–9.
36. See chapter 1, p. 4.
37. Benjamin, Walter (1973), *Understanding Brecht*, London: New Left Books, p. 93.

INDEX

absence/presence 92, 137–8

Adorno, Theodor 32, 168, 171, 232

Aeschylus 93

aesthetic discourse 6–8, 31–2, 34, 123, 147–63, 165, 188–9; and universal valuing subject 152–4, 160–1, 165

Althusser, Louis 10–11, 20, 22, 31–2, 121, 129, 131, 145, 147; on ideological conceptions of history 63, 65–6

Anderson, Perry 28, 31, 120; Marxism as self-critical theory 24–5

Arnold, Matthew 179, 204, 219, 221–2, 224, 230–1, 238; on literary criticism 193–4

Aronson, Ronald 25

articulation 253–5, 258–9, 262–5

Attridge, Derek 274–8; on etymology and history 276–7; on Saussure 274–5

Auerbach, Erich 201

Austen, Jane 91, 204

Bachelard, Gaston 203

Bakhtin, Mikhail 104; critique of Russian Formalism 128–9, 133; on genre 95–8

Baldick, Chris 204, 230, 241

Balzac, Honoré de 91, 95, 124

Bann, Stephen 292–3n

Barthes, Roland 52, 100, 126–7, 130, 201, 285; approaches to literature 3–5; structuralism and history 273–4

base/superstructure metaphor 9, 19, 41, 45, 52

Benjamin, Walter 14, 29, 32, 62, 189, 201, 228, 232, 287

Bennington, Geoff 43, 53

Bourdieu, Pierre 151, 209, 241; disinterestedness and the aesthetic 158–9

Brecht, Bertolt 120, 163, 165–6, 228, 287

Bromley, Roger 137

Bunyan, John 89, 93

Bürger, Peter 173–4, 181–2; art as institution 172; art's autonomy 168–71; sociological fallacy 80

Burgin, Victor 272

Caudwell, Christopher 13

Cervantes, Miguel de 83, 95

Chandler, Raymond 100–1

Chaucer, Geoffrey 89

Christie, Agatha 100

Churton-Collins, John 210

Cobbett, William 149

Cohen, Hermann 143

Colletti Lucio 31

Conan-Doyle, Sir Arthur 100–1

Copernicus 66

Corris, Peter 100

Cousins, Mark 55–6; representations of events 56